"Howell and Paris have provided an introductory text for [anthro]pology that is not only well-written, informative, and int[eresting but] unique in bridging the gap between this secular discipline [and faith.] Theological excursions into subjects relevant to Christians, devotional exercises for contemplating the full significance of human life in biblical terms, and personal accounts of the paradoxes of the working life of Christian anthropologists are interwoven with clear and penetrating explanations of anthropological concepts. In all this, the authors are faithful both to Christianity and anthropology. This book will provide much food for thought to Christians interested in discovering the value of anthropology for life, ministry, and practice."

—**Eloise Hiebert Meneses**, Eastern University

"The authors provide a concise and clearly written text that examines cultural anthropology from a Christian standpoint. Each chapter presents the subject matter in a form that preserves conventional scientific perspectives while viewing the subject through a Christian lens. This book fills a niche within the panoply of anthropological textbooks not previously addressed by the profession."

—**Paul Langenwalter**, Biola University

"For Christian students just starting their journey into anthropology, this is a good place to start. Written to be a text for undergraduate courses, *Introducing Cultural Anthropology* is short, readable, interesting, and covers the territory quite well. The final chapter will be especially helpful for those wondering whether or not anthropological study is helpful as a part of preparation for life."

—**Charles Kraft**, School of Intercultural Studies, Fuller Theological Seminary

"*Introducing Cultural Anthropology* provides an exceptional resource for helping students contextualize sometimes difficult anthropological topics such as culture, sexuality, and power with Christian faith. This integrative book updates previous offerings in anthropology, and does so in a way that is eminently readable and accessible to the student. Each author brings a distinct voice to the text which helps the reader feel they are on a collegial journey with excellent guides. Highly recommended!"

—**Matthew S. Vos**, Covenant College

"Finally—an anthropology textbook with a balanced Christian approach that covers all the basic anthropological topics in a captivating yet academic manner. Professionally written and well presented to enhance learning, I eagerly await this new textbook and plan to use it in my introductory anthropology classes."

—**Jon Arensen**, Houghton College

Introducing Cultural Anthropology

A CHRISTIAN PERSPECTIVE

Brian M. Howell & Jenell Williams Paris

Baker Academic

a division of Baker Publishing Group

Grand Rapids, Michigan

Published by Baker Academic
a division of Baker Publishing Group
P.O. Box 6287, Grand Rapids, MI 49516-6287
www.bakeracademic.com

Printed in the United States of America

Library of Congress Cataloging-in-Publication Data

Howell, Brian M.
    Introducing cultural anthropology : a Christian perspective / Brian M. Howell & Jenell Williams Paris.
       p. cm.
    Includes bibliographical references and index.
    ISBN 978-0-8010-3887-7 (pbk.)
    1. Christianity and culture. 2. Culture. 3. Anthropology. I. Paris, Jenell Williams. II. Title.
BR115.C8H69 2011
261.5—dc22
                                                             2010025385

15 16 17   7 6

Contents

Preface

The Story of a Book

Some time ago, a colleague asked me (Brian) for resources that would help her teach the concept of culture to her French class. She was teaching about modern French film and wanted students to learn how terms like "popular culture" and "subculture" were distinct from "culture." She also wanted her students to reflect on how Christians might engage film, literature, and other media in their society.

At the time, I knew of many resources written for secular colleges, and many aimed at professional anthropologists, but I could not offer her just what she needed: a book that would explain the culture concept in both academic and Christian terms, without assuming the reader has a professional anthropologist's training for sorting through theoretical and technical issues.

After that conversation I envisioned authoring a short book—perhaps eighty pages—that would address the culture concept in Christian perspective. I even had a title: *Culture: A Primer for Christians*. Similar small booklets had been published by presses such as Oxford and others, and it seemed potentially useful for Christians teaching many subjects—even modern French film.

As my sabbatical approached, I revisited this idea, but now I imagined a slightly longer book—perhaps 120 pages—that would address a cluster of key topics in addition to culture. I wanted a coauthor, and was glad Jenell saw the value of the project for all the same reasons I did.

In the end, the project grew larger than our initial vision, from a modest primer to a more sizable textbook. When we approached Baker Academic, we pointed out that the anthropology textbooks written by and for Christians are now more than twenty years old. Although they had stood as excellent texts, it was time for something new that would speak to contemporary audiences and incorporate current terminology, theory, and examples. We also pointed out that while anthropology has long had a strong relationship with foreign missions, it has grown in Christian higher education to support general education, cross-cultural ministry, anthropology (or anthropology and sociology) majors and minors, Teaching English as a Second Language programs, intercultural studies, and many other academic programs. There was a need for a textbook that presented anthropology as a discipline in its own right and not only as a tool to support foreign missions or other explicitly cross-cultural work.

About the Authors

Combined, we have taught Introduction to Anthropology for more than twenty years. We enjoy encountering new ideas (or revising good ones) with our students, and seeing students stretch their own sense of humanity, culture, and God. We see this book as an opportunity to share what we've learned in the classroom and to provide resources that encourage an even stronger presence of anthropology in Christian higher education. Although we came to anthropology through different paths (described below), we have both embraced our roles as teachers and see this book as an extension of that call.

Jenell Williams Paris

My areas of interest include urban anthropology, race, gender, and sexuality. My path to anthropology (partly described at the beginning of chap. 1) began as an undergraduate at Bethel University in Minnesota. In addition to majoring in sociocultural studies, I did a month of fieldwork in Amsterdam and a semester program in Washington, D.C., both of which exposed me to cultural diversity, urban life, and social science scholarship. I also spent two summers doing urban ministry in Philadelphia with KingdomWorks (now Mission Year), which was the strongest motivator for further studies in urban anthropology.

My dissertation research at American University was on political activism and community formation in a low-income neighborhood of Washington, D.C. Since then, I've continued to research race and poverty and have expanded my interests to include contraception, gender, and sexual identity. My articles and books have appeared in secular and Christian journals aimed at scholars, as well as magazines such as *Christianity Today* and newspapers such as the *Los Angeles Times*. Before this book, I published two others: one about urban ministry (*Urban Disciples*, coauthored with Margot Eyring), and one about birth control (*Birth Control for Christians*).

As a professor, throughout my nine years at Bethel University in Minnesota and now at Messiah College in Pennsylvania, I often mentor students in research and writing as well as in spiritual and personal growth. I want to connect my teaching, scholarship, mentoring, and calling as a public intellectual. This book is an important step in that journey.

Brian M. Howell

I have worked primarily in the areas of globalization, global Christianity, and, to a lesser extent, race and religion in the United States. As I tell in my own short biography at the beginning of chapter 1, I attended Wesleyan University in Connecticut, a good liberal arts school that has long since severed ties with its Christian past. While I got a wonderful education in social theory and economic history, there was little to help me connect my intellectual life with my faith. God provided one professor, Richard Elphick, a historian of South African Dutch missions, as a mentor. He modeled for me the life of a faithful Christian and rigorous scholar. Although God eventually drew me to anthropology rather than history, Professor Elphick showed me how important it is for Christians to connect the life of the mind with life in Christ.

Since earning a master's degree at Fuller Seminary and then a PhD in anthropology from Washington University in Saint Louis, I have taught at Wheaton College in Illinois for nine years. Teaching anthropology in this setting provides the same joys and challenges my colleagues everywhere face. My students find anthropology inherently fascinating. It helps them to make sense of short-term mission experiences, multiculturalism, or their own backgrounds as missionary kids, ethnic minorities, or simply people who question cultural assumptions. In the face of a discipline that emphasizes cultural and social explanations, however, these very issues sometimes raise questions about the universality of faith or the nature of God. I have found no greater reward than helping students connect the insights of anthropology with their faith.

Like Jenell, my publishing has been in both the scholarly and popular venues. My books have addressed global Christianity, with my primary field site in Baguio City, Philippines. (Hence the many Philippine examples throughout the book!) In addition to global Christianity, my research has also been in areas of race in U.S. churches and short-term missions. I have enjoyed encouraging students in their own research and have even copublished with students in the past.

We both see this book as an opportunity to share what we have learned in the classroom and to provide a resource that encourages the development of anthropology in Christian colleges.

Using the Book

The book relies on a time-honored organizational schema. Chapters cover the aspects of culture and analytical categories common to the discipline and are grouped according to what some call "cultural subcategories." The text could be taught in exactly the order in which the chapters present the material, corresponding to a standard U.S. semester. At the same time, the chapters make reference to one another, making it easy to teach or read the chapters in any order.

We kept the book midlength in order to keep it affordable for students and flexible for teachers. In reaching that goal, we left some areas of cultural anthropology less developed, such as cultural aspects of aesthetics and art, medical anthropology, and cross-cultural psychology. The material on theory and the history of the discipline could easily be twice as long. In maintaining a focus on cultural anthropology, the book's treatment of biological anthropology and archaeology is, by necessity, cursory.

We anticipate professors using ethnographies, ethnographic film, and other primary sources to highlight particular areas of interest. With various topics, ethnographic and commercial ("Hollywood") films can be used to highlight the concepts in the text.

Although it is primarily geared to an undergraduate course in introductory anthropology, the book also may contribute to mission courses about the history of mission, practical ministry, and ministry in both cross-cultural and domestic contexts. With devotional materials and Christian theology integrated throughout, it could serve as a helpful text for short-term mission preparation courses and cross-cultural ministry classes at local churches.

Imagining an Audience

Every author imagines who will read his or her book. This imaginary audience helps the author to choose the "voice" of the book, the examples to be used, and overall style. Every author hopes that many other people read the book as well, but it often helps the reader to know the primary audience the authors had in mind. In this case, both of us tended to picture our own students: undergraduates at Christian colleges in the United States. Many of our students are European American English speakers who were born and raised in the United States, but others are from various racial and ethnic groups. Others are international students pursuing college degrees in the United States, and some are the children of missionaries or military personnel who have lived most of their lives outside the United States. Some of our students are well-traveled and culturally conversant, while others have very little familiarity with cultural diversity.

Drawing on our experiences, we have worked into the text many of the questions and issues that have arisen for us throughout the years. Some relate to a Christian perspective, while others are more about the particular cultural background many of our students bring to the table. Because both of us have done the bulk of our teaching in the United States (and were both born and raised in the United States), the book's examples tend to draw on U.S. cultural norms and practices. Many illustrations come from our lectures and from our students. Several ideas, ethnographic examples, and biblical explanations come from colleagues who have been kind enough to allow their words to appear here (with citation).

Many seminaries and colleges around the world offer courses in anthropology, of course, and we sincerely hope this book can be of service internationally. We hope the examples, though relative to the North American context, will be helpful for students everywhere as students and faculty adapt the book to various contexts through class discussions, lectures, films, and the like.

Acknowledgments and Thanks

This book has been encouraged along at several points and has benefited from the gracious help of many colleagues, students, and editors. We're thankful to Baker Academic and Bob Hosack, in particular, for believing in the text and encouraging us in our work. I (Brian) especially appreciated his arranging a much-needed advance during my reduced-salary sabbatical. We were thrilled when the book quickly became collaborative, drawing on the expertise of Christian anthropology colleagues, many of whom are part of the Network of Christian Anthropologists. For expert review of chapter drafts and other contributions, we thank Miriam Adeney, Kevin Birth, Katrina Greene, Mike Jindra, Diane King, Sherwood Lingenfelter, Eloise Hiebert Meneses, Sue Russell, John Schaefer, Dan Shaw, Sarah Tobin, Christa Tooley, Todd Vanden Berg, and Steve Ybarolla. Special mention must go to Njeri Bene, who read two chapters and provided detailed editorial and substantive comments that were very helpful and much appreciated. For photographs, we thank Elinor Abbot, Dean Arnold, Jeff Deal, Calenthia Dowdy, Katerina Friesen, Katrina Greene, Tom Headland, Tony Kail, Adam Kis, Bruce Privratsky, John Schaefer, and Steve Ybarolla. For cartoon illustrations, we appreciate James Marohn's artistry and generosity.

We relied on student assistance from Messiah College students Samantha Moore, Karli Davis, and Caitlin Kruse. Messiah College students in my (Jenell's) Introduction to Cultural Anthropology courses in fall 2009 and spring 2010 tested the book, providing excellent critique.

Josh Walton, my (Brian's) teaching assistant at Wheaton College, came to the project toward the end but read the entire manuscript and aided immensely in creating graphs, charts, and other editorial work. Muchas gracias. We are grateful to Wheaton College for providing me (Brian) the sabbatical time to work on a project such as this. We're thankful for Kim Phipps and Sue Hasseler at Messiah College, both of whom supported me (Jenell) and this project in practical ways, including course release time. I (Jenell) also thank the Pinklings, my writing group, for support and critique.

We are both grateful to our families, as well.

Brian: Marissa, thank you for your unflagging support. A shout-out to Hannah (14), Sam (10), and Ben (7), who actually saw a bit more of me during sabbatical even though I was sometimes distracted by projects such as this one. Thank you for not letting me become too distracted.

Jenell: James, thank you for believing in me as an anthropologist and as a writer. Wesley (4), Oliver (4), and Maxwell (3), thank you for believing in me as a mother. Someday (after you learn to read!) I hope you'll enjoy your mother's writings.

The Discipline of Anthropology

After studying this chapter, you should be able to:

1. Describe the four fields of anthropology and explain how they relate to one another.
2. Articulate the methods and concepts that distinguish cultural anthropology from related disciplines such as sociology.
3. Explain how Christians have contributed to the discipline of anthropology as well as how anthropology can contribute to specifically Christian work such as missions.

Finding Cultural Anthropology

Jenell's Journey

After a summer of urban ministry in Philadelphia, I returned to my suburban Christian college in Minnesota and searched the academic catalog for classes related to race, poverty, and cities. The Department of Anthropology and Sociology offered the most classes related to my emerging areas of passion, so I signed up as a major. Later, after I spent a month in Amsterdam, Holland, in a college class doing anthropological research about church planting for Youth With a Mission, I decided to become an anthropologist.

Jenell socializes with a key informant at a neighborhood gathering.

For me, anthropology has always been intertwined with urban life and ministry. My doctoral fieldwork involved four years of life, ministry, and research in a neighborhood in the northwest quadrant of Washington, D.C. From my bedroom window I could see the U.S. Capitol, as well as the profound poverty and racial segregation that exist just blocks from that global symbol of freedom and democracy. My research question was about ghetto formation and resident activism—how urban spaces become racially homogeneous and economically disadvantaged, and how residents work for neighborhood betterment. My research was motivated by faith—specifically by the question, "Who is my neighbor?" I hoped the research itself would be an act of neighborliness, telling the story of a neighborhood from residents' perspectives. My participant observation included being an involved citizen and church member while living at Esther House, a Christian community house of women committed to neighborhood betterment. I came to see that the methodology of anthropology—living among people and listening to their stories—could be a Christian practice.

Brian's Journey

I got my first taste of anthropology when I was developing an undergraduate thesis project at my New England college in a program that combined government, economics, history, and social theory. I decided to do research on missions in the Philippines, since both my best friend and my girlfriend (now wife) had Philippine ancestry. I had not taken a single course in anthropology, but I knew I wanted to travel and could not see myself working in an

Brian and a student pose with Parno, a coconut seller in Puncak, Indonesia.

archive; I wanted to talk with actual people. With my background in social science and a lot of enthusiasm, I spent a summer doing fieldwork in a small mountain village in the northern Philippines, interviewing people and learning about the process of social change following the widespread conversion to Christianity some thirty years earlier. Writing my thesis was the first time in my secular education that I really connected the social, theological, and cultural aspects of Christianity.

I wanted to continue the research in graduate school, but did not know which discipline would work best. I considered history and political science, but neither discipline seemed a good fit. At the time, I lived near Fuller Seminary in Pasadena, California, where I found anthropologists in the school of intercultural studies. After a few trial classes, I realized that cultural anthropology would allow me to consider all the aspects of life I found interesting. My research was also motivated by my faith as I sought to bring to the wider academic world an understanding of Christianity that is scholarly and critical but not hostile to Christians. During my fieldwork, I taught courses at the Philippine seminary where my family and I lived. There I came to see anthropology as a vital mode of thought for the church as well as the world.

Eventually we met each other in the relatively small world of Christian cultural anthropologists. After years of talking at conferences and even working on a colleague's book project together, we became convinced that anthropology had many important insights for Christians.[1] Drawing from nearly twenty combined years of teaching Introduction to Anthropology in Christian college and seminary classrooms, and many other courses as well, we have put together our knowledge of the discipline with our understanding of the particular questions and emphases Christians often bring. Thus, in addition to presenting the discipline of cultural anthropology generally, this text addresses distinctively Christian concerns, acknowledging points of tension and highlighting ways in which the discipline of anthropology can contribute to the work of Christians and the church.

What Is Cultural Anthropology?

On the first day of class, we often ask our students, "When you tell people you're taking a cultural anthropology class, what do they think you're studying?" The answers range from the study of dinosaurs, to images of Indiana Jones hunting down priceless (and magical) artifacts, to radical cultural relativists who think there is no truth. The first of these guesses is understandable, but wrong; the second is flattering, but not a very realistic portrayal of a different branch of anthropology; the third gets to a bit of truth, although as we discuss in chapter 2, this unfortunate characterization comes from particular anthropologists rather than from the discipline itself.

The truth is that *cultural anthropology* is the description, interpretation, and analysis of similarities and differences in human cultures. It is a diverse discipline encompassing a wide variety of topics related to human beings. Cultural anthropologists often differentiate themselves by referring to areas of interest and expertise such as economic anthropology, urban anthropology, or anthropology of religion, to name just a few.

As the personal stories at the beginning of this chapter demonstrate, anthropologists come to the discipline in a variety of ways and study an array of topics, but they share a commitment to a common perspective and method. The *anthropological perspective* refers to an approach to social research that seeks to understand culture from the point of view of the people *within* that cultural context. *Ethnographic fieldwork* is anthropology's hallmark research method, based upon the anthropologist's direct experience in a culture.

What often draws Christians to the discipline is the realization that the anthropological perspective and method enable us to serve the world by better understanding it. For me (Jenell), that has included urban ministry and

1. Robert Priest and Alvaro Nieves, eds., *This Side of Heaven: Race, Ethnicity, and Christian Faith* (New York: Oxford University Press, 2006).

community development, as well as college teaching. For me (Brian), anthropology has shaped my ability to teach and write about global Christianity, short-term mission, and church organization. Many Christians find a career in anthropology studying topics that have little obvious relationship to their faith, even while the calling to do research and scholarship provides an opportunity for faithfully using the gifts God has given them. Ultimately, most anthropology students do not become professional anthropologists, yet all Christians can benefit from understanding the methods and concepts of the discipline and connecting anthropology to matters of evangelism, social action, theology, church life, and the role of culture in our own understanding of the gospel.

In this chapter we present an outline of the four branches, or subfields, of anthropology. We then elaborate on the branch that is the focus of this text, cultural anthropology, giving an overview of its distinctive methods and concepts and distinguishing it from other social sciences. Finally, we discuss the contributions an anthropological understanding can provide Christians in our efforts to live faithful lives as members of the local and global body of Christ.

The Four Subfields of Anthropology

Simply breaking down the word "anthropology" into its parts reveals the breadth of the discipline. *Anthro* comes from the Greek *anthropos*, meaning "human," and *-ology* from *logos*, or "study." The term *anthropology* is extraordinarily broad because the discipline as a whole encompasses several distinct but related modes of research. Anthropology has traditionally been divided into four subfields: archaeology, linguistics, physical or biological anthropology, and cultural or social anthropology.[2] The four subfields are very different from one another in method and theory, yet all share the anthropological perspective on human life and culture. Today some add a fifth branch of anthropology—*applied anthropology*—in which practitioners use anthropology in the service of particular social concerns. Others argue that applied anthropology is not a subfield because application is an integral part of each subfield, and because applied anthropologists usually earned their degrees in one of the traditional four subfields. In this text, we discuss applied anthropology as it occurs in each of the traditional four subfields and do not categorize applied anthropology as a fifth subfield.

2. As explained later in the chapter, the terms *social* and *cultural* anthropology refer to British and American emphases. Today, the terms are virtually interchangeable, with some graduate programs using the term "sociocultural" to avoid the distinction. We will use the term "cultural" throughout the chapter to refer to this fourth branch of anthropology.

Fig. 1.1 The Four Subfields of Anthropology

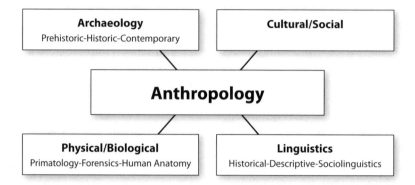

Archaeology

Archaeology is the study of material artifacts to understand a people's culture or society. This could be the people of the ancient past understood through the simple stone tools or fire pits they left behind, or it could be the relatively recent past of the last century or even contemporary communities. Archaeologists have studied everything from the Underground Railroad by which enslaved people in the southern United States escaped to the North, to Mayan empires in Central America, to the historicity of biblical narratives, to consumption patterns of Americans based on their garbage.

The primary data collection method of archaeologists is *excavation*, a rigorous method of extracting artifacts from underground, though they may also study visible structures such as pyramids, footprints fossilized into rocks, or cave paintings. By interpreting artifacts, archaeologists are able to draw conclusions about how the people connected to those artifacts lived. For example, before Europeans arrived in what is now North America, a civilization known to us only as the *Mound Builders* constructed massive mounds in various places throughout the Great Plains and southeastern United States. Archaeologists digging into these mounds and analyzing bits of pottery, metal, animal bones, microscopic pollen, and the composition of the soil have been able to posit social hierarchies, trade relationships, patterns of settlement, daily diet, religious beliefs, and a great deal more. All of this comes only from the material remains; the Mound Builders left no written accounts of their lives.

Archaeologists may combine the analysis of material life with information taken from contemporary populations, a form of study known as *ethnoarchaeology*. Comparing the past (as seen in a material record) to the present (understood through the ethnographic methods described below) provides information about cultural change even when no written records of the past exist. Similarly, archaeologists have used artifacts to gain information about contemporary populations that is not easily accessible through ethnographic or other interactive methods.

One famous project by William Rathje involved the study of garbage in the midsized Arizona city of Tucson.[3] Rathje and his team gained permission to go through the city's garbage, comparing what they found with what people said about their own patterns of consumption and disposal in surveys and interviews. Due to the preservative qualities of landfills, they were even able to go back decades, finding perfectly preserved papers from the 1950s and earlier. What they learned was that surveys—like the people who answer them—are not always as reliable as the archaeological record. When asked how much beer they drank per week, or how much food they threw away, respondents often gave answers that differed greatly from the material data. Rathje disseminates his findings in scholarly venues for archaeologists, and also writes for the public in ways that heighten people's awareness of their consumption and disposal habits. Archaeology is a nonreactive measure of human behavior, meaning it does not cause subjects to change behavior in response to the research. Thus, archaeology provides another means of understanding culture that is an important part of the discipline.

Linguistics

A second subfield of anthropology, *linguistics*, involves the study of language. In some universities, it remains a distinct field of study, particularly where language is studied primarily as a system of sounds and rules. Where language is studied primarily in relation to its use within larger cultural and social systems, it is known as sociolinguistics and is integrated with the study of cultural anthropology. William Leap is a sociolinguist who studied how language was used by both teachers and students in schools on the Ute Reservation in Utah. Conflicts between standard English-speaking teachers and students who spoke both Ute and a Ute-specific dialect of English could be understood and sometimes resolved by highlighting the power dynamics present in both verbal and nonverbal language.[4]

Many Christians have heard of linguistics through the work of Wycliffe Bible Translators and its academic sister organization, SIL International, formerly known as the Summer Institute of Linguistics. Wycliffe and SIL International deploy hundreds of linguists and anthropologists to translate the Bible into the thousands of languages around the world. Some do technical linguistic analysis, creating systems of writing and codifying the grammar of oral languages. Others engage directly with sociolinguistics, working out

3. William Rathje, *Rubbish! The Archaeology of Garbage* (New York: Harper Collins, 1992).

4. William Leap, *American Indian English* (Salt Lake City: University of Utah Press, 1993).

Christianity, Science, and Evolution: Francis Collins and the Human Genome Project

Francis S. Collins (b. 1950) was professor of internal medicine and human genetics when he was appointed to lead the Human Genome Project in 1993. This multibillion-dollar project brought together the world's top scientists to map the human genome. With the potential to discover genetic causes and cures for hundreds of genetically rooted diseases, it was an enormous honor and a testimony to the high stature Collins had among his peers.

Collins committed his life to Christ after earning a PhD in chemistry from Yale and an MD from the University of North Carolina. Although his work as a geneticist was built on the theory of evolution and genetic relatedness, Collins never felt there was a conflict between his work as a scientist and his Christian faith. In 2006 he published *The Language of God: A Scientist*

Presents Evidence for Belief, in which he proposed the idea of BioLogos, arguing that all natural processes, including evolution, are an expression of God's character and will.[1]

Collins has become a very public witness for faith in the scientific community, although biblical scholars hold various opinions about his theology. Bringing the Human Genome Project to completion ahead of schedule and under budget, Collins resigned his leadership in 2008. In 2009, he was appointed as the head of the National Institutes of Health (NIH), where he oversees a multibillion-dollar research budget and serves in one of the most strategic scientific organizations in the world.

1. Francis Collins, *The Language of God: A Scientist Presents Evidence for Belief* (New York: The Free Press, 2006).

---

the proper metaphors, concepts, images, and poetics of the target language in order to faithfully translate Hebrew and Greek Scriptures into a new linguistic context.

Today sociolinguistics is often considered a part of cultural anthropology, since both subfields focus on the study of meaning and culture. Linguistics, and anthropological approaches to language in general, are significant for the study of culture and society. We devote an entire chapter to it (see chap. 3).

Physical/biological anthropology

Physical or *biological anthropology* involves the study of human anatomy, nonhuman primates (*primatology*), and human origins. Physical anthropology as connected to archaeology, linguistics, and cultural anthropology illuminates how the study of physical qualities relates to the ways humans organize social life. Physical anthropologists often employ their expertise in medical schools, teaching courses in gross anatomy and embryology. Physical anthropologists may apply their work to medical care, using comparisons of human growth patterns to understand nutrition and physical variation within a community and to otherwise aid medical practitioners in providing good care.[5] Forensic anthropology is a rapidly growing applied branch of physical

5. For an example of this application of physical anthropology to medical and cultural concerns and nutrition, see Katherine Dettwyler, *Dancing Skeletons: Life and Death in West Africa* (Long Grove, IL: Waveland Press, 1993).

anthropology in which anthropologists interpret human remains, usually for legal purposes. Clea Koff is a forensic anthropologist who exhumed remains from sites of mass killings in Rwanda and the former Yugoslavia.[6] Her work contributed to legal processes and to healing for survivors who were finally able to identify the deceased.

Physical anthropology is, for many Christians, the most controversial subfield of anthropology. For Christians, Jews, Muslims, and other religious people who believe God created the world, the scientific study of human origins often raises difficult issues. For many Christians, their interpretation of Genesis precludes the idea that humans are descended from other life-forms. Others point to Romans 5:12, where Paul speaks of sin entering the world through "one man," meaning Adam must have been created separately from other animals. Even the idea of God selecting preexisting hominids in order to create God's image in them strikes many Christians as incompatible with scriptural accounts.

Other Christians believe that Genesis teaches theological truth but that it does not provide scientific or historical accounts of creation. These Christians, including biblical scholars and theologians, as well as scientists and other scholars, believe the questions addressed by evolutionary theory are distinct from those answered by Genesis.[7] Today some Christians find their calling by working in areas of physical anthropology and primatology. They feel they can accept the mechanism of evolution as God's means of creating the world without compromising the authority of Scripture.

Understanding the relationship of creation to human development involves many fields of study, including theology, biblical exegesis, hermeneutics, geology, cosmology, genetics, and paleontology, as well as anthropology. Many excellent treatments of these issues from a variety of perspectives can address specific questions in much more depth than we can undertake here.[8] For this book, with a focus on cultural anthropology, it is not necessary to settle these questions in order to understand how physical/biological anthropology fits within anthropology generally. Nor should questions about evolutionary theory be an insurmountable barrier for Christians to fully engage the discipline of cultural anthropology.

Cultural anthropology

The fourth subfield, and the focus of this text, is cultural anthropology. Many people in the United States have never heard of anthropology or have

---

6. Clea Koff, *The Bone Woman: A Forensic Anthropologist's Search for Truth in the Mass Graves of Rwanda, Bosnia, Croatia and Kosovo* (New York: Random House, 2005).

7. See Dorothy Chappell and David E. Cook, *Not Just Science: Questions Where Christian Faith and Natural Science Intersect* (Grand Rapids: Zondervan, 2005).

8. See, for instance, ibid.

only a vague notion of what it is. However, most of the topics and methods of cultural anthropology are ones that people find immediately interesting and may have encountered in other ways.

Cultural anthropology began from eighteenth- and nineteenth-century reports from missionaries and colonialists about the unfamiliar people and customs they encountered in their travels. Studying anthropology, even today, remains a form of scholarly travel through which people encounter the lives of others. Anyone who enjoyed reading about people around the world in high school social studies, or dreamed of traveling to faraway places in order to learn about how people live, has taken a step toward cultural anthropology.

Several disciplines involve detailed understandings of social organization and cultural difference, of course, including history, geography, and sociology. While the differences between those disciplines and anthropology will become clearer throughout the text (see below for a contrast between cultural anthropology and sociology), one of the most distinctive features of cultural anthropology is the primary method anthropologists use in their research: ethnographic fieldwork.

Ethnography and Fieldwork

Ethnography [*ethno* = people, *graphy* = writing] refers to both the activity and the product of cultural anthropology. Cultural anthropologists engage in ethnography by studying multiple aspects of life in a particular place or among a group of people to create a picture of how those people understand and live in the world. Anthropologists write up their research in accounts called *ethnographies*, rich descriptions and analyses that include the anthropologists' experiences of "being there." It is often said that "being there" is the ethnographic standard for legitimate anthropological knowledge.

When Elliot Liebow was preparing for fieldwork among urban African Americans in the United States, his supervisor said, "Go out there and make like an anthropologist." Anthropologists have made a career out of hanging out. In fact, ethnographic research consists of living in a way that allows the anthropologist to become as integrated into daily life as possible. Even when fieldwork appears to be just hanging out, as Liebow did for months on Washington, D.C., street corners, the anthropologist is always purposeful, observing and participating with care and taking notes (either on the spot or later) that will be used for analysis.[9]

Emerging in the early twentieth century, the importance of long-term fieldwork reflected the belief that understanding complex social and cultural life

9. Elliot Liebow, *Tally's Corner: A Study of Negro Streetcorner Men,* 2nd ed. (New York: Rowman & Littlefield, 2003).

necessarily involves observing and interacting with people as they go about their daily lives, and that this goal takes a long time to reach. Anthropologists often spend one to two years in the field, sometimes making repeated field trips over the course of their careers to correct errors, observe changes over time, and pursue new areas of interest. Unlike earlier scholars who relied on secondhand information or direct interviews with individuals outside their own social context (see chap. 2), anthropologists became committed to the notion that research on culturally identifiable groups required that the anthropologist learn the languages and customs of people he or she wished to understand and spend significant time observing daily life as well as events of special social significance.

Participant observation is the primary method associated with ethnographic research. Picture a continuum with full participation at one end and detached observation at the other. *Participant observation* involves moving around on the continuum throughout fieldwork; it is an approach to research that combines participation and observation in various ways to optimize understanding of the culture being studied. Standing back and taking a good look around is often the way an anthropologist begins, and detached observation yields good insight. But simultaneously and self-consciously, the anthropologist moves toward participation.

For me (Jenell), participant observation meant living, worshiping, socializing, and even holding my wedding in a low-income African American neighborhood of Washington, D.C. At times, I stood back and observed—for instance, at a heated meeting of community activists when I didn't yet understand the issues at hand. At other times I fully participated—having my say at community meetings, hosting community gatherings at my home, and joining a local church. Though people knew I was doing research, as I engaged in the daily activities of life, they came to trust and understand me even as I understood them.

In my research on congregations in the Philippines, I (Brian) spent eighteen months participating in three congregations.[10] Having graduated from a seminary and being in a place where relatively few people were able to earn such advanced degrees, I was frequently invited to preach and lead Bible studies in congregations. Participating in this way gave me a role and position that people could understand more easily than "anthropologist." More importantly, sharing my faith and contributing to Christian life in these ways created *rapport*, a relationship of conversational ease with individuals and groups. For all of us, good rapport allowed us to talk more honestly and intimately about our lives and perspectives on issues of culture, faith, community, and context.

10. See Brian Howell, *Christianity in the Local Context: Southern Baptists in the Philippines* (New York: Palgrave Macmillan, 2008).

For some anthropologists, participant observation may take the form of holding a job in the organization being studied, taking on an official leadership position, or even adopting a role that makes them appear to be a typical member of the community. Adopting multiple roles can be difficult since anthropologists in the United States embrace the American Anthropological Association's code of ethics, which does not allow researchers to misrepresent themselves or trick people into participating in research.[11] Yet even when anthropologists are forthcoming about their identity and research interests, it is still possible for them to become part of a community and for people to get used to the presence of an outsider. In some cases, particularly when anthropologists do not stand out in some obvious way, they can become insiders of a sort. They can occupy a place in the daily routines of life in the community they have come to study. It is through these everyday interactions that anthropologists gain insights into culture and social life.

Within the general method of participant observation, anthropologists employ a variety of techniques for obtaining information and increasing their understanding. *Ethnographic interviews* involve purposeful, documented conversation with research participants. They may be formal, including recording an interview based on a list of questions, or very informal, with questions generated on the spot and note-taking done later. Anthropologists may conduct *focus groups*, a type of interview in which small groups of people are asked to discuss a particular topic while the anthropologist takes notes. Other methods that complement participant observation include *mapping* (diagramming geographical space or human interpretation and use of space), recording a *life history* (an interview or series of interviews that document the trajectory of a single life), and conducting a *survey* (a standardized set of questions applied to numerous individuals or places).

These methods, as well as participant observation, are increasingly used in short-term research projects. Long-term fieldwork requires great personal and financial commitment, and many researchers wish to glean as much benefit as possible from ethnography even when they don't have time or funding for years in the field. A recent development in research methodology that makes the benefits of the anthropological approach more accessible to more people is *rapid ethnographic assessment procedures* (REAP), or the time-compressed use of focus groups, ethnographic interviews, mapping, and other methods within a framework of participant observation. REAP projects can occur over a period of weeks, days, or even hours. REAP researchers must always account for ways in which the short-term nature of the research limits the validity of findings, as well as ways in which ethnographic methods enhance

11. The American Anthropological Association's code of ethics can be found at www.aaanet.org/issues/policy-advocacy/Code-of-Ethics.cfm.

Anthropologist Michael Jindra (in baseball cap) discussing "death celebrations" with a group of village elders in Njindom, Cameroon.
Photo: Michael Jindrz

their findings beyond what a simple questionnaire or detached observation could yield.

Participant observation and its related methods highlight the extent to which cultural anthropology focuses on small-scale cases—villages, clubs, neighborhoods, congregations, families. The anthropologist draws on many aspects of life to create a holistic understanding of the situation. A *holistic understanding* assumes that all parts of human life—from birthing practices to the economy to warfare to art—are interconnected. From that very local and specific perspective, the anthropologist then discusses how the processes, features, and particularities of the case reveal something about human life more generally.

The Anthropological Perspective

Anthropologists believe that culture is a part of everything human beings do and think, often in ways hidden from those immersed in it. The anthropological perspective, as we stated earlier, refers to the attempt by the anthropologist to explain a cultural context from the *inside*, understanding the motives, actions, and beliefs of others in their own terms. This does not mean anthropologists are trying to become different kinds of people, to "*go native*" and be completely submerged in a new culture. Rather, it means they learn the context and culture to the point that they can explain how the people of a particular culture or context understand the world, and how diverse aspects of their lives come together. The methodology of long-term fieldwork is designed to allow the anthropologist to understand this complexity by spending enough time among a people to not only observe what they do but to understand why they do it. The central concept of culture (defined in detail in the next chapter) connects every aspect of human life, from the way people raise children, to how they dress, to how they classify the colors they see. Rather than isolating particular features of social life, such as political institutions or economic decision making, anthropologists seek to understand how these interrelated aspects of life function in shaping how people live; how those people *think* about those features; how they relate to the other aspects of human life found in community. Margaret Mead (1901–78), an anthropologist who became a major public figure of the twentieth century, once said, "The world is my field—it's all anthropology."[12]

It is in understanding those different from ourselves—the *Cultural Other*—that cultural anthropologists believe we can best understand ourselves. When we realize that many things we take for granted other people construe quite differently—such as what makes a person beautiful, or how many colors there are—we can more easily examine our own culture. Christians, in particular, may find this helpful as we explore our own cultural assumptions that may help or hinder a faithful walk with Christ.

Anthropology and Sociology

Because cultural anthropology draws together history, economics, politics, religion, family, and psychology to understand people's social and cultural lives, it overlaps with several disciplines, but none more than sociology. The simple answer to the question, "What's the difference between sociology and anthropology?" is that historically, sociologists have focused mainly on Western societies and used *quantitative research methods*: that is, measurement-based approaches that rely on mathematics, statistics, and hypotheses for producing and interpreting data. Anthropologists more often turned to small communities outside the West and used qualitative methods to develop holistic portraits of cultural life. *Qualitative research methods* are interpretive approaches that use participant observation, interviews, document analysis, and other methods to understand the nature and meaning of phenomena. In the contemporary world, many sociologists and anthropologists use mixed-method approaches that strategically rely on both quantitative and qualitative methods to best explore a research question.

Sociology and anthropology have a number of other distinctive features as well. Anthropologists are more likely to study cross-culturally than sociologists. Even when studying their own culture, anthropologists compare their findings cross-culturally and employ concepts built from the ongoing comparison of cultural differences. Anthropologists are more committed to the

12. Winthrop Sargeant, "It's All Anthropology," *New Yorker*, December 30, 1961, 31.

use of culture as a central concept to any analysis, while sociologists are more likely to use society and institutions (see chaps. 2 and 4) as the key organizing ideas. Christians can rely on anthropology more to understand mission and the relationship between gospel and culture, at home and abroad. Sociology proves more useful for Christians seeking a big-picture view of religion and social life on a national or regional scale.

In U.S. universities and colleges, sociology and anthropology are sometimes blended in an academic department, or sociologists may teach an introductory class in cultural anthropology. Because both disciplines explore social life, cultural diversity, and group behavior, this compatibility makes good sense. Historically, the two disciplines come from some of the same philosophers and social theorists who began thinking about rapid changes in European life in the eighteenth century and the increasingly apparent differences found among people around the world (see chap. 11).

In the end, what makes anthropology distinct from all social sciences is anthropology's focus on the Other. As historian of anthropology William Y. Adams has written, "After more than a century of existence, anthropology has only just begun to understand its proper role among the social sciences. It is, we now recognize, the systematic study of the Other, whereas all of the other social disciplines are, in one sense or another, studies of the Self."[13]

Anthropology and the Christian Witness

In the first one hundred years of the discipline, anthropologists and Christians not only worked well together; they were often one and the same. Early anthropologists such as Maurice Leenhardt (1878–1945) conducted anthropological research in conjunction with missionary work.[14] After spending twenty-four years in New Caledonia as a Protestant missionary, Leenhardt took over the prestigious chair in social anthropology at the Ecole Practique des Hautes Etudes, a leading French university, where he taught what he had learned during his missionary travels. Later missionary anthropologists and linguists made significant contributions to the discipline from work that flowed directly from their Christian work in Bible translation and evangelism, even establishing scholarly journals such as *Anthropos* and *Missiology* (formerly known as *Practical Anthropology*) with the express purpose of bringing together anthropology and missiology.

The relationship between Christianity and anthropology has not always been smooth and harmonious. Anthropologists working in various parts of

13. William Y. Adams, *The Philosophical Roots of Anthropology* (Stanford, CA: CSLI Publications, 1998), 1.

14. See James Clifford, *Person and Myth: Maurice Leenhardt in the Melanesian World* (Durham, NC: Duke University Press, 1992).

the world have documented both the inadvertent and conscious cooperation of missionaries with colonial rulers, in which mission work became part of a "civilizing" and subjugating process. Christians, including Christian anthropologists, have pointed out secular assumptions often implicit in anthropological work that seem to make religious belief incompatible with anthropological research and theory. There may be some necessary tension between Christianity and anthropology, but we believe it can be a generative, creative tension for people of either group, and even more so for individuals like us who belong to both groups. Christians are often uncomfortable with anthropology for a variety of reasons. Some Christians' discomfort has centered on the issue of human origins and evolution. For others it comes from the particular kind of relativism espoused by some anthropologists that denies the truth of Scripture (for more on different kinds of relativism, see chap. 2). But at the same time, Christians have successfully integrated the study of anthropology into their colleges, universities, seminaries, and missions training programs. Wheaton College was one of the first liberal arts colleges of any kind to have a cultural anthropology major. Biola University has established a master's degree program in cultural anthropology. Many other educational institutions use anthropology to teach cross-cultural understanding, mission, intercultural studies, or just anthropology in and of itself.

Anthropology and Missions

Missionaries often engage in multiple tasks simultaneously. In addition to serving in pastoral positions, they may have medical duties, educational work, economic development projects, and more. In order to be effective, they must understand how to communicate and live effectively in the culture. Anthropology is often an important part of that understanding. First, many missionaries spend time studying the anthropological research on a particular group or place before they go. They learn not only about history, customs, traditions, beliefs, and values, but they also are able to read about daily life, community dynamics, and processes of change that will be critical in introducing the gospel or strengthening the church.

Second, missionaries often study anthropological theory and method so they will be equipped to study the context personally. No matter how well-researched a particular place or people may be, cultural change and local specificity make it imperative that missionaries are equipped to do their own anthropological research. A number of the largest North American seminaries have one or more anthropologists teaching in their mission education programs. Missionaries can become expert ethnographers, using participant observation, ethnographic interviews, surveys, and other research techniques to learn about another culture. They apply their research to their mission work and sometimes also publish it in anthropology journals. In this way, Christian anthropologists are actively involved in helping missionaries become more effective in their calling.

Anthropologists have long been involved in missionary organizations such as Wycliffe Bible Translators and SIL International (formerly known as the Summer Institute of Linguistics), the Christian and Missionary Alliance church network, and many others. Some of the earliest missionaries took anthropological research to heart in thinking about how the new converts in the places they worked could become Christians while maintaining their own cultural identities. This notion, which has come to be called "contextualization" or "indigenization," grew out of the interaction of anthropology and missiology as Christians throughout the world understood how effective communication and practice of the Christian faith relies on cultural understanding (see chap. 12).

Many Christians going into anthropology find themselves having to defend or correct the views some anthropologists have about missionaries. In some cases anthropologists have encountered missionaries who lack sensitivity to culture and work in ways that ignore or denigrate cultural differences. Other anthropologists have formed opinions of missionaries based on stereotypes and rumors. Certainly, for anthropologists who are not Christians, the idea of missionaries working to change the religious commitments of non-Christians can be seen as "destroying culture."

Missionaries themselves often acutely experience the creative tension between anthropology and Christianity. Some missionaries have had experiences with anthropologists who provide negative examples of the discipline. For missionaries, who often work alongside local Christian leaders for better health care, political rights, and human dignity, the commitments of some anthropologists to "leave people alone" can be seen as a despicable lack of concern for real human needs.

Despite these difficult conflicts, however, anthropology has made profound contributions to mission work, and many missionaries find that the tensions produce a sharpened ability to explain the Christian faith, to live peaceably with those of other faiths or no faith, and to acknowledge the failures and mistakes Christians have made. As the church grows and develops outside European and North American contexts, the need for cross-cultural understanding on the part of Christians will only continue to grow.

Christians and Basic Research in Anthropology

Many Christians come to anthropology with interests other than mission and participate in the discipline as scholars, professors, and applied scientists. Christian anthropologists have become world-renowned experts in areas of

Participant observation circa 1970—Agta man trying to teach Thomas Headland how to hunt with bow and arrow, here showing the ethnographer how to lie in wait in a tree to ambush passing deer. No game shot that day!
Photo: Thomas Headland

anthropological research that seem far from explicitly Christian concerns. Thomas Headland, an ecological anthropologist trained at the University of Hawaii and affiliated with SIL International for many years, conducted research on people living in the forests of the Philippines that became central to understanding the forest ecosystem and human life for ecological anthropologists everywhere.[15]

Dean Arnold, who studied at the University of Illinois and taught at Pennsylvania State University prior to teaching at Wheaton College, conducted research on potters and cultural change among Yucatec Mayan communities in Mexico. He published his research in 1986 in a book with Cambridge University Press that became a key text for archaeologists and cultural anthropologists working with economic change and social life among indigenous people of Latin America.[16]

Our own research on such topics as race, global Christianity, and anthropological theory has been published with secular publishers and journals, speaking to larger anthropological discussions.[17]

Christians in anthropology have published work on everything from craft production among the ancient Mesoamerican people of Tarasco to the lives

15. Thomas Headland and John Early, *Population Dynamics of a Philippine Rainforest People: The Ildefonso Agta* (Gainesville, FL: University of Florida Press, 1998).

16. Dean Arnold, *Ceramic Theory and Cultural Process* (New York: Cambridge University Press, 1988).

17. See, for example, Brian M. Howell, "The Repugnant Cultural Other Speaks Back: Christianity as Ethnographic Standpoint," *Anthropological Theory* 7, no. 4 (2007): 371–91. Also Jenell Williams Paris, "'We've seen this coming:' Resident Activists Shaping Redevelopment in Washington, D.C.," *Transforming Anthropology* 10, no. 1 (2001): 28–38.

Dean Arnold studying clay used in the production of pottery among Mayan potters in the Yucatan in 2007. Photo: Dean Arnold

of market women in contemporary India. Like all scientific research, however, the importance of this knowledge is not always obvious in its immediate application to social problems.[18] Similar to the work Christians do in chemistry, biology, history, or literature, this research becomes the foundation on which future scholars build.

Anthropology and the Global Church

As Christians, we are practicing a faith born in an ancient Middle Eastern context, first preached in a language (Aramaic) we do not speak, originally recorded in yet a different language (Koine Greek), developed among a multicultural religious minority in a now-extinct empire, passed through multiple European, African, and Asian cultures over thousands of years, and finally interpreted among the technological complexity of the twenty-first century. In other words, simply being a Christian is a cross-cultural experience.

18. See Amy Hirshman, "Tarascan Ceramic Production and Implications for Ceramic Distribution," *Ancient Mesoamerica* 19, no. 2 (2008): 299–310. Also Eloise Hiebert Meneses, *Love and Revolutions: Market Women and Social Change in India* (Lanham, MD: University Press of America, 2007).

Traditional ritual ceremonies, called *kanyaw*, are seldom practiced nowadays. Due to economic and religious changes, most Ikalahan host Christian prayer services, or *gimong*, which continue many of the elements of kanyaw ceremonies, such as providing food for the whole community.
Photos: Katrina Friesen

This truth is amplified by the cultural diversity of the global church today. Christians worship in thousands of different languages, use myriad instruments and musical forms, and pray in ways that can seem strange to their Christian brothers and sisters in other places. This diversity is a gift and part of God's plan for the church, but it poses challenges for being unified (as Jesus prayed in John 17:21).

The movement of God around the world is reason for Christians everywhere to rejoice, but without the ability to relate with one another, we may become suspicious and isolated. It is all too easy to misinterpret unfamiliar practices of other Christians and to assume they are unbiblical. Christian house blessings in the Philippines, for example, in which the blood of a sacrificed pig is painted above the door, initially may appear to some Christians outside this context to be syncretic remnants of a pre-Christian past.

From such a perspective, it would be easy to think these practices will pass away as people become "mature" Christians, or even that such ceremonies reflect a lack of understanding of Christian theology. In fact, among the Ikalahan, these ceremonies are revivals of traditions that have not been practiced for decades. They reflect the desires of some younger Ikalahan, including many with theological training, to reconnect with their culture while strengthening their Christian identity. While Christians everywhere (including U.S. Christians) do things that are not in line with Scripture, without a clear understanding of why differences exist, what they mean, where they came from, and how they fit with other parts of culture, we risk misunderstanding and unnecessary division. Anthropology develops the abilities to ask the right questions, observe more critically, and think more deeply about the differences and similarities we will encounter as the church continues to grow and diversify.

Terms

anthropological perspective: the approach to social research that seeks to understand culture from the point of view of the people *within* that cultural context.

anthropology: the holistic study of humankind.

applied anthropology: branch of anthropology in which practitioners use anthropology in the service of particular social concerns.

archaeology: the study of material artifacts to understand a people's culture and society, usually in the past.

cultural anthropology: the description, interpretation, and analysis of similarities and differences in human cultures.

Cultural Other: a term used to refer to the subjective experience of difference at the cultural level; identifying "us/me" and "them/you" through cultural symbols and markers.

ethnoarchaeology: an approach to archaeology that combines the analysis of material life with information taken from contemporary populations.

ethnographic fieldwork: anthropology's hallmark research method, based upon the anthropologist's direct experience in a culture.

ethnographic interviews: purposeful, documented conversation with research participants that may be formal or informal.

ethnography: a rich description and analysis of a culture that includes the anthropologist's experience of "being there."

excavation: a rigorous method of extracting artifacts from underground; the primary data collection method of archaeologists.

focus groups: a type of interview in which small groups of people are asked to discuss a particular topic while the anthropologist takes notes.

"go native": an expression referring to a phenomenon in which an anthropologist fully affiliates with the culture being studied.

holistic understanding: the view that all parts of human life—from birthing practices to the economy to warfare to art—are interconnected.

life history: an interview or series of interviews that document the trajectory of a single life.

linguistics: the subfield of anthropology devoted to the study of language.

mapping: diagramming geographical space or human interpretation and use of space.

Mound Builders: a Native American group known for their burial mounds.

participant observation: an approach to research that combines participation and observation in various ways to optimize understanding of the culture being studied.

physical (or *biological*) *anthropology*: the study of human anatomy, nonhuman primates (primatology), and human origins.

primatology: the study of nonhuman primates.

qualitative research methods: interpretive approaches that use participant observation, interviews, document analysis, and other methods to understand the nature and meaning of phenomena.

quantitative research methods: measurement-based approaches that rely on mathematics, statistics, and hypotheses for producing and interpreting data.

rapid ethnographic assessment procedures (*REAP*): the time-compressed use of focus groups, ethnographic interviews, mapping, and other methods within a framework of participant observation.

rapport: a relationship of conversational ease with individuals and groups.

survey: a standardized set of questions applied to numerous individuals or places.

Devotion 1

Jesus the Participant Observer

Jesus went through all the towns and villages, teaching in their synagogues, proclaiming the good news of the kingdom and healing every disease and sickness. When he saw the crowds, he had compassion on them, because they were harassed and helpless, like sheep without a shepherd. Then he said to his disciples, "The harvest is plentiful but the workers are few. Ask the Lord of the harvest, therefore, to send out workers into his harvest field." (Matt. 9:35–38)

The first time Matthew describes Jesus as being moved with compassion is after Jesus spent time traveling, teaching, and healing. Jesus's compassion was stirred when he *saw* the crowds. His love was not abstract or distant; Jesus lived among people, saw them, touched them, and loved them.

For Christian anthropologists, participant observation can be a spiritual practice. Anthropological research is never distant or detached. Like Jesus's ministry, anthropological research involves being close to people, speaking their language, eating their food, participating in their weddings and funerals, and caring about their concerns. In a sense, Jesus could even be described as God doing participant observation. In Jesus, God came to live among us and experience our lives as we do. Of course, just as the anthropologist retains elements of her or his own distinctive identity, so Jesus was still "Other" (divine), even as he shared fully in our humanity. Although an anthropologist never "incarnates" from one context to another, like Jesus, anyone can draw closer in understanding and love through participating as fully as possible in another's world. Jesus's life and ministry provides wonderful inspiration for anthropologists doing fieldwork.

Devotion 2

Fulfilling the Great Commission

Then the eleven disciples went to Galilee, to the mountain where Jesus had told them to go. When they saw him, they worshiped him; but some doubted. Then Jesus came to them and said, "All authority in heaven and on earth has been given to me. Therefore go and make disciples of all nations, baptizing them in the name of the Father and of the Son and of the Holy Spirit, and teaching them to obey everything I have commanded you. And surely I am with you always, to the very end of the age." (Matt. 28:16–20)

Jesus gave his disciples the monumental task of making disciples of all nations. They took up the challenge, spending the rest of their lives spreading the gospel. Jesus's message is meant for all other believers as well, and Christians today are as challenged by the Great Commission as the eleven men who heard it spoken by Jesus.

What Jesus did not mean was to go and make some disciples *in* each country (although such a thing is not contrary to the spirit of the passage). The word translated "nations" here (*ethnos*) refers to the culture of a people, an ethnic group. Jesus was calling his disciples, then and now, to help everyone understand how the gospel is meant to penetrate all our ways of thinking, living, acting, and relating. Jesus was calling his followers to make disciples of all *ethne*. The gospel must become intimately entwined with the ways we all live, even as it calls us to transformation.

Sharing Jesus's message with people of all *ethne* requires travel, language skills, and cross-cultural understanding. We must work hard to think with people in a different culture about what it would mean for them to become disciples of Jesus. Cultural anthropology helps us fulfill the Great Commission by preparing Christians to go to all *ethne* and speak and live effectively.

The Concept of Culture

After studying this chapter, you should be able to:

1. Define culture and describe its development within anthropology.
2. Distinguish between the three major types of ethnocentrism.
3. Evaluate common metaphors for culture.
4. Appreciate culture as a good part of God's creation.

Introduction

The term "culture" is used so often today, in phrases such as "multicultural-ism," "cultural diversity," and "the culture wars," that culture often seems like a real thing that exists as a taken-for-granted part of our world. Culture is an idea created to describe a reality that people experience, the behaviors and assumptions common to a group that distinguish one group from oth-ers. Scholars who would come to be called cultural or social anthropologists became more aware of the similarities and differences between these behav-iors, assumptions, and patterns, and realized that what seemed "natural" or simply "human" in one place was often different or even completely unknown in another. The idea of culture—and later, cultures—helps explain human similarities and differences.

The culture concept is both central and controversial in anthropology. It is an indispensable part of the discipline, but one that can cause confusion and disagreement. Whenever anyone—anthropologist or not—talks about culture, the question must be asked: What exactly are we talking about?

In this chapter, we first critique a common way of defining culture, the "ethnic fair" model. Then, we recount how anthropologists have defined culture over the course of the discipline's development. Next, we describe related concepts: cultural relativism and the varieties of ethnocentrism. Finally, we conclude with a look at contemporary definitions of culture and metaphors for culture. Throughout, we consider ways in which the culture concept can be beneficial for Christians.

The Ethnic Fair

Imagine you are invited to participate in an ethnic fair. Your ancestors come from the Philippines, so you decide to introduce the fairgoers to "Philippine culture." What do you put in your booth? You might start with the flag, hanging it prominently on the back of the booth. Then you may set out a CD player with traditional Philippine folk songs. Next, you put up a photo of a Philippine landscape, perhaps something tropical, maybe rice fields or a coastal fishing scene. Of course, you'd also want a picture of the distinctive Philippine *jeepney*, the common mode of transportation throughout the islands. Some lists of facts—population, the number of islands (more than seven thousand!), and a few historical notes—might appear. Finally, you'd display some food, probably *lumpia*, the fried Filipino egg roll that people everywhere find delicious.

Now what if you're asked to represent the United States? No problem; just set out McDonald's hamburgers instead of *lumpia* and play country music instead of folk songs. But what about jazz? Or bluegrass? Or hip-hop? Those are all distinctively U.S. musical genres too. And if you're going to show scenery, do you choose the Grand Canyon or the Appalachian Mountains? New York City or rural Iowa? Which foods, music, or landscapes really represent "U.S. culture"?

When people think about their own "culture," they often become aware of the differences between regions and individual experiences that make generalizations difficult. You may be a vegetarian who listens to indie British rock and have no interest in the Grand Canyon or New York City. Does that make you less of a U.S. American? What is real "U.S. culture"?

The same issues arise with Philippine culture. The millions of Philippine citizens who live in the high mountains of the north do not traditionally eat rice and fish, but sweet potato and wild deer. Many in the south are Muslims whose style of dance and art resembles that performed in Jakarta, Indonesia,

The colorful Philippine jeepney is an expression of cultural identity, even though many Filipinos own their own cars, ride bicycles, or take the bus to work.
Photo: Brian Howell

rather than Manila. Furthermore, millions of people living in the major cities are more comfortable at Starbucks than in a rice paddy behind a *carabao* (water buffalo). And every day, millions of Filipinos enjoy McDonald's hamburgers. So which is the true "Filipino culture"?

Ethnic fairs are enjoyable and educational to some extent, but this approach to culture has several problems. First, it implies that culture is primarily expressed through decorative material items like food, clothing, and holiday trinkets. With an ethnic fair display, it is difficult to convey how profoundly culture shapes all parts of life. Second, it leads us to think of culture as a fixed and bounded entity, one that can be easily judged as "authentic" or "inauthentic." For this reason, culture change is often seen as culture loss, particularly for so-called traditional people. This is not to say that change is always good, or that cultures are indefinable, but the notion of culture as a fixed entity within specific boundaries contradicts the anthropological view of culture as dynamic and fluid. Third, it implies that each individual belongs to only one culture, when in fact many people are bicultural or multicultural, blending cultural elements into their lives and families in various ways.

History of the Culture Concept

The English word "culture" comes from the German *Kultur*, meaning to develop or grow. It is the root of words such as "agriculture" and "horticulture." As a more abstract concept referring to the advance or growth of "spirit," "mind," or "civilization," it was present in Greek philosophy and resurfaced among German idealist philosophers such as Immanuel Kant, Georg Hegel, and Johann Herder in the eighteenth and nineteenth centuries. In spite of these early roots, however, contemporary anthropological notions of culture as the total way of life of a group of people did not emerge until the latter half of the nineteenth century.

Victorian-era British anthropologists began comparing reports from colonial administrators, explorers, and missionaries around the world to discern patterns of behavior and belief among disparate groups. (For more on these early anthropologists, see chap. 11.) These first anthropologists are now often called *armchair anthropologists* for their gathering of data from travelogues and books rather than from their own direct research. They were most interested in explaining why groups were so different from one another. Building on the biological theories of evolution advanced by Charles Darwin and others, these scholars assumed all societies moved from simple to complex forms in progressive evolutionary stages. They developed an idea of Culture as a singular capacity that all human beings possessed to greater and lesser degrees. These anthropologists did not talk about different cultures, only the differences in Culture, with a capital C. In this view, all cultural development followed a single path, or line, from simple to complex.

This view developed into the theory of *unilinear cultural evolution*, which stated that all cultures evolve from simple to complex along a single trajectory of progress. "Higher development" was manifested in social and political systems such as market economies or democracy, technological innovations such as metallurgy, and complex religious beliefs in which the highest form was no religion at all but a commitment to scientific atheism.[1] Not surprisingly, the northern European scientists who developed the theory defined northern Europeans as having progressed to having the "most Culture," while non-European people were seen as less evolved, living in a simpler, less civilized state.

For decades, European and U.S. anthropologists used Culture to classify societies as higher or lower on a scale of cultural development. This notion is not only repulsive to most people today but has been thoroughly discredited by anthropologists themselves. U.S. English does retain a remnant of this view, however. References to a person as "cultured"—meaning he or she has expensive, fancy, or rarified tastes ("We're going to take you to the opera and get you some culture!")—refers to this older idea that an individual can have more or less Culture than someone else.

Though it would ultimately lead to negative consequences for both Christians and anthropologists, many nineteenth-century Christians accepted the

---

1. See Edward Tylor, *Primitive Culture: Researches into the Development of Mythology, Philosophy, Religion, Language, Art, and Custom*, 2 vols. (1874; repr., Whitefish, MT: Kessinger Publishing, 2007).

theory of unilinear cultural evolution. For Christians, the unilinear theory was important because it contradicted the idea of *polygenesis*, the widely held nineteenth-century theory that different groups of humans appeared on earth or were created separately. In other words, the unilinear theory fit with the view that all humans originate from a single creation of God (*monogenesis*).

Although unilinear cultural evolution seemed to support the Christian belief in all humans originating from a single creation, it also supported *cultural superiority*, the idea that people of one culture are more enlightened, advanced, civilized, or intelligent than another and *racism*, the belief that humans are organized into race groupings that are different from one another in intelligence and worth. The question raised by the unilinear theory was why some groups remained at lower levels of development while others advanced. Linking with earlier theories of racial hierarchy, the unilinear theory seemed to provide scientific support for biological explanations of difference. Put simply, many argued that some races were inherently superior to others, seen in their higher levels of Culture. For decades, anthropologists and other scientists used race theories to explore supposed biological differences between culturally distinct groups. Proponents of slavery and discrimination, advocates for eugenics, and even the Nazis used these theories to support their views. Many Christians fought vigorously against such movements, yet often inadvertently advanced the idea that cultural differences should be ranked as higher and lower. Thus, for some Christians, to follow Christ also meant to adopt "advanced" Culture.

Fortunately, in the early twentieth century, even though some anthropologists still worked to bolster racial theories and the unilinear notion of culture, others began to critique it. Around the turn of the century, anthropologists moved out of their armchairs and began promoting ethnographic fieldwork as the best, if not the only, method for truly understanding different societies (see chap. 1). By immersing themselves in other cultures for long periods of time, anthropologists found that supposedly simple societies actually had complex social and cultural lives. Lacking systems of elections or political office, for instance, did not mean a lack of structure, power, or authority. Supposedly racially inferior people had complex organizational systems and cultural norms that took anthropologists years to understand—hardly strong support for racial inferiority or cultural simplicity. Such discoveries led anthropologists to advance the idea that differences between groups were not linked to biological predisposition. Cultural diversity, then, was not the manifestation of Culture at different stages of development, but evidence of fully developed cultures that had taken different paths based on particular historical and environmental contexts.

This new theory, which would come to be called *historical particularism*, argued that each culture is a unique representation of its history and context.

This theory discarded Culture in favor of cultures, and it supported research that looked at various cultural groups as complex and sophisticated adaptations to particular challenges. Over time, some anthropologists used materialist theories (often rooted in Marxist political economy) to explain contemporary cultures. Others focused more on psychological needs and pressures, linguistic constructs, or cognitive categories as the key to understanding how and why people in one place developed ways of thinking and living so different from people in another. (More detailed information on these theories can be found in chap. 11.)

Today, in light of globalization, communication technologies, and urbanization, anthropologists emphasize the importance of seeing cultures as complex, with permeable boundaries, instead of as isolated, bounded entities. At one time, anthropologists deliberately sought out seemingly bounded societies. Several of the first well-known anthropological studies were of groups living on islands in the South Pacific; each group seemed literally bounded, surrounded by ocean. It seemed very obvious where the limits of the "culture" existed. Even then, however, these boundaries were anthropological fictions, drawn according to features of language or identity the anthropologist saw as important. Connections existed even among seemingly separate cultures; for example, regional exchange systems linked island societies through regular interactions of economic interdependence. In later years, the constructed nature of these boundaries would become even clearer as members of these societies traveled and communicated in the global community. The "ethnic fair" assumptions about cultures as neatly bounded and highly homogeneous entities simply didn't withstand scrutiny.

In addition to the internal complexity of cultures, anthropologists now emphasize power dynamics: the ways in which differences in wealth and prestige (or access to wealth and prestige) shape the human experience. A village in the Yucatan might seem peaceful and serene, but even there, older men may dominate younger men and women; religious specialists may use their knowledge to control nonspecialists; those with charisma may exploit others not so gifted. Anthropologists employ postmodern theories of language and power to conceptualize culture as an arena where individuals and groups of individuals *within* a particular society advance their own interests.

This understanding of culture—as plural, porous, and power-laden—has led anthropologists to reevaluate the meaning of cultural differences. If there is no singular direction to "progress"—if cultures change in response to historical events, environmental issues, and power dynamics—cultural differences must be evaluated on their own terms. In other words, cultures can only be understood relative to the historical, ecological, and social context in which they developed. This is the foundational anthropological concept of cultural relativism.

Cultural Relativism

Cultural relativism is the view that cultural practices and beliefs are best understood in relation to their entire context. A symbol, belief, or behavior may make little sense or even be offensive when understood from an outsider's cultural perspective. When viewed holistically, in light of its own economic, historical, political, and religious contexts, what at first seemed nonsensical will appear sensible. Thus, culture is relative to context.

The idea of cultural relativism is one of the most important principles of cultural anthropology, but it is often misunderstood, particularly among Christians. The word "relativism" may raise worries about secular scholars attacking Christian truth claims, or any truth claims at all. Understood correctly, however, cultural relativism poses no conflict for Christians. Cultural relativism is not a value judgment but an empirical reality. That is, everywhere in the world people find ways to live in response to changing conditions. In fact, as we explain below, cultural relativism affirms deeply held Christian values and is an important aspect of life in the global church.

Cultural relativism does not imply that any particular belief is right or that a specific action is good simply because it is part of a culture. For example, I (Brian) recall a class in graduate school in which my professor was showing slides of the Kofyar, a people who raise grains in the high plateau of Nigeria. In one photo, a man was working alone, obviously struggling to lift the large sheaves of sorghum[2] into the high rack used for drying. As we stared at the anomalous photo, the professor remarked, "Oh yeah, this guy has to work alone. He's a Protestant." My curiosity was piqued about the connection between working alone and being a Protestant. I learned that these particular Protestants are Baptists who believe drinking alcohol of any kind is taboo for Christians. Of course, many Christians throughout the world affirm the same teaching. The problem for Kofyar Christians is that this belief sets them apart as inhospitable and isolated from community. Kofyar beer is a thick, carbohydrate-rich sorghum beer only available during the harvest season. Women prepare large vats of the rich brew to share with neighbors and relatives who come to help with the harvest. Beer provides both the energy to work all day and the festive atmosphere enjoyed by the community during the days of hard labor. Beer is a symbol of hospitality and community; all the men drink from a common vessel. Without an offering of this drink, the Protestants generally cannot get anyone to come help them with their harvest. As a result, they are seen as abandoning values of hospitality and community. They end up somewhat isolated, which puts them at a serious economic disadvantage.

2. Sorghum is a tall grain used as animal feed and in making beer and sorghum molasses for human consumption.

Understanding the relationship between beer and work does not imply that drinking beer is good or bad. In many places, alcohol consumption causes social problems; domestic abuse, alcoholism, and traffic fatalities are linked to beer consumption in many societies. In some of these places beer is as much a symbol of domineering masculinity—not conducive to family life—as it is a symbol of productive community. For these reasons (and others), some Christians may teach that drinking is prohibited.[3] What is missing in the Kofyar case, however, is an understanding of how beer ties into economic and social life. Without an understanding of what beer consumption means in economic and social terms, Christians may misunderstand the consequences giving up beer will have on important areas of life.

Cultural relativism is distinct from moral relativism or epistemological relativism. *Moral relativism* is the idea that something is only right or wrong according to context-specific criteria. This notion is incompatible with Christian faith and ethics, and also is virtually impossible to put into practice. Virtually all anthropologists, Christian or not, make moral judgments when they see human rights violations such as genocide or torture. If they are not Christian, they may rely on humanistic values—that is, principles common to most humans—or the ethical code of the American Anthropological Association to evaluate right or wrong in cross-cultural contexts. Few, however, would say everything is morally neutral.

Epistemological relativism is the belief that the validity of knowledge itself is limited to the context in which it was produced. This is the idea that some things are "true for you, but not true for me," or even "real for you, but not real for me." The epistemological relativist would argue that truth in the world of the Kofyar is different from, say, truth among suburban U.S. Americans. Though the Kofyar and the U.S. American may experience the world quite differently, the Christian theology of revelation—that God has revealed knowledge to everyone—says that reality is not merely a reflection of experience. The triune God and the world God made exist independent of human perception or perspective and we can know these things through revelation, perception, and reflection. Though our knowledge may always be partial, it is not relative.

Cultural relativism does not demand the acceptance of either moral or epistemological relativism. We can hold to Christian ethics and morality while still acknowledging that cultures can best be understood in relation to themselves. When cultural relativism is not practiced, people typically use the

3. Some Christian traditions point to biblical injunctions against drunkenness and to contemporary research on addiction in order to support a position against consuming alcohol of any kind. Others believe that only drunkenness is prohibited, while consumption is a matter of Christian freedom. See, for example, the Southern Baptist resolution on alcohol (www.sbc.net/resolutions/amResolution.asp?ID=1156); in contrast, see the Presbyterian (USA) statement (www.pcusa.org/101/101-alcohol.htm).

standards of their own culture to understand others, which invariably leads to misunderstandings rooted in ethnocentrism.

Varieties of Ethnocentrism

Ethnocentrism is the use of one's own culture to measure another's, putting one's own culture (*ethno*) at the center (*centrism*) of interpretation and typically devaluing the other culture. Ethnocentrism is inevitable because humans are socialized to see their way of life as normal, natural, and often superior. Nonetheless, it is important to identify ethnocentrism in ourselves and in the world and work toward reducing it.

Anthropologists may distinguish between three types of ethnocentrism: xenophobia, cultural superiority, and tacit ethnocentrism.

Xenophobia

Xenophobia is an intense, irrational dislike of people from other countries or cultures. Xenophobia is sometimes expressed in anti-immigrant views or even discrimination or violence against Cultural Others. The most pervasive expression of xenophobia in the world today is racism. As we noted before, racism is the belief that humans are organized into race groupings that are different from one another in intelligence and worth. Racism asserts the superiority of some people over others, as expressed by such U.S. groups as the Ku Klux Klan or the World Church of the Creator. Despite efforts against it, xenophobia continues to motivate massive harm around the world in expressions ranging from genocide to political oppression to hate crimes to verbal assault. Fortunately, many people around the world have become increasingly sensitive to this bigotry and speak out against it.

Cultural superiority

The second type of ethnocentrism, *cultural superiority*, is the belief that one culture is more enlightened, advanced, civilized, or intelligent than another. It is often expressed with patronizing comments such as, "Those people just don't know any better," or, "If we can teach these people how we live, then they can become as advanced as we are." Cultural superiority can be found all over the world; no society has a monopoly on cultural arrogance. Cultural superiority has devastating effects when a group of people has sufficient power and privilege to impose their ethnocentrism on other groups. For example, European colonial governments in North America, Africa, Asia, Australia, and elsewhere imposed their European educational systems and languages on indigenous people, suppressing many important cultural and subsistence practices. At times, this was motivated by xenophobia ("their ways are bad, wrong, immoral, or

Is the United States a "Christian Culture?"

It is not uncommon to hear someone refer to the United States as a "Christian nation." They might be thinking about the history of European settlers and the importance of Christianity to them. They might be thinking of the prominence of Christian symbols and phrases in public life. Or they may say that the United States has a "Christian culture." But can a culture be Christian?

First, it's important to note that to refer to the United States as "a culture" is to confuse national and cultural categories. As described earlier, the United States has a great deal of cultural diversity. But to the extent that there are widespread norms, shared understandings, and familiar symbols among many U.S. Americans, can't we say that, on the whole, the U.S. is a Christian culture?

We must keep in mind that to be a Christian is to follow Christ. A culture cannot choose to give its life to Christ. Only people can do that. Certainly a place where many people have lived as Christians for a long time has adopted more Christian symbolism in language, law, education, and other aspects of society than a place that doesn't; but this does not make the culture, as a whole, a follower of Jesus.

But isn't it true that the United States has a more Christian culture than, say, communist China? More non-Christians in the United States might be better informed about Christianity than non-Christians in China, but it is not true that an entire culture can be more Christian than another. Indeed, U.S. culture, for all its Christian history and symbolism, also values sexual freedom, individual autonomy, and materialism. Secular culture in China reflects values of social connectedness, family loyalty, and spirituality. So is China "more Christian" than the United States?

Some aspects of U.S. culture connect strongly to biblical teachings. For example, the individual autonomy prized in the United States resonates with the biblical call for people to abandon their lives to follow Christ. Those of us raised in the United States may find it easier to turn from the teachings of a non-Christian family or non-Christian friends for the sake of Christ. At the same time, the family loyalty of China may make it harder for some to leave the religion of their families, but it may also make it easier for Christians there to understand and practice the biblical metaphor of the church as family. Christians in *every* culture find themselves at odds with some things in their background, while other aspects of the same culture help them to live more faithfully with Christ.

immature") and at other times by paternalistic cultural superiority ("we need to teach everyone to live like we do, so they can be civilized too"). Either way, the result was the devastation of indigenous cultures worldwide.

Today most Christians reject these ethnocentric attitudes because they are in opposition to the gospel. Indeed, in the book of Acts, Paul opposed his own people's (Jews') ethnocentrism toward non-Jewish converts. Across time, God has empowered brave Christians who risked their lives to lead movements against racism and xenophobia in societies around the world. But even those opposed to xenophobia and cultural superiority may still harbor the third kind of ethnocentrism: tacit ethnocentrism.

Tacit ethnocentrism

Tacit ethnocentrism is the assumption that one's own way of life is just normal, not cultural. Tacit ethnocentrism is present, for example, when a person does not see anything particularly cultural about liking ice in a glass of water, or finding a mountain lake beautiful, or wanting a soft bed off the floor. He might understand that many people from India *don't* put ice in their water but easily assume it must be because they are poor and do not have ice-makers or have simply never experienced how wonderful cold water is. He may not hold it against them, but he might still think not wanting ice is different, interesting, and maybe a little weird. In a perspective shaped by tacit ethnocentrism, the curiosity is why they do not like ice, not why we do. One's own culture (*ethno*) takes center stage (*centrism*), and the other culture is understood in terms of how it is not like one's own.

As an example, consider camping. Many people in the United States find camping or other encounters with nature to be profound spiritual experiences. We Christians often find that nature stirs our souls to ponder our smallness in the face of God's grandeur. We may interpret these feelings as natural and human, as the testimony of creation pointing to the Creator (Job 12:7–11).

Such scenes may not produce these feelings at all, however, for people who actually live close to nature. They may know their lake intimately—how to spot wind or water currents, when and where fish congregate, the most likely spots for turtles' nests—and they may respect and cherish this resource, but they may not have anything like a soulful, spiritual response. They may also see the world as pointing to God as Creator, but in terms of how nature provides for human life rather than in sublime feelings of awe.

Similarly, people from urban subcultures in the United States often express frustration that some (usually from the dominant ethnic/racial group) insist that *everyone* should love camping—that everyone can "naturally" see God better in the woods; you just have to try. One urban African American student at a Christian college expressed it this way, "You know, in my neighborhood, people do not go camping. They say, 'I have a house. Why do I want to live in a little tent in the woods and have bugs crawling on me and eat in the dirt?' But my friends here say there's something wrong with me, that I just don't get it. I'm tired of people telling me that they're right and I'm wrong just because I don't see it that way."

This student did try camping, and in many ways he learned to enjoy it as his friends did. His frustration came from the fact that these friends did not see the differences as cultural but rather as a flaw in him. They seemed to believe that *everyone* should love to experience nature as they do; surely that is just natural—a God-given response to creation. Actually, a spiritual experience in nature is a culturally conditioned response. It is surely connected to something beyond culture—God and creation—but it is not the only, the best, or the "natural" response.

In addition to blinding us to our own culture, tacit ethnocentrism can take the form of someone saying, "I have no culture. I'm boring. I'm just a normal, average person." This might seem like a compliment to those deemed to *have* culture, but those who call themselves cultureless tacitly suggest that the ways they feel—their judgments, tastes, and reactions to the world—are just normal, human ones. "Others are different; I'm just normal." "Others are ethnic; I'm just me." The anthropological view of culture emphasizes that everyone is ethnic, because everyone is shaped by culture. Certainly biological responses are real; you touch a hot stove, you pull your hand back. But what do you say? "Ouch"? "Aahhh"? Or, if you're in the Philippines, "Aray!" Even an instantaneous, unthinking response such as this is cultured.

Imagining human beings without culture does not paint a picture of a "pure" human. Our ability to interact with the world through culture is the very thing that *makes* us human. Human beings in the garden, before the fall, had language and were living in a world filled with cultural meaning. Adam alone, without society, was declared "not good." God gave humans relationships, language, names, and an identity distinct from the rest of creation; this is culture, part of God's good creation. It is not the barrier to understanding God; it is the means through which God becomes known to us.

The problem is when one particular cultural expression (all of which are now tainted by the fall) is seen as normal, natural, and human, and anything different from it as substandard, aberrant, or sinful. Combating ethnocentrism is a place where anthropology and Christian values come together. Acknowledging how tacit ethnocentrism plays into our assumptions should humble us into acknowledging the strengths and limitations of our vantage point on God's world.

The Culture Concept Today

Culture is the total way of life of a group of people that is learned, adaptive, shared, and integrated. Each of these four characteristics—learned, adaptive, shared, and integrated—reflects important elements of the culture concept.

Learned

People learn culture from other people, usually by being raised in a culture or by extended exposure to a new one later in life. Affirming the learned aspect of culture allows anthropologists to focus on such things as the socialization of children, the production of knowledge, and culture change. Anthropologists agree that ethnographic data provide no support for the notion that cultural differences come from biological differences or predisposition. Brain studies suggest that our brains take shape, to some degree, in response to our social and physical environment, but at birth every brain is ready to learn any culture. Stereotypes such as "Japanese people are quiet" or "People in the United States smile a lot" may reflect widespread cultural norms, but there is no demonstrable link between particular cultural forms and the biology of the people who practice those forms.

Adaptive

People's ways of life are adapted to their environments. Language, values, and behaviors may be understood as related to their economic, political, geographical, and historical contexts. Sometimes journalistic reports of societies in the rain forests of the Amazon or Southeast Asia describe them as "living unchanged since the beginning of time." This is flat-out wrong; all cultures have changed and continue to change. Some of these changes are dramatic and rapid. Some are imposed by outsiders. But even people living relatively remote and independent lives experience culture change in response to problems and opportunities in their environment.

Shared

There is no such thing as individual culture. There is variation among individuals, but culture can never be private. You may wake up one morning and decide to throw off the oppressive structure of English, bursting out of your room declaring, "Amtanzafna! Moockano v Stinana!" If no one else shares this particular pattern, it cannot be called a language, which by definition is a form of communication. If no communication occurs, you just have random sounds. Unless others share your understanding of these symbols, they do not constitute a language or a culture.

Integrated

Any aspect of culture relates, in some way, to other parts of that culture. As demonstrated by the example of the Kofyar and their beer, some missionaries have thought that changing religion or giving up certain rituals, food, or drinks was a relatively simple thing. They have argued that in converting to Christianity, "culture" did not need to change, as long as these few key things changed. It is a mistake, however, to think that some aspects of culture can change without having unforeseen consequences on other aspects of culture.

It is important, when encouraging change in one's own culture or another, to recognize that change in one part of life will influence the whole.

Affirming the integrity of culture does not mean that any culture is perfectly or completely integrated. Within any culture, different individuals have different levels of knowledge and understanding, may agree or disagree with various aspects of their society, and may be working for or against change. Changes are often unpredictable and complex, unfolding over many years and among different subgroups.

Metaphors for Culture

People often use metaphors to describe culture and how we relate to it. Some metaphors are used by anthropologists, and others are popular with Christians or other groups in society. Though each has its strengths, each of the common metaphors for culture obscures an anthropological understanding.

Culture as the water in which we swim

In an effort to make the point that culture is pervasive, largely unconscious, and intrinsic to our very humanity, anthropologists have sometimes portrayed people as fish, constantly swimming in their culture. It goes with the old brainteaser, "Does a fish know it's wet?" This metaphor makes clear the important idea that culture is not a thing that we humans simply add on to our lives. Just as a fish needs water to survive and get around, so too human beings need culture.

The downside of this metaphor is that unlike fish, which cannot change water, humans can change their culture. For instance, fish cannot say, "With all these ships coming through, I think it would work better to change the chemical composition of water from H_2O to something less dense so these boats will sink. Let's try that out and see if it catches on." But human beings can devise ways of changing their culture. Thus, discussions of culture must include agency—how individuals and groups respond, adapt, and innovate within a cultural context resulting in intentional and unintentional changes to the culture itself.

Culture as the lenses through which we see the world

The idea that culture is like a set of glasses affecting how people see the world has been a favorite of missiologists for some very good reasons. Mission scholars and trainers want students to understand that cultures are not just different from one another but that cultural assumptions profoundly affect how we perceive the world.[4] Often coupled with the idea of worldview, this metaphor also highlights the pervasive nature of culture. If a man has trouble seeing (and this metaphor seems to assume universal astigmatism), he needs glasses to get around. Without any glasses at all, he's pretty limited. Culture is like that. Without culture, we don't see more clearly; we can't see much at all. However, we have to be aware that one set of "cultural glasses" is not the same prescription as others; thus one culture will have a different view from another.

The positive element of this metaphor is that it helps us become aware of our glasses and to consider what it would mean to view the world through someone else's glasses. We do not have to be "mono-glassical" (i.e., monocultural). Changing glasses is not easy, but it can be done. For anyone wanting to understand another, learning to see through that person's glasses seems to be a prerequisite to good communication.

This metaphor also contains several problems. First, it assumes that "American glasses" or "Korean glasses" will fit everyone of that description. We know there are more variations *within* contexts than this suggests, as well as variation over time. Second, the glasses image (and the idea of worldview) assumes culture exists inside someone's head before interacting with the material world. For example, in U.S. society, most people would recognize that cars are part of the culture. Owners often give them names and customize them, while the government builds neighborhoods and cities around the use of them. But did the United States come to value cars because of the idea or view of cars, or did a love of cars follow the development of cars themselves? The glasses metaphor does not capture well the dynamic interaction between the material world and our views or understandings of the world.

Last, the glasses metaphor limits discussion of power and change. When an optometrist makes a set of glasses, she cannot push a political, religious, or social agenda through the prescription. She is simply making the right glasses for her patient. The patient, for his part, can put them on or take them off as he chooses, without worrying about what the optometrist thinks or might do to him if he doesn't wear the glasses. Glasses are inert objects that do not change us; nor can we change them. They do not reflect the political, social, or economic interests of those making or wearing them. And it is hard to imagine glasses being affected by sin in the ways culture is.[5]

4. See, for example, Paul Hiebert, *Anthropological Insights for Missionaries* (Grand Rapids: Baker Books, 1986), 31; also Duane Elmer, *Cross-Cultural Conflict: Building Relationships for Effective Ministry* (Downers Grove, IL: InterVarsity, 1993), 12–20.

5. This is not to say that all those using the glasses metaphor (or any of the others) are endorsing these weaknesses or are unaware of the dynamics of culture we discuss here. By using the metaphor, however, they risk others misunderstanding the nature of culture as they employ the metaphor themselves.

Christ and culture

Perhaps more than any other theologian, H. Richard Niebuhr influenced the way Christians think about engaging culture with his categories: Christ against culture, Christ of culture, Christ above culture, Christ and culture in paradox, and Christ transforming culture.[6] This may not seem like a metaphor, but it is. By typologizing the different ways Christians have interacted with social institutions and cultural norms in various times and places, Niebuhr made both Christianity and culture seem more concrete. This has helped Christians become aware of how they and their traditions tend to approach culture—with a stance of appreciation, rejection, or control—and to understand why other Christians see the issues differently.

As helpful as his work has been, however, Niebuhr's metaphor conceptualizes Christianity and culture as separate, discrete entities, like balls on a pool table bouncing against each other in occasional interactions. In fact, Christianity is, by definition, the expression of the gospel in a cultural context. There is no such thing as a nonspecific, free-floating "Christianity," existing apart from a particular time or place in which it is expressed. While the risen Christ does exist beyond a particular cultural context, our understandings of him occur in concrete cultural terms. Thus, regardless of which strategy for engagement a Christian may choose, this metaphor of Christ and culture is misleading in that it encourages Christians to think of themselves as existing outside culture, with unencumbered choice as to how they interact with culture. Anthropologists emphasize that all people, and all religions, exist within cultures and are influenced by culture in ways they are often unable to perceive.

Other metaphors—culture as the rules of the game, culture as a map, culture as a many-layered onion with surface features and deep features (or maybe culture as a parfait, since not everyone likes onions), highlight some features of the culture concept. All of them, however, tend to omit these vital facts: cultures are internally diverse, always changing, and affected by power.

Culture as a Conversation

Our preferred metaphor is culture as a conversation. In real life, a conversation has many of the qualities anthropologists affirm as aspects of culture. For example, like culture, a conversation is shared. At the same time, a conversation is dynamic. In any conversation different individuals, from moment to moment, respond to power, intention, use, and context. This reflects the dynamism anthropologists understand as part of the culture

6. H. Richard Niebuhr, *Christ and Culture* (1951; repr., San Francisco: Harper San Francisco, 2001).

concept. Just as people might make up a new word in the course of a conversation ("Dude, that was a great speech! Total Ska-doosh!"), individuals can "play with" their culture to express something others understand in new ways. These innovations may or may not catch on, but they are always possible.

Body language, facial expression, tone of voice, and word choice are all critical aspects of communication. If you meet the president of the United States or the prime minister of Thailand, you are probably going to use different words (you might not say, "What up, Dawg?"), a different tone of voice, and even different body language than if you were speaking to your roommate. In any conversation, one person can subtly communicate superiority (a tone of voice, a patronizing hand on the shoulder) without saying it. It is not unusual to be put off by the way some people speak, even if what they say is not offensive. At the same time, all these choices—to be friendly, to convey superiority, to modify one's words to be more respectful, even to use certain language—are constrained by the meanings of words, grammar, symbols, and shared assumptions existing prior to the conversation. Individuals have freedom to shape the conversation, but this creativity is both enabled and limited by the context (i.e., culture) in which the conversation occurs.

The metaphor of culture as conversation captures the learned, adaptive, shared, and integrated aspects of the culture concept, while also allowing us to see how it is laden with power relationships and is open to individual creativity. In culture, as in conversation, there is improvisation and innovation. Individuals take what exists in order to accomplish or even imagine things they want to do, including innovative and novel things. People are limited by culture, in that they cannot do or even think absolutely anything. Yet culture is the medium that enables people to do what they want. As individuals interact through culture, they accomplish individual purposes through shared means. Understood this way, culture is not so much a *thing* that people *have* as it is an *activity* they *do*. Culture is a practice. Whether we're making conversation, pancakes, or a film, we are living within a culture while simultaneously making culture.

As Christians, then, we should not simply ignore the culture in which we find ourselves, as that invariably results in an unthinking acceptance of the status quo. Nor should we try to reject culture, becoming "just Christians" without any culture. God's truth is revealed to us through specific cultural forms. We then use our own cultural forms to understand that revelation. Sometimes we try to strip away the medium by which God communicates to us to get the "pure message" underneath. But God gave us different cultures so that we can understand God. The incarnation was God's statement that creation—culture, society, the human body—is a good thing that will be redeemed, not a necessary evil we must tolerate or repress until Christ comes again. Without culture, we have no language, no symbols, no revelation, and no community.

We are always Christians in particular times, places, and cultures. We were designed, from the beginning, to interact with God and each other through culture. As we do culture, we should be aware of the ways in which our particular culture falls short of reflecting God's character and priorities. As those creating culture all the time, we do have the ability to change and adapt our own cultures in positive ways. The reality that all cultural contexts are twisted by sin should make us even more determined to understand our own and others' cultures. With the anthropological perspective, we can understand the contours of our own (and others') cultures better, thus making us intentional about preserving or changing them.

In the book of Revelation, John provides a vision of the New Jerusalem, a city in which God rules over the diverse nations of the world, in which the kings bring their splendor before God (Rev. 21:24). Culture, and cultural diversity, will not be wiped away, but redeemed. This suggests that culture, in all its present diversity, is not a problem to be overcome but a blessing that will be present for eternity. It only makes sense that Christians would learn to understand it now.

Terms

armchair anthropologists: early anthropologists who gathered data from travelogues and books rather than from their own direct research.

cultural relativism: the view that cultural practices and beliefs are best understood in relation to their entire context.

cultural superiority: the belief that one culture is more enlightened, advanced, civilized, or intelligent than another.

culture: the total way of life of a group of people that is learned, adaptive, shared, and integrated.

epistemological relativism: the belief that the validity of knowledge itself is limited to the context in which it was produced.

ethnocentrism: the use of one's own culture to measure another's, putting one's own culture (*ethno*) at the center (*centrism*) of interpretation and typically devaluing the other culture.

historical particularism: an early anthropological theory that argues that each culture is a unique representation of its history and context.

monogenesis: the view that all humans originate from a single creation of God.

moral relativism: the idea that something is only right or wrong according to context-specific criteria.

polygenesis: the theory that various groups of humans appeared on earth or were created separately.

racism: the belief that humans are organized into race groupings that are different from one another in intelligence and worth.

tacit ethnocentrism: the assumption that one's own way of life is just normal, not cultural.

unilinear cultural evolution: an early anthropological theory that states all cultures evolve from simple to complex along a single trajectory of progress.

xenophobia: an intense, irrational dislike of people from other countries or cultures.

Devotion 1

Culture: The Pattern of This World

Therefore, I urge you, brothers and sisters, in view of God's mercy, to offer your bodies as a living sacrifice, holy and pleasing to God—this is true worship. Do not conform to the pattern of this world, but be transformed by the renewing of your mind. Then you will be able to test and approve what God's will is—his good, pleasing and perfect will. (Rom. 12:1–2)

Culture is the total way of life of a group of people that is learned, adaptive, shared, and integrated. It also could be called the pattern of this world, the way of life we learn to be conformed to through enculturation. This passage encourages us to become critical thinkers, especially with respect to our own culture. When the Holy Spirit renews our minds, we are better able to engage our culture critically rather than simply living from its values without even recognizing them. This won't lift us out of culture, but will move us toward living with wisdom and discernment, always testing what is good, pleasing, and perfect. How might we, as Christians, encourage critical engagement with our own culture? What about others' cultures?

Devotion 2

Culture as Part of God's Good Creation

Then the Lord God said, "It is not good that the man should be alone; I will make him a helper as his partner." So out of the ground the Lord God formed every animal of the field and every bird of the air, and brought them to the man to see what he would call them; and whatever the man called every living creature, that was its name. The man gave names to all cattle, and to the birds of the air, and to every animal of the field; but for the man there was not found a helper as his partner. So the Lord God caused a deep sleep to fall upon the man, and he slept; then he took one of his ribs and closed up its place with flesh. And the rib that the Lord God had taken from the man he made into a woman and brought her to the man. Then the man said, "This at last is bone of my bones and flesh of my flesh; this one shall be called Woman, for out of Man this one was taken." Therefore a man leaves his father and his mother and clings to his wife, and they become one flesh. (Gen. 2:18–25 NRSV)

Genesis 1 and 2 describe God's creation before the fall. In this passage, we see elements of social organization that anthropologists later would call "culture." Marriage and kinship are present in the relationships between Adam and Eve and their descendants. Work and leisure are portrayed in Adam and Eve's responsibility to steward and enjoy the garden. Even with a world of only two people, they needed culture: shared understandings and ways of life that would allow them to thrive as human beings. Genesis 3 presents the fall, and the impact of sin as pervasive in human culture from then up through the present. But God created culture as a context for human flourishing so that we may work toward its redemption and enjoy its goodness. How do we identify the ways in which our own cultures reflect the Fall? How do they reflect God's goodness in creation? How might we pursue the latter while seeking redemption of the former?

3

Language

After studying this chapter, you should be able to:

1. Compare and contrast historical linguistics, descriptive linguistics, and sociolinguistics.
2. Name the major theories of language in anthropology.
3. Describe the relationships between culture, language, and society.
4. Discuss the importance of language ideology in reading Scripture.

Introduction

In the beginning was the Word, and the Word was with God, and the Word was God. He was in the beginning with God. All things came into being through him, and without him not one thing came into being. What has come into being in him was life, and the life was the light of all people. The light shines in the darkness, and the darkness did not overcome it. (John 1:1–5 NRSV)

Jesus is called the "Word" (*logos*). God created the world by speaking it into existence. At Pentecost, the Holy Spirit appeared as "tongues of fire," enabling the apostles to speak in the multiple languages of the people assembled in Jerusalem. Throughout Scripture, language and images of language are central to how God reveals truth and moves in the world. Therefore, it is not surprising that language is a fundamental element of human life as well.

Language is a system of verbal and nonverbal symbols used to communicate. As with culture, anthropologists ask many questions about language. How different are the various languages of the world? Are some languages more developed or sophisticated or just more suitable for particular activities? How and why do languages change? These are just some of the questions linguists pursue.

In this chapter, we present the field of linguistics. After presenting significant theories of language, we provide a discussion of *sociolinguistics*, the study of how language is used by people in society, and the political context of language. We conclude with a consideration of how linguistics provides profound insights for Christians in understanding Scripture as God's revelation.

Historical Linguistics

Historical linguistics is the study of how languages develop and change over time and how different languages are related to one another. European scholars first began to systematically study language by collecting writing samples from India, China, sub-Saharan Africa, and elsewhere and by exploring connections between various languages. Sir William Jones, a British scholar living in eighteenth-century India, noticed relationships between Sanskrit and classical Greek, Latin, and modern European languages. Sanskrit was no longer spoken in Jones's time, but a number of ancient Sanskrit texts had been preserved. By studying *linguistic morphology*, the patterns and structures of words in a language, Jones and other scholars connected different languages into language families. A *language family* is a group of languages that derives from a common ancestor language. Each language family traces back to a *protolanguage*, the ancient language from which all the members of a particular language family are derived.

Jones's work illustrated the principle that languages are constantly changing. Consider the following Bible passage in Old English: "forþam todæg eow ys hælend acenned. se is drihten crist on dauides ceastre."[1] The grammar, syntax, and spelling (including letters no longer in use) are so different that no speaker of contemporary English could read it without specific training. The same passage taken from the Wycliffe translation approximately four hundred years later is a bit clearer to the modern eye, but with a great deal of unusual spelling: "for a saueour is born to day to vs, þat is crist a lord in þe cite of dauid."[2] Even the King James translation of 1611 has many words spelled incorrectly by today's standards. "For vnto you is borne this day, in

1. Luke 2:11 as taken from the Wessex Gospels, www.bible-researcher.com/engchange.html (accessed January 5, 2009).
2. Luke 2:11 as it appears in The Wycliffe Bible of 1382. See H. W. Robinson, *The Bible in its Ancient and English Versions* (Westport, CT: Greenwood Press Publishers, 1970).

Fig. 3.1 The Indo-European Language Family

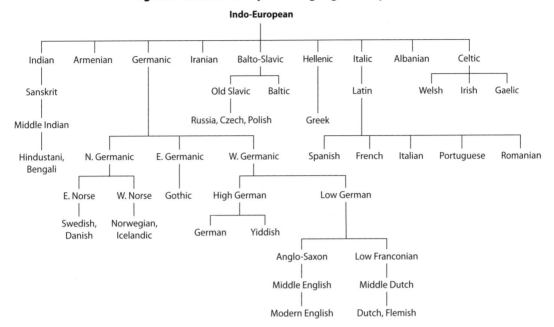

the citie of Dauid, a Sauiour, which is Christ the Lord."[3] Of course, there is nothing wrong with any of these versions. Each was written according to the linguistic standards of its time, and each represents different stages in the development of English.

This focus on language change over time, known as *diachronic* research, allowed scholars to consider how changes in social life, politics, and so forth were reflected in language. Today, many people who do historical linguistic research call it *philology*, the study of societies through their texts. This distinguishes them from those doing descriptive linguistics, described below.

Descriptive Linguistics

After the initial development of historical linguistics, some scholars began to focus less on how languages change over time and more on how languages are patterned at a given moment in time (*synchronic* research). *Descriptive linguistics* is the study of specific features of individual languages, such as patterns of grammar and sounds.

3. Luke 2:11 as found in The Holy Bible, 1611 edition, King James Version; a word-for-word reprint of the First Edition of the Authorized Version presented in roman letters (Nashville: Thomas Nelson, 1993).

Missionary Linguist and Academic Innovator

Kenneth Pike, who served with Wycliffe Bible Translators and the Summer Institute of Linguistics (now called SIL International), made as profound an impact on the field of linguistics as any individual in the twentieth century. Born in 1912, Pike attended Gordon College in 1929 as preparation for mission work, but he was turned down in his first application to China Inland Mission. In 1935, he joined the founder of Wycliffe Bible Translators, William Cameron Townsend, in southern Mexico, where Pike began studying the Mixtec (mish'-tek) language. The following year, Pike was already working as an instructor in Wycliffe's linguistic training program, teaching his method for learning, transcribing, and translating unwritten languages.

With a love of linguistics ignited by his experience in the field, Pike went to the University of Michigan and earned his PhD in 1942. The next year his dissertation was published. That publication, entitled *Phonetics: A* *Critical Analysis of Phonetic Theory and Technic for the Practical Descriptions of Sounds*, would be the first of twelve books and innumerable articles. His work has become canonical reading in the field of descriptive linguistics.

Pike was hired by the University of Michigan as a professor in 1954, elected president of the Linguistic Society of America in 1961, honored with the Distinguished Faculty Achievement Award in 1966, and awarded the Charles C. Fries Professorship in Linguistics, which he held from 1974 until 1979, when he retired.

Throughout this time, Pike continued to speak at missionary conferences, work for SIL International and Wycliffe, and share his faith in public settings around the world. His work left an enduring impact on the field of linguistics, while his faith left an eternal legacy for the kingdom.

Descriptive linguistics relies heavily on phonetics and phonemics. *Phonemics* is the study of specific structures and sounds in a particular language. *Phonetics* is the study of all possible structures and sounds humans use in language. Together, these two areas of study are known as *phonology*.

Any language in the world only uses a subset of the possible sounds humans can make. The sounds available in any particular language are known as the *phonemes* of that language. For example, the <th> sound, found in most dialects of American English, is a phoneme: a unit of sound without meaning on its own. Many languages do not use this sound at all, making it very difficult for those learning English to pronounce it. A few phonemes do carry meaning. For example, <i>, with the long vowel sound, is a single sound (phoneme) that has meaning when it functions as the singular, first-person pronoun.

In any language, most phonemes must be combined with other phonemes to create what are called *morphemes*, or units of language that carry meaning. Morphology includes the study of how languages make meaning from phonemes. In English, many morphemes are simply words (e.g., the distinct phonemes—b, a, t—combine to make one morpheme—bat). There are some "inseparable morphemes" in English, such as "–ed" attached to a verb making it past tense, or the "-s," which creates plural nouns. In other languages, however, many or even most morphemes are not words, per se, but must be combined with other morphemes to create meaning. For example, in Tagalog, the prefix *magpa-* means "to have _____ done by someone else." To fill in the blank, *magpa-* must be affixed to a root morpheme, such as *gupit*, meaning "to cut." *Magpagupit*, then, means "to have someone cut [your] hair" or "to get your hair cut [by someone else]." Concepts that in English require lots of separate morphemes (i.e., words) to express are communicated in Tagalog through the combination of morphemes that never stand alone.

Morphemes get organized according to particular rules of use known as grammar and syntax. Grammar, in a linguistic context, is different from how most U.S. Americans use the term. In school, many learn grammar as the rules most people do not actually know and must learn in order to speak "correctly." For the linguist, however, *grammar* refers to the rules that people actually use to organize their speech. Understood this way, there really is no such thing as incorrect grammar as long as communication occurs.

For example, the following sentence will make sense to any native English speaker: "You'll be able to quickly finish your work." "Proper grammar" would say this sentence is incorrect; official rules in English state that infinitive verbs (in this case "to finish") should not be split by another word or phrase ("quickly"). While a school teacher may say this is an error, the linguist would say that since this usage is understood by speakers of the language and is considered by most people to be normal language, it is an example of how grammar changes over time. A statement such as, "I ain't got no time for that" is "incorrect" according to official rules, but is grammatically correct (i.e., has a clear meaning and common usage) in most dialects of American English (see "Social judgments of languages and dialects" below).

Syntax refers to the order in which morphemes appear. In any English sentence, speakers can choose several orders of words. "The girl threw the ball." "The ball was thrown by the girl." "By the girl the ball was thrown." Each communicates the same event but with different syntax.

Like grammar, the rules of syntax are adaptable and continually changing. Oral languages tend to change faster than those with literate traditions, because writing helps preserve consistency over time. *Official languages*, languages sanctioned by a ruling body and defined and protected by powerful interests such as royal courts or other governmental institutions, tend to change more slowly than those used by populations less strongly tied to the state, such as rural and poorer groups.

Descriptive linguistics is what many missionary linguists do, particularly those affiliated with SIL International and Wycliffe Bible Translators. Two of the most prominent U.S. linguists of the twentieth century were missionary linguists Kenneth Pike and Eugene Nida. They developed conceptual and methodological tools for the study of language that are widely used in linguistics today.

Language Theory

Much of what drove the move from historical linguistics and philology to the descriptive study of language came from scholars thinking about the nature of language itself. These philosophers of language developed *language theory*, or explanations about what language in general really *is*. One of the most influential thinkers in the development of language theory was Swiss scholar Ferdinand de Saussure (1857–1913).

Structuralism

Like many scholars of his day, Saussure wanted to study human phenomena with the same rigor and methods as natural scientists studied the natural world. Language, he argued, could be studied by separating the human forms of speech (what he called *parole*) from the underlying rules on which these utterances were based (the *langue*). Parole could change with each speaker, reflecting idiosyncratic pronunciation, *kinesics* (body language), or even the certain qualities applied to particular words such as volume, tone, or emphasis, features known as *paralanguage*. What did not vary, Saussure argued, were the rules—the structure—that organized the meanings of words in relationship to one another.

The structure of every language, Saussure observed, was based on word pairs and oppositions, in which the meaning of one word came from the meaning of its opposite. In English the word "hot" only makes sense if the listener also knows the word "cold" (i.e., "not hot"). A "stool" can only be identified in relation to what it is not—a chair, bench, sofa, and so forth. Because meanings were rooted in this oppositional structure, the sounds themselves (words or signs) of this system were arbitrary symbols with no necessary connection to the thing to which they referred. (A *symbol* is something that stands for something else.) A *chair* in English is an *upuan* in Tagalog and a *chaise* in French, though each sound refers to the same object. What gives *chair/upuan/chaise* a meaning is not the object but that sign in relation to other signs in the language. This principle of arbitrariness was later argued to be a *design feature* of language, or an element that is common to all languages. In particular, this feature meant language always had openness, allowing people to innovate language to express new ideas or reference new objects.

Saussure's emphasis on the systemic structures of language gave rise to the term *structuralism* to refer to his theory of language that says all languages share an underlying binary structure. Structuralism would later be extended to the study of culture generally (see chap. 11). For both language and culture, structuralist theory meant that each could be studied as a system of signs unto itself. For linguistic structuralists, the social life of the people speaking became important only as it revealed the underlying structure governing the language. Linguist Noam Chomsky further developed structuralist linguistic theory in the 1950s and later. He also referred to language as having two parts: surface structure and deep structure. The surface structure, corresponding to Saussure's notion of *parole*, referred to the language coming out of people's mouths. Spoken language provided the empirical data a scientist would use to unravel the "generative grammar," or deep structure, that provided the rules determining what could and could not be said in the language. Moving from the surface structure to the deep structure, Chomsky believed linguists could apply mathematical principles to determine the range of possible utterances a particular grammar would allow in a particular language. By comparing linguistic systems, Chomsky believed linguists could uncover principles of human thought generally.

This theory of language has had a tremendous influence on anthropology as scholars began using the ideas of surface and deep structure to understand culture as well as language. But even as Chomsky was elaborating on Saussure's theory and publishing to wide acclaim, other linguistic anthropologists developed an alternative. Following the work of early U.S. anthropologist Franz Boas, linguistic anthropologists like Dell Hymes, Edward Sapir, and Benjamin Whorf argued that the speech of real people was not simply a reflection of a deep structure but that language and culture exist in a dynamic relationship of mutual influence.

The Sapir-Whorf hypothesis

The *Sapir-Whorf hypothesis* posits that language shapes people's perceptions, thoughts, and views of reality. Edward Sapir, a student of Boas's at Columbia, studied Native American languages and became particularly interested in the relationship between language and culture. His student, Benjamin Whorf, elaborated Sapir's ideas as he developed on his own work among the Hopi of the southwestern United States. Whorf noted that while English has many markers of time (such as present and past tense and markers of future intention), Hopi speakers expressed things as ongoing processes without clear linguistic categories of past, present, and future. Whorf argued that where English speakers saw discrete units of time (today, tomorrow, five days), the Hopi saw an ongoing process (the day that is happening now, the time that is coming). Thus, where English speakers saw a break with a new beginning, the Hopi perceived actions as connected to the past and future. Whorf wrote, "One might say that Hopi society understands our proverb, 'Well begun is half done,' but not our "Tomorrow is another day.'"[4]

4. Benjamin Whorf, "The Relation of Habitual Thought and Behavior to Language," in *Anthropological Theory: An Introductory History*, 4th ed., ed. J. L. McGee and R. Warms (New York: McGraw-Hill, 2008), 150.

This hypothesis posed an intriguing idea about the relationships between language, society, perception, and reality. Those who became interested in the specific language-culture complexes around the world developed an approach known as *ethnosemantics* (or *ethnoscience*), the study of the culturally and linguistically specific ways people make sense of the world. Advocates of the Sapir-Whorf hypothesis believed that as they compared societies, they would find that linguistic categories and terms profoundly shaped or even determined how individuals viewed the world.

Subsequent ethnosemantic research on language and perception has not supported the extreme version of the hypothesis. Research on color categories, for example, has demonstrated that although some languages offer only two words for colors, they are almost always the same categories: one label for colors in the blue-green-violet spectrum and another for the yellow-red-orange spectrum. Those who have three categories pull out red as the third color (by whatever name), and so on, in a consistent pattern. This suggests that humans physically respond to light spectrum in the same ways—they see the same things—although those with fewer linguistic categories will have less interest in differentiating between, say, shades of red, orange, and yellow.[5]

Even while physical perception does not seem determined by language, however, linguistic determinism pushed many anthropologists to argue that language, particularly the performance of language, was more than just a reflection of a deep grammar. Through attention to the social use of language and its cultural settings, these scholars supported the idea that language use, as it is modified and shaped in real social contexts, potentially shapes how people think and behave. In other words, culture is not just a reflection of language; culture *changes* language.

Sociolinguistics

In the 1960s, linguist William Labov became interested in social influences on language. He observed that American racism perpetuated the segregation of African Americans in neighborhoods, workplaces, and churches, and that segregation contributed to the development of distinctively African American forms of speech. Additionally, racism influenced speakers of standard American English to devalue African American Vernacular English (AAVE) as an improper and less sophisticated way of speaking English. Labov and his students argued that AAVE is not deficient English but a legitimate dialect of English, with its own coherent grammar, syntax, and lexicon (vocabulary). This work was part of the founding of sociolinguistics as a sub-

5. Brent Berlin and Paul Kay, *Basic Color Terms: Their Universality and Evolution* (Berkeley: University of California Press, 1969).

discipline of anthropology, one that addresses the mutual influences between culture and language.[6]

Sociolinguists often apply their research in social settings with the goal of improving human relationships by enhancing communication. For example, Diana Eades researched how Aboriginal people tell their stories in courtroom settings. The expectations for coherence, structure, and consistency set by Australian courts don't always match the cultural norms for storytelling in Aboriginal culture, and so Aboriginal defendants are often at a disadvantage in court cases. Eades described the issue and also suggested approaches to story-telling and story listening that could enhance justice in Australian courts.[7]

Eades's work exemplifies sociolinguistics in that it highlights contextual issues like ethnic stratification, social inequality, and political representation. When historical linguists study similar issues, they acknowledge context but focus more on changes in and relationships between the languages themselves. Descriptive linguists explore the relationship of language design and cultural context, but often without much emphasis on change, political context, or social power. With their focus on language and culture in mutual interaction, sociolinguists are most interested in change, context, and culture. Three issues of importance to sociolinguists include social judgments of languages and dialects, multilingual societies, and language contact.

Social judgments of languages and dialects

In studying dialects, sociolinguists use formal linguistic skills to study language structure and use, and ethnographic skills to describe how power dynamics shape social judgments of various dialects. Distinct but mutually intelligible forms of a single language are called *dialects*. English has many dialects, such as Jamaican, African American Vernacular, Standard American, Appalachian, Kenyan, Australian, and varieties of British, all of which maintain particular rules of grammar, words, and pronunciation.

In practice, however, the categorization of one language as a distinct "language" while another is called a "dialect" is often more of a social judgment, reflecting how a particular dialect is valued by speakers of another dialect. For example, in the Philippines there are eight major languages and dozens of smaller languages. Yet in addition to the colonial language of English, Tagalog emerged as the most prestigious Philippine language. As the language spoken in the areas around Manila (the most important Philippine city), Tagalog became the second official language of the country. Though the languages of the Philippines are related (the way Spanish and French are related), Tagalog

6. See William Labov, *Language in the Inner City: Studies in the Black English Vernacular* (Philadelphia: University of Pennsylvania Press, 1973).

7. See Diana Eades, *Courtroom Talk and Neocolonial Control* (New York: Walter de Gruyter Press, 2008).

Language Hierarchies

Although the Philippines was colonized by Spain for four hundred years, the Spanish had a policy of *not* allowing Filipinos to learn Spanish (in contrast to Spain's Latin American policy). When the United States assumed colonial control in 1898, English became the official language for education, government, and business. As the country prepared for independence, it created a national language based on Tagalog (first called "Pilipino" and later "Filipino").

Today, the medium of instruction in public schools is supposed to be Filipino until high school and university, at which point most subjects are taught in English. This creates difficulties in areas where fluent Tagalog/Filipino speakers are hard to find. Through much of the island nation, people grow up speaking other languages. When they become teachers, it is much easier to teach children in the language everyone understands than to use a language everyone is learning.

The imposition of Tagalog has created some resentment among speakers of other languages.

Language hierarchy, the system by which some languages or dialects have ranked political, economic, and social status, exists in many countries. Kenyans speak dozens of different languages, but Swahili (a language indigenous to a small group on the coast) and the colonial language English have become prestigious languages. In India, an enormous country of over a billion people, more than eighteen languages are recognized as official regional or national languages. Yet Hindi and English remain the most prestigious.

Where hierarchies exist, those who are raised speaking the more prestigious languages, or who have the resources to learn favored languages fluently, gain social advantages over speakers of less-prestigious languages.

speakers cannot understand Filipinos speaking Ilokano, Cebuano, or any of the other many languages of their nation. These are separate languages, yet the vast majority of Filipinos refer to these less prestigious languages as "dialects."

Conversely, some fluent or native speakers of Spanish say they can understand Italian or Portuguese and even learn to speak those languages relatively easily. Yet it is rare to hear someone refer to Italian as a "dialect" of Spanish (or the other way around). The difference has nothing to do with the languages of Spanish, Italian, Tagalog, or Ilokano; the difference is in the relationship of Spaniards to Italians as opposed to Tagalogs and Ilokanos. Spain recognizes Italy as a separate country with its own history and value. Tagalog and Ilokano have been placed in the same country as a result of colonialism. Today Tagalogs, and particularly urban people in Manila, tend to look down upon speakers of other languages as being provincial or backward. That the speakers of languages other than Tagalog have adopted the terminology of "dialects" for their own languages reflects how they have accepted the judgment that their languages are less worthy of respect than Tagalog and English; again, the use of this terminology is not due to features of the languages but is instead a consequence of politics and history.

Referring to someone else's language as a "dialect" becomes a way of marking that language as less important, less developed, or derivative of a more important language. By placing a language into the category of "dialect,"

it becomes easier to argue that it should not be taught in school or used in literature or news media, or that it is even a degraded form of another more "pure" language.

Language hierarchy can even portray certain languages as intrinsically superior to other languages. Many who speak dialects of European languages have come to view their version of the language as "lower" than the version spoken in the original country. Throughout Latin America, people often refer to the Spanish spoken in Spain as "pure" Spanish or "good" Spanish. Even between very different languages, particular languages are sometimes ranked as better than others. For example, while some might argue that English is a superior language for business or German is more suited to theology, linguists believe there is no such thing as "superior" or "advanced" languages. Some languages do have relatively larger *lexicons* (i.e., all the morphemes of a language) than others. In the case of English (a language with an exceptionally large lexicon), this is due to the willingness of English speakers to borrow words from other languages, alter pronunciations, and adopt them as English. Speakers of other languages may be less willing to adopt words from another language or may have vocabularies developed more specifically around local concerns, but every language *can* express anything a speaker of that language wants to express.

For example, Ilokano, a language of the northern Philippines, has grown and changed to reflect the concerns of the speakers. In Ilokano there are many words to refer to rice. Rice to be used for seed is called *bunubun*. Cooked rice (about to be eaten) is *inapoy*. If you leave the pot on the stove too long, the burned layer at the bottom is *itip*. There are specific terms for rice that has been harvested but not threshed, rice that has been planted but without the seeds yet formed, cold rice left over from the day before, and so on. It would be unfair to think that English is an inferior language for our lack of specificity when it comes to talking about rice. Because of the less-than-central role of rice in the diets of English-speaking populations, the English language has not become as specific on the topic of rice as Ilokano has.

Multilingual societies

While languages are not inherently better or worse than one another, where many languages are used in a single society, there are always political dynamics in which the use of various languages becomes hierarchically arranged. Some languages may come to dominate some spheres of life such as home and church, while other languages are used in school and politics. How people negotiate the relationships of these languages and their use is called the sociology of language.

In most countries today, multiple languages are spoken even where an official language is mandated by law. In the United States, although English is widely spoken and has been declared an official language in twenty-eight states, Spanish is widely spoken throughout the country, along with French in the Northeast, Norwegian in the Midwest, Gullah in several Eastern sea islands, and numerous other languages, particularly in areas where new immigrant populations are concentrated. Other countries, such as South Africa, India, and many others, have encompassed dozens or even hundreds of different languages from their inception.

Some multilingual societies may not have many multilingual individuals, as languages tend to be separated into various regions. In Switzerland, German, French, and Italian are spoken in different regions of the country, making it a multilingual state.[8] Yet many individuals are monolingual (speaking only one language) in the language of their region. In other cases, such as the Philippines, where the official languages of English and Filipino are spoken alongside seven major and dozens of minor languages, most individuals are multilingual themselves, often growing up speaking three or more languages daily.

Language contact, pidgins, and creoles

When speakers of different languages come together in one place, they may develop a *creole*, a type of language formed when speakers of different languages combine their languages. Haitian Creole is a combination of French and the West African languages spoken by people brought to the plantations of Hispaniola. The Creole of Louisiana is also a French-based language, drawing on Native American, Spanish, and English. In other situations, instead of combining language influences, speakers in a multilingual context use a simplified form of one language (often a colonial language) as a common language across a region or group. The simplified language, known as *pidgin*, may become a second language for speakers of older, more com-

8. Romansh, the language of the Roma minority, is also considered a language of Switzerland, although it is spoken by an ethnic minority and not associated with a region of the country.

Anthropologist Steve Ybarrola (on right) with the pastor of the church he attended in Donostia (San Sebastian), the Basque Country, Spain. They are having *comida* (lunch) after the Sunday morning church service. Most of those in the background look Latin American—because they are. The evangelical churches in the Basque Country are now filled with immigrants, the impact of which Ybarrola is currently researching.
Photo: Steve Ybarrola

plex languages, or eventually replace those languages. Linguists working in Bible translation note that biblical Greek took on characteristics of a pidgin language, reducing its grammatical complexity as it became widely spoken among formerly non-Greek speakers of the ancient world.[9]

Pidgin languages often developed as a result of colonial rule, but not all colonized people adapted the languages of the colonizers. Some societies have responded to political and linguistic domination through *linguistic nationalism*: the use of language to promote nationalist ideologies. One example is the Basque community of northwest Spain and southwest France. Members of this community have been struggling against Spanish and French rule, sometimes violently, for decades. One potent symbol of their identity and their struggle has been their language, Euskara. Anthropologist Steve Ybarrola noted that when fascist Francisco Franco came to power in Spain, he made the speaking of Euskara (and other minority languages) illegal. Correspondingly, as the Basque nationalists of the region began to resist, they emphasized the centrality of speaking Euskara as the most significant marker of being or becoming Basque. Living among the Spanish within the border of the Spanish state, they insisted immigrants learn Basque to integrate into "their" (i.e., Basque)

9. Other linguists argue that the simplification of Greek was a distinct process from the formation of pidgin languages. The point here is not to settle the definition of these terms but to point out how simplification of grammar tends to follow as a language spreads across linguistically diverse populations. For a more detailed description of pidgin versus other forms of simplification, see Eugene Nida, *Language Structure and Translation: Essays by Eugene Nida* (Palo Alto, CA: Stanford University Press, 1975), chap. 7.

A demonstration in a fishing town in the Basque Country. One of the complaints Basques have had with the Spanish state is that Basque prisoners (most in prison for activity in ETA—Euskadi ta Askatasuna, the Basque Country and her Freedom) are not being held in Basque prisons, which they claim is required by the Spanish constitution, but are rather dispersed throughout the Spanish state. The families view this as a form of state harassment. The banner reads "Basque prisoners returned to the Basque Country NOW!" (in Euskara, not Spanish). Also seen are several people holding placards with photos of their imprisoned family members, as well as some with a map of the Basque Country with red arrows pointing into the territory indicating, once again, that Basque prisoners must be returned to the Basque Country to serve their terms. Photo: Steve Ybarrola

society. As the nationalist movement developed, language continued to play a central role, with some arguing that "the Basque language encourages distinct sentiments, values, and beliefs within a person."[10] In other words, speaking Euskara made you into a certain kind of person. In this way, emphasizing the Basque language—and forcing people to learn and speak it—became integral to creating Basque identity.

When sociolinguists study issues of social judgment, multilingual societies, and language contact, they often focus on contextual factors such as ethnic stratification, social inequality, and political representation to understand how language and culture affect each other. Linguistic anthropologist Jane Hill has studied how English speakers in the United States often speak Spanish in particular settings and for reasons that tend to diminish the integrity of the Spanish language.[11] Using what she calls "mock Spanish," English speakers may use Spanish in joking ways—throwing out a casual "Hasta la vista, baby!" when saying goodbye to a friend—spoken with a strong U.S. English accent. She argues that by using Spanish in a "slangy way," it has the (probably unintentional) effect of making that language appear less important or seem less sophisticated than English. Since English speakers tend to be wealthier, in positions of power, and members of the majority, the use of "mock Spanish"

10. Cyrus Zirakzadeh as quoted in Steven Ybarrola, "Identity Matters: Christianity and Ethnic Identity in the Peninsular Basque Country," in *Power and Identity in the Global Church: Six Contemporary Cases*, ed. Brian Howell and Edwin Zehner (Pasadena, CA: William Carey Library, 2009), 111.

11. Jane Hill, "Language, Race, and White Public Space," *American Anthropologist* 100, no. 3 (1999): 680–89.

Code Switching

Sociolinguist Dell Hymes noted that within any given speech community—meaning any concrete group of individuals that interact verbally on a regular basis—there are actually a number of varieties of language being used. Some of these are *regional dialects*, accents and word choices related to geography, while others are *social dialects*, ways of speaking connected to class, such as the pronunciation of "Park the car" ("Pahk the cah") of south Boston compared to the British-sounding accent of the Back Bay area of the city. *Social registers* are also important—ways of speaking related to specific settings such as a sporting event, institution of higher learning, or religious community.

An individual's competency with these various dialects and registers comprises his or her verbal repertoire. Some individuals are adept at *code switching*, which is the practice of keeping particular forms of speech separate in their lives, using one in one setting (with friends and peers, for example) and another in another setting (in the classroom, on the job). Truly multilingual people code switch with completely different languages, but even monolingual speakers often become adept at knowing which form of their language to use in which settings. Those fluent in more than one code or language are described as practicing diglossia.

Currently, some university scholars and grade school teachers advocate teaching the concept of code switching to urban African American children. Instead of labeling AAVE "deficient" and standard English "superior," teachers help students recognize grammatical differences between home speech and school speech. With both dialects treated as valid, students learn to successfully code switch, discussing how, when, and in what contexts to use AAVE or standard English.

---

can become a way that Spanish speakers themselves are made to feel less a part of the society or inferior to English speakers.

Language and Scripture

For Christians, an essential question about language and language theory concerns how we read and understand Scripture. God provided revelation through language, and the written Scriptures are central to our understandings of the Divine. Anthropology can help us better understand what the Bible is and how to read it. Both language theory and sociolinguistics offer important insights into approaching and understanding Scripture.

Many Christians refer to the Bible as "the Word of God," but it's important to retain the supremacy of the Trinity. When Scripture refers to the eternal Word, it refers to Jesus, not the Bible.[12] For this reason, the Bible, in a theological sense, is the *words* of God, while Jesus is the Word.

This is not to lower the authority of Scripture in any way. Throughout Scripture, particularly in the Psalms, there are references to God's Word, referring to the law and the prophets (Ps. 119:9–11, 105). Jesus affirms the authority of this law (Matt. 5:18) and the apostles of the early church stress

12. In addition to John 1:1ff., see also Psalm 119:89.

the Scriptures as central to Christian life (Heb. 4:12; 2 Tim. 3:16–17). At the same time, one of the most profound Scriptures about the Word is the one that opens this chapter from John 1:1: "In the beginning was the Word." The "Word," in this case, is not the Bible, but Jesus himself.

This makes the Christian Bible very different from the Muslim Koran. The traditional theology of the Koran teaches that the angel Gabriel dictated the words in classical Arabic to the prophet Mohammed, who wrote them down verbatim. For this reason, most Muslims affirm the teaching that while the Koran may be translated into various languages, only the classical Arabic is authoritative. In contrast, the Bible's authority is not seen by Christians to be limited to a particular language. Even in the original writings, there were different versions of Hebrew in the Old Testament. Jesus spoke Aramaic (another iteration of Hebrew), but his followers wrote his words in Greek. Some parts of the New Testament only survive in the Latin Vulgate. Most Christians throughout the centuries have never read the Bible in its original languages yet have come to a saving knowledge of Christ. It is part of the beauty of Christianity and the character of God that the gospel can be spoken in any language, any culture, and any time; through the Holy Spirit, it has the power to change lives.

There is no sacred language for Christians; no language is more suitable or appropriate for Scripture than any other. According to structuralist theories, the meaning of language is found in the code—the grammar—behind the form. Figuring out what the Bible "means" is to get behind the words (the *parole*, or the form) to the unchanging meaning (the *langue*, or deep structure and meaning). This is a useful way to understand why Christians should accept the translation of Scripture. Saussurian linguistic theory supports the notion that every human language has the ability to communicate the same deep or universal meanings even as they are expressed in the various surface structures of languages around the world.

While these ideas of language are useful for understanding translation, however, some theologians have also emphasized the importance of social and cultural context for the writers and readers of Scripture. Thus, contemporary evangelical theologians also draw insight from sociolinguistics. Stanley Grenz and John Franke, for example, refer to the "cultural-linguistic" approach to Scripture as a way to understand the dynamic between what Scripture says and how it is read in context.[13] They emphasize how the meanings of Scripture are always linked to the text itself as well as to the *use* of them in context. Theologian Jonathan Wilson describes how Jesus's disciples learned through *doing* his words, not simply hearing or reading

13. Stanley Grenz and John Franke, *Beyond Foundationalism: Shaping Theology in a Postmodern Context* (Louisville: Westminster John Knox, 2001).

Names and Metaphors of God

The limits of language become quickly apparent when humans try to speak about God. Old Testament Hebrews, and observant Jews today, do not speak the divine name. They may substitute *Adonai* (my Lord) or *Elohim* (God) for YHVH, the Hebrew convention for writing God's name. This taboo symbolizes respect for the sacred nature of God, and also reminds people of their tendency to make an idol out of a symbol, something that stands for God but is not God.

Scripture contains hundreds of names and metaphors for God. Christians in various societies use certain names more than others, emphasizing particular characteristics of God. God as King, for instance, makes a powerful statement in a monarchical society. Contemporary praise and worship music relies on "You," "Father," "Jesus," and "Lord," all basic words for God that encourage personal intimacy between God and the worshiper.

Other names and images for God, though just as biblical as the familiar ones, fall into disuse. God's fury and power are highlighted when God is described as a woman in labor (Isa. 42:14), and God's protectiveness is emphasized when God is described as a hen (Matt. 23:37) or as a seamstress making clothes for Israel to wear (Neh. 9:21). Sociolinguistics helps us see how culture shapes our preferred words and metaphors for God and how repeated use of that language, in turn, shapes our understanding of God.

A famous hymn asks, "What language shall I borrow?" to thank and praise God. Whether we speak of God with a single name, many different names, or refuse to speak God's name at all, it's important to be aware of how language simultaneously illuminates and constrains our understanding of God.

them.[14] The truth of Scripture is not limited to a code underneath the printed words but exists as the church *lives* according to Scripture.

Sociolinguistic views stress how interactions between culture and language shape the creation of meaning. Taken too far, attention to context may make some think that the meaning of Scripture is *dependent* upon the cultural context, just as the Sapir-Whorf hypothesis said perception of reality was *dependent* upon linguistic categories. Historic Christianity teaches that God has revealed truth through Scripture that humans can understand in any time and place, through any language. While these truths are not *dependent* on context, cultural contexts still matter. Through the Bible, God continues to reveal truth as the gospel is taken up in new cultural and historical contexts. As God's people live out the Scriptures, God continues to reveal the riches of God's revelation. In terms of sociolinguistics, this is the interaction of the text with the community in which new possibilities of meaning emerge. As Christians, we know this process is guided by the Holy Spirit, and among the many manifestations of Christianity around the world, we can see how the Spirit works with cultural forms such as music, dance, speech, language, and more in forming the many expressions of the global church.

14. Jonathan Wilson, "Toward a New Evangelical Paradigm of Biblical Authority," in *The Nature of Confession: Evangelicals and Postliberals in Conversation*, ed. Timothy Phillips and Dennis Okholm (Downers Grove, IL: InterVarsity, 1996), 151–62.

Terms

code switching: the practice of keeping particular forms of speech separate in one's life, using one in one setting (with friends or peers) and another in another setting (in the classroom or on the job).

creole: type of language formed when speakers of different languages combine their languages.

descriptive linguistics: the study of specific features of individual languages, such as patterns of grammar and sounds, as they exist at a given moment in time.

design feature: an element that is common to all languages.

diachronic: studies that focus on change over time.

dialect: distinct but mutually intelligible forms of a single language.

ethnosemantics (or *ethnoscience*): the study of the culturally and linguistically specific ways people make sense of the world.

grammar: the rules that people use to organize their speech.

historical linguistics: the study of how languages develop and change over time and how different languages are related to one another.

kinesics: body language.

language: a system of verbal and nonverbal symbols used to communicate.

language family: a group of languages that derive from a common ancestor language.

language hierarchy: the system by which some languages or dialects have ranked political, economic, and social status.

language theory: an explanation of the general nature of language.

lexicon: all the morphemes of a particular language.

linguistic morphology: the patterns and structures of words in a language.

linguistic nationalism: the use of language to promote nationalist ideologies.

morphemes: units of language that carry meaning.

official language: language sanctioned by a ruling body.

paralanguage: certain qualities applied to particular words, such as volume, tone, or emphasis.

philology: the study of societies through their texts.

phonemes: the sounds available in any particular language.

phonemics: the study of specific structures and sounds in a particular language.

phonetics: the study of all possible structures and sounds humans use in language.

phonology: the study of language sounds, including phonemics and phonetics.

pidgin: language formed when speakers in a multilingual context use a simplified form of one language (often a colonial language) as a common language across a region or group.

protolanguage: the ancient language from which all the members of a particular language family are derived.

regional dialect: an accent and word choice related to geography.

Sapir-Whorf hypothesis: a hypothesis that posits that language shapes people's perceptions, thoughts, and views of reality.

social dialect: a way of speaking connected to class.

social register: a way of speaking related to a specific setting such as a sporting event, institution of higher learning, or religious community.

sociolinguistics: the study of how language is used by people in society.

structuralism: a theory of language that says all languages share an underlying binary structure.

symbol: something that stands for something else.

synchronic: studies that focus on a given moment in time.

syntax: the order in which morphemes appear.

Devotion 1

Language and the Image of God

In the beginning God created the heavens and the earth. Now the earth was formless and empty, darkness was over the surface of the deep, and the Spirit of God was hovering over the waters. And God said, "Let there be light," and there was light. (Gen. 1:1–3)

The phrase "And God said" introduces each day of creation in Genesis 1. God spoke light, darkness, water, ground, and all living things into existence. The power of language, seen in God's creation of the world, is also reflected in the *imago Dei* that is present in each person. Humans use language in powerful ways to create and shape human culture. The words of a wedding vow speak a marriage into existence. Cruel or hateful words can destroy a relationship. Affirming words shouted by a coach to a player in a game can generate ambition, energy, and strength that wouldn't otherwise be present.

The ability to communicate with language and our reliance on language for culture transmission is a distinctive characteristic of humans that sets us apart from all other created beings. Language is one important way in which we bear the image of God. Though language often fails us in our fallen world, we can give thanks for the many ways in which language—in particular and in general—is a blessing for and from the people of God.

Devotion 2

Jacob's Multilayered Language

Jacob went close to his father Isaac, who touched him and said, "The voice is the voice of Jacob, but the hands are the hands of Esau." He did not recognize him, for his hands were hairy like those of his brother Esau; so he blessed him. (Gen. 27:22–23)

Genesis 27 records the story of Jacob and Esau. In one episode, Jacob disguised himself as Esau, dressing and speaking like his brother. Jacob conned their father, Isaac, into giving him the blessing that was intended for Esau.

Sociolinguistics offers tools for interpreting the many layers of communication at play in this story. The words spoken, both the trick and the blessing, were just one layer of language. Language is also present in kinesics, the body language Jacob used when he covered his hands and neck with goatskins so they would seem hairy like Esau's. Jacob relied on paralanguage to alter the tone and quality of his voice to sound more like Esau. He used a kiss as a symbol that, in their culture, stood for loyalty and truthfulness.

True to his name, which means "supplanter," Jacob manipulated all of the major elements of human communication—words, body language, vocal style, and symbols—to get what he wanted. Interpreting the story with the use of linguistic tools illuminates the full dimensions of truthfulness: that is, that honesty is about more than just words.

4

Social Structure and Inequality
in Race, Ethnicity, and Class

After reading this chapter, you should be able to:

1. Define social structure and related concepts (status, role, inequality).
2. Understand race, ethnicity, class, and caste.
3. Explain how race, ethnicity, class, and caste structure inequality.
4. Appreciate practical ways Christians can be involved in addressing inequality.

Introduction

In the United States, people love an underdog. Hundreds of films, songs, books, and plays tell of the outsider who pulls himself or herself up by the bootstraps, works hard, and becomes a success. Whether it's Rocky Balboa's fictional rise from the streets of Philadelphia to boxing glory, or Oprah Winfrey's true-life rise from poverty to prominence, these stories affirm basic U.S. values: that everyone is equal, that opportunity is there for the taking, and that anyone can make it to the top through talent and hard work.

What makes these stories so compelling are their common starting points: these individuals, by virtue of who they are, began with less access to wealth, education, and power. Anthropologists refer to this unequal distribution of social resources as *social stratification*, meaning the organization of people into ranked groups, or hierarchies, based on particular characteristics. In addition to inequalities of wealth, these hierarchies are often organized around cultural categories believed to be rooted in biology, history, or family—qualities over which individuals seem to have no control. Social stratification is present in varying degrees in all societies. Even the most egalitarian bands make distinctions, if only temporarily, between individuals' skills in gathering, hunting, healing, or decision making. Social stratification is more extreme and consequential for individuals' life chances in chiefdoms, kingdoms, and states (see chap. 7).

Related to social stratification, the term *social inequality* refers more specifically to the differential access to economic resources, political power, or social prestige that results from stratification. In some societies, inequalities are conscious and widely affirmed; this was the case in feudal, medieval Europe, where royals, nobles, and serfs occupied distinct places in the social order. In other societies, social inequalities are officially prohibited, as in most democratic, constitutional states today where all citizens are equal under the law. Even when legal (*de jure*) discrimination may not exist and cultural ideologies favor equality and open opportunity, in practice (*de facto*) some people have less access to economic, political, and social power based on their social group.

In this chapter we discuss social inequality. We start with a discussion of social structure and key concepts of status, role, stratification, and inequality. We then explore areas in which inequality is often expressed, specifically race, ethnicity, class, and caste. Finally, we ask how Christians should think about and respond to social inequality.

Social Structure and Inequality

Social structure (also called *social organization* or *social order*) refers to the ways people coordinate their lives in relation to one another at the level of society. Like culture (see chap. 2), social structure is often difficult to perceive. In many democratic states, particularly in the West where individual accomplishments and identity are prized, ideologies of equal opportunity and individualism make social structure nearly invisible. In the United States, for example, we are socialized to believe that the same social opportunities are available to every individual. In reality, however, there is more to the stories of Rocky Balboa, Oprah Winfrey, or our own personal histories than a hardworking individual being successful in a neutral world. Race, class, gender, religion, language, dialect, and citizenship are just a few important elements of social structure that influence an individual's life chances. Anthropology acknowledges the importance of individual motivation, effort, and limitations in how easily a person can accomplish his or her goals. At the same time, an anthropological understanding of social structure highlights ways individuals find themselves—through birth, their own choices, or the choices of others—with advantages and disadvantages in life.

In this way, social inequality does not just refer to how much someone has—that is, being rich or poor—but refers to differential access to valuable resources. Sociologist Max Weber (see chap. 11) identified three related areas of social stratification: *wealth*, or economic status; *power*, or the ability to influence others; and *prestige*, or the social affirmation and approval given to some members of society.

Fig. 4.1 Three Related Areas of Social Stratification

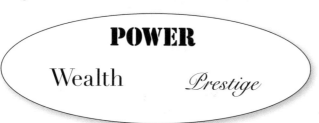

These three areas of social stratification work together, such that wealth may bring power and prestige, or higher levels of prestige may provide access to wealth. For example, many college students in the United States are "poor"; that is, they do not have a lot of disposable income. At the same time, simply by being in college, students have access to higher levels of prestige. When they graduate, they will have access to jobs with higher incomes. Through *cultural capital*—cultural knowledge, including linguistic skills—they will be able to navigate bureaucratic institutions more successfully in order to get mortgages and buy homes, access credit, or invest in the stock market.[1] In fact, simply by having college degrees (regardless of current income), they will find it easier to get credit. This makes it easier to live in the neighborhood of their choice, get their children into better schools, and give their children relatively more access to wealth, power, and prestige.

Societies often organize individuals into groups that experience these unequal relations to power, wealth, and prestige, though it becomes more pronounced in communities integrated into states, kingdoms, and chiefdoms than in tribes and bands. Within every society, differences in age, gender, race, ethnicity, and many other categories become social statuses arranged in hierarchical systems. Yet social stratification is not a consequence of difference alone; it forms around the ways those differences are given relative value in society.

1. For a thorough discussion of cultural capital, see Pierre Bourdieu, *The Logic of Practice* (Stanford, CA: Stanford University Press, 1990).

Status

Status refers to any position a person may occupy in a social structure. Like the common English phrases "high status" or "low status" suggest, anthropologists emphasize hierarchy and stratification when they study status.

There are two types of status: achieved and ascribed. An *achieved status* is one that a person chooses or becomes associated with due to behaviors or skills. Occupations like student or farmer are achieved statuses because people aren't simply born into them; they have to make choices and learn skills in order for their status to be socially recognized. An *ascribed status* is given to an individual through no choice or action of her or his own; it is a status granted by circumstances of birth. Examples of ascribed status are son, Southerner, or female. Statuses may be linked—for example, a person cannot be a wife without another being her husband—or they may be independent.

Each person has multiple statuses at any time, and people typically change statuses frequently throughout their lives. Often one status becomes more important in one setting than another, such as being a child at home and a student at school. Each person likewise often has one status, sometimes known as a *master status*, that tends to be most important in shaping his or her life. For the leader of a chiefdom, for instance, the fact that he is the chief would likely be more fundamental to his identity than his being an uncle or neighbor.

Statuses often change with setting. Someone who is a son at his mother's house is a father when he goes home to his own children. If his mother comes over to visit, he is simultaneously a son and father. Even ascribed statuses that may seem permanent can be altered by culture and context. In some patrilineal cultures (see chap. 8), when a daughter marries, she is no longer part of the family into which she was born (her natal family). For example, in the Hebrew Scriptures, in Ruth's declaration of allegiance to her mother-in-law Naomi, she proclaimed herself no longer a Moabite. This was an affirmation that upon marriage she had relinquished her previously ascribed status and had become an Israelite (see Ruth 1:16–17).

When a cluster of statuses is organized around a common focus, such as education, law, or art, it functions as an *institution*. A political institution, for instance, involves achieved statuses such as voter, representative, president, lobbyist, and legal aid, and ascribed statuses such as citizen or noncitizen.

Statuses are usually ranked, which means some become elevated above others. In an institutional setting, this hierarchy may be built into the system. For example, teachers, students, administrators, office assistants, and resident advisors are all statuses organized hierarchically in a university. All may be respected, but some are granted more resources, social recognition, and influence. In society at large, people may deny that status hierarchies exist, yet in practice people experience and understand some statuses as more advantageous than others. The status of man, woman, black person, white person, Native American, New Yorker, or inner-city resident officially has no bearing on an individual's access to wealth, power, or prestige. Yet, statistically, it is clear that particular statuses correlate with varying degrees of access to employment, education, security, health care, and more. Linguistically, although individuals may affirm the equality of men and women, say, status hierarchies are revealed in such expressions as, "You throw like a girl." In U.S. English, it is rarely an insult to call someone a man, or suggest someone is doing something "like a man." To "take it like a man" is, in fact, a virtue showing strength and character. But accusing someone of doing anything "like a girl" or a "woman" (to say nothing of specifically gendered curse words) are common insults directed at both men and women.[2]

Role

A *role* prescribes expected or required behaviors for those who occupy a particular status. Some statuses, particularly those defined by institutions, have clear roles. Students, for instance, are to enter the classroom, sit in the desks, listen carefully, take notes, ask informed questions, and send many gifts and notes of appreciation to their professors. (OK, maybe just a few gifts. . . .) Other statuses, such as child, grandmother, Midwesterner, or urbanite, may have vague or widely variable roles even within a single society, but the existence of stereotypes suggests shared understandings of roles that are associated with these statuses. In this way, there are cultural expectations for people to behave in ways corresponding to their status.

Roles contribute to the organization of society by reducing ambiguity or confusion as to "who does what." When social organization changes abruptly, people may become distressed and even violent as role expectations change. The civil rights era in the United States, for example, changed roles for African Americans as well as for European Americans. Whether based in paternalism and charity, or violence and superiority, European American race role expectations of the pre–civil rights era were no longer valid. The role expectation for African Americans to be subservient, undereducated, and politically and socially marginalized also changed. People of all races in the United States had to quickly reorganize their understanding of the roles associated with racial statuses.

Though individuals everywhere have multiple statuses at once, in large-scale societies encompassing many thousands or even millions of people, the

2. It could certainly be insulting for a woman to be told that she "walks like a man" or otherwise does not live up to a feminine ideal. However, to "be one of the boys" is often a high compliment given to a woman who is friendly and at ease with groups of men. To tell a man he's like "one of the girls" would seem odd, at best, and likely insulting.

multiplicity of statuses increases, often becoming more distinct (separating work from family, for example) and more rigidly stratified. People experience *role conflict*, or *role strain*, the stress that occurs when the behavioral expectations from various roles come into play simultaneously. For instance, at a family reunion a man may be, simultaneously, a husband, father, son, uncle, nephew, and also an employee (available to his employer by cell phone or email). He experiences role conflict when he is expected to play a game with his niece, put his own baby down for a nap, talk with his father, and complete workplace tasks via email all at the same time.

Analyzing manifestations of inequality requires an understanding of all the relevant statuses and roles at play. For example, around the time this text was published, in the western Chicago suburb of Wheaton, Illinois, an older teenager could earn $7–12 per hour to babysit children. For mowing a lawn, the going rate for the same age group was at least $25. Even with breaks, using a push mower, and not working particularly fast, most of the lawns in Wheaton could be mowed in well under an hour. This works out, in some cases, to over $30 per hour. Though pay is not dependent on the sex of the worker (males and females earn the same for babysitting or lawn mowing), the different wage rates reflect the value placed on a traditionally female role (child care), versus the stereotypically male work of lawn care. It is hard to imagine that many people would say that their lawns are more important than their children. The difference, it would seem, is rooted in a social value given to the different gender statuses and the value of associated roles, rather than in the job itself.

People disagree, often vehemently, about the importance of social variables like race, ethnicity, and class when discussing social inequality. Even the examples included in this chapter—teenage employment, gendered insults, and rags-to-riches stories—may incite debate. Because social structure is invisible, it is difficult to interpret precisely the ways in which an individual's experience is shaped by social forces that produce inequality. Anthropology doesn't settle the question once and for all, but it provides important concepts like social structure, status, and role that help cultivate discernment in perception and clarity in communication about how society influences individual experience.

The following sections present several categories—race, ethnicity, class, and caste—that are particularly important in understanding social structure. Gender is important, as well, and is the focus of this book's next chapter. Not all the concepts in this chapter function solely to structure inequality in society. Ethnicity, for example, is one category that is not always linked to social inequality. Race, class, and caste are primarily (if not exclusively) elements of social inequality, and in the contemporary world, ethnicity is frequently part of the same processes. In each case, it is only by understanding the history, meaning, and arrangement of these categories that we can begin to view and critique them.

Race

During the 1980s, a common daytime talk show topic was something like, "People who look white but are actually black." A guest would appear who seemed white by all common measures—skin color, hair texture, facial features. Then a sister or mother or father would come out and the audience would see a black person. The audience would gasp a little and the conversation would usually revolve around why the person who was "actually black" was trying to deny his or her "real identity."

Today this topic would undoubtedly seem oddly out-of-date, because it is more common to see so-called mixed race families in which members of a nuclear family have various features indicative of different racial identities. Racial categories and their meanings change over time. In U.S. society, over just a few decades, the talk show guest who once was pushed to identify as "white" or "black" may now self-identify as "mixed race." In 1997, golfer Tiger Woods, whose mother is from Thailand and father was a U.S. American of African, European, and American Indian descent, famously described himself as "Cablinasian," incorporating his Caucasian (white), American Indian, black, and Asian heritage into his self-identity. But it is not only racial categories and meanings that change over time; race itself is a cultural construction that hasn't always existed, doesn't exist in all cultures, and changes over time in cultures that are race-based.

Race is a cultural category that divides the human race into subspecies based on supposed biological differences. Unlike gender, in which the basic biological difference between men and women is universally acknowledged (albeit in very different ways), the physical features used to identify races are arbitrary in terms of their biological or genetic value. Biologically speaking, there is no more reason to group people according to hair texture, skin color, or eye shape than by any other biological feature.

Humans do vary from one another due to geography, culture, and "breeding pools" (this is the phrase used to describe the "gene pool" from which a person finds a mate). But some differences are infused with social meaning, while others are not included in social hierarchies. Geographer Jared Diamond notes that many human populations have biological distinctions by which they could be grouped.[3] For example, lactose intolerance (the inability to digest

3. Jared Diamond, "Race without Color," reprinted in *Applying Cultural Anthropology: An Introductory Reader*, 5th ed., ed. Aaron Podolefsky and Peter Brown (Mountain View, CA: Mayfield Publishing Company, 2001), 107–14.

milk products) is extremely frequent among the Japanese and most Native American groups. Ninety-nine percent of people in these groups cannot digest milk without taking a supplement of some kind. On the other hand, among the Fulani, a West African pastoral society, there is virtually *no* instance of lactose intolerance; nearly all adults can drink milk comfortably. The only other group with such a low rate of lactose intolerance is Swedish people. Lactose intolerance is a biological reality and makes a meaningful difference in people's lives, yet it is not considered a "racial" trait. Instead of having one race of black people, one of white, and another of Asian, it would make as much sense to say that one "race" of people are the Milk People, comprising the very dark-skinned African Fulani and the blond, blue-eyed Swedes, while the other "race" is the Lactose Intolerant, made up of Japanese and Native Americans.

Racial categories are described as neutral, scientific categories that simply reflect real biological and genetic human differences, but this is not true. The biological claim is really the ideological justification for racial categories that support particular systems of economic and political inequality.

The creation of racial categories

During the colonial period, when European countries began controlling the resources and populations of places in Africa, Asia, and Latin America, the development of plantation systems and immigration made it advantageous for those in positions of power (landowners, European rulers) to keep laborers and slaves from banding together. In the early days of the plantation systems in the Caribbean and North America, poor whites from Europe and poor blacks from Africa worked together, often marrying and living in the same communities.[4]

As these populations grew, it became clear that it was to the advantage of the European settlers and landowners to keep the poor European servants on their side, while keeping those of African descent under control as permanent labor. By adopting the idea of racial difference and racial superiority, the European colonialists and their supporters in Europe had a seemingly natural reason to keep Africans enslaved, while preventing poor European servants from finding common cause with poor African laborers. These processes are seen in historical documents such as journals, plantation records, and church records that began referring to people by color.

Scientists were influenced by these emerging popular sensibilities and encoded them in the seemingly objective and neutral language of science.

---

4. Native peoples were used as laborers also, but European diseases killed the vast majority of them, leaving the colonialists without labor. For a comprehensive history, see Thomas Gossett, *Race: The History of an Idea in America*, 2nd ed. (New York: Oxford University Press, 1997).

Anthropologists and Race

As early anthropologists encountered human physical and cultural diversity they had never seen before, many relied on their contemporary cultural sensibilities about the need for slavery, the inferiority of enslaved people, and the supposedly civilized, progressive, evolved status of European society. They didn't see how this ethnocentrism influenced their scientific work, so racial science "proved" the legitimacy of the very stereotypes and prejudices that were believed in the first place.

Franz Boas [1858–1942] was an early American anthropologist who challenged race theory. He studied biological changes in Europeans who immigrated to the United States, showing that dramatic biological change can occur due to culture and diet, not genetic change. Some anthropologists followed Boasian theory and sought to disprove racial theories, but many continued to believe in race theory.

Today, "The American Anthropological Association's Statement on 'Race'" represents the profession's official point of view. It states that:

"'Race' thus evolved as a worldview, a body of prejudgments that distorts our ideas about human differences and group behavior. Racial beliefs constitute myths about the diversity in the human species and about the abilities and behavior of people homogenized into 'racial' categories. The myths fused behavior and physical features together in the public mind, impeding our comprehension of both biological variations and cultural behavior, implying that both are genetically determined. Racial myths bear no relationship to the reality of human capabilities or behavior."[1]

1. American Anthropological Association, "AAA Statement on Race," www.aaanet.org/stmts/racepp.htm.

Contemporary categories of race began in scientific classification systems emerging in Europe in the eighteenth century. Scientists such as Carl Linnaeus, who devised the Latin naming system used by scientists today, thought the biological categories that applied to butterflies and birds (phylum, genus, and so forth) could be applied to human beings as well. These scholars used many different ways to classify human beings, but they did not agree on which characteristics (cranial capacity? height? body hair?) were most important, nor on how many racial categories there ought to be. A change in economic systems that developed during colonialism was the reason that the physical features of skin color and hair texture, along with notions of national heritage, coalesced as our contemporary understandings of race.

Despite claims that they are permanent and scientific descriptions of actual human differences, race categories vary dramatically across societies. A person labeled "colored" in South Africa could be "white" in the United States. A "white" person in parts of South America could be "black" in the United States. Based on the notion of *hypodescent*, the belief that race is inherited from one's ancestors, the United States imposed legal definitions of race that often had little to do with appearance but reflected only "blood." People in other countries, such as Brazil, identify members of the same nuclear family as different "races" (*tipos*) if those family members have different skin tones, hair texture, and eye color.

At the same time, the commitment to racial separation in the United States did not prevent some groups from "changing" race over time. Some European immigrant populations of the early twentieth century, such as Jews and Irish, were once not considered white. Later, as these groups assimilated culturally and as white groups felt more threatened by newer immigrants from places such as Puerto Rico or China, Jews and Irish people became "white." Categories such as Asian and Latino have emerged for political and economic reasons as well, mirroring the use of facial features and continental heritage as the primary determinants of race.

Race and inequality

W. I. Thomas stated a foundational principle of sociology with his theorem: "If men define situations as real, they are real in their consequences."[5] It is this process that makes race "real," even if the supposed biological divisions are not. Because people believe race is real, it exists as a powerful social category that has been, and continues to be, used to support social inequality.

First, in the United States, and in many countries throughout the world, people continue to use racial categories to explain, if not justify, social inequality and other phenomena. Books such as *The Bell Curve*, published in 1994, argue that race and intelligence are directly correlated, with some racial groups inferior to others. In the same way, some people root supposedly positive stereotypes of racial minorities (such as "Asians are good at math," or "Blacks are superior athletes") in racial categories. Though they seem positive, these racial stereotypes minimize the accomplishments of individuals by suggesting they had a biological advantage. Even medical research sometimes still uses racial groups (e.g., White and Asian women are more likely to get osteoporosis), rather than breaking out more fine-grained data around economic, social, or political realities. Racial oversimplification makes it more difficult for public health workers to identify environmental, economic, and social roots of disease.[6]

Second, in many places, including the United States, race correlates with social problems such as poverty, unemployment, violence, and imprisonment.

5. Known as the Thomas Theorem, this quotation was first published in William I. Thomas and Dorothy Swaine Thomas, *The Child in America: Behavior Problems and Programs* (New York: Alfred Knopf, 1928), 571–72.

6. Characteristics such as athletic ability and mathematical talent do have biological components. Biological anthropologists argue that some populations have advantages, particularly in specific athletic tasks such as sprints, high jumps, and the like. Attributing these abilities to racial categories such as "black," however, rather than much smaller population groups, grossly distorts the variation. For more discussion about athletics and race, see the American Anthropological Association's web-based curriculum, *Understanding Race*, www.understandingrace.org/lived/index.html.

Is Interracial Marriage Unbiblical?

Just as scientists absorbed racial prejudice from society into science, so did many believers transfer racial thinking from society into Christian theology. Concerns for interracial marriage have been important to Christians for hundreds of years. Passages such as Ezra 9:12 ("Therefore, do not give your daughters in marriage to their sons or take their daughters for your sons. Do not seek a treaty of friendship with them at any time, that you may be strong and eat the good things of the land and leave it to your children as an everlasting inheritance") are sometimes still used today to argue that God wants people to marry within racial groups.

Anthropology contributes to a better interpretation of Ezra 9:12: that God's concern in marriage is with the faith of his people and the purity of their worship of him, not genetics or race. The term "race" does not appear in Scripture except in versions in which the Samaritans are called "half-breeds," a term added by later commentators.[1] Defenders of racial ideology and a notion of purity have used the tower of Babel to suggest that God wants races to be separate. However, there is nothing in the story to suggest that the nations created by God were physically (racially) distinct. Nor is there anything to suggest that God wants these people to remain separate as individuals. The inclusion of Rahab (a Canaanite) and Ruth (a Moabite) into the line of Jesus suggests quite the opposite. God's covenant was not limited to a racial group, but to those—of any background—who would faithfully follow his commandments.

Concerns about children who are "half-breeds," "half-caste," or "mixed race" have nothing to do with an innate quality of people whose parents belong to different racial categories. The only challenges such individuals face come from dealing with a racial classification system that suggests individuals should belong to one race or another (and answering the common and annoying question, "So, what are you, anyway?").

God's promise calls all people to be part of a common family united in worship of God. It is not a promise for a genetic subset of humans to maintain their purity through selective reproduction. As Paul said to the people of Athens, "From one ancestor he made all nations to inhabit the whole earth, and he allotted the times of their existence and the boundaries of the places where they would live, so that they would search for God and perhaps grope for him and find him. . . . For we too are his offspring" (Acts 17:26–28 NRSV).

1. Tite Tiénou notes that while many seem to assume that Jewish enmity toward Samaritans had something to do with their "mixed blood," this was an idea brought to the Bible by later readers who assumed mixing "races" was bad. See Tite Tiénou, "The Samaritans: A Biblical-Theological Mirror for Understanding Racial, Ethnic, and Religious Identity?" in *This Side of Heaven: Race, Ethnicity, and Christian Faith*, ed. Robert J. Priest and Alvaro Nieves (New York: Oxford University Press, 2007), 211–23.

In the United States, though the majority of poor people are white, disproportionately high percentages of black and Hispanic people are poor. People from several racial minority groups, especially men, are overrepresented in prison. The likelihood of going to a substandard school, living in an under-resourced or environmentally degraded neighborhood, or experiencing abusive behavior from the police rises dramatically for some racial minority groups in the United States.

Third, because the ideology of race has supported the separation of individuals, families, and communities, some racial groups have developed their own cultural traditions. These ways of speaking, artistic expressions, worship practices, educational styles, naming of children, and other cultural phenomena related to nonwhite races are often stigmatized as less appropriate, inferior, or low-class. Members of these communities receive the message that if they want to fully participate in social life and have equal access to social resources, they should repudiate the well-established and rich cultural traditions that have developed among those racial groups kept separate for so long. Today, as racial categories are deconstructed and critiqued, people face the unique challenge of maintaining valued cultural practices and beliefs even while they reject the racial classifications that once organized society.

Challenging racial hierarchies means repudiating race as a valid scientific category while valuing and celebrating the cultural diversity that has emerged from the shadow of racial ideology.

Ethnicity

In 1990, the U.S. Census Bureau classified all U.S. residents according to four racial categories—"Black," "White," "American Indian or Native Alaskan," and "Asian and Pacific Islander." In 2000, the new categories made "Asian" its own group, put "Native Hawaiian" and "Other Pacific Islander" together, added "African American" to the category "black," and included the option "Some Other Race." While these categories were meant to identify biological heritage, after choosing a race, each person was asked to identify their ethnicity: "Hispanic or Latino" or "non-Hispanic or non-Latino."[7] Hispanic, the argument goes, refers to people who come from a Spanish-speaking country of Central or South America, and may be of any racial group, including Asian. It is a confusing distinction that people regularly debate. What is the difference between race and ethnicity? Where does one category stop and the other start?

Anthropologist Eloise Hiebert Meneses notes that, "in everyday conversations, people [in the United States] are inclined to use the terms *race* and *ethnicity* as functionally synonymous, with the former emphasizing biological connections within a group, and the latter, cultural connections within the same group."[8] As the previous section demonstrates, the biological connections indicated by race are actually cultural constructions themselves. Ethnic identities usually involve more tangible practices such as a common language, relationship to a particular place, or common cultural practices. Ethnic identi-

7. The U.S. Census Bureau changed these ethnic categories from "Hispanic," to "Hispanic or Latino" (and "non-Hispanic or non-Latino"). The reason for the addition of Latino is not clear from the explanation of the change, but may reflect changes in self-identity among people in the United States from Spanish-speaking countries.

8. Eloise Hiebert Meneses, "Science and the Myth of Biological Race," in *This Side of Heaven: Race, Ethnicity, and the Christian Faith*, ed. Alvaro Nieves and Robert J. Priest (New York: Oxford University Press, 2007), 33–46.

ties tend to be more complex in their definitions than racial categories, rooted in a wider variety of characteristics than simply physical appearance. However, anthropologists argue that, like race, ethnic categories are based on cultural "markers" in which members of one group distinguish themselves from others. *Ethnicity* is a category based on the sense of group affiliation derived from a distinct heritage or worldview as a "people." Most ethnic identities are believed to be linked to heritage or "bloodlines." At the same time, particular cultural features—language, religion, even occupation—may also be considered indispensable elements of the identity. The relative importance of cultural, biological, and historical criteria depends on the context.

Some anthropologists argue that the experience of ethnicity is a basic human impulse. *Primordialism* is the view that ethnic identity, like race, is a naturally occurring and immutable feature of human life. Primordialist scholars stress that the experience of belonging to a group—knowing who is part of that group and who is not—is found among people all over the world.

A White Guy Considers His Ethnicity

As a European American, I (Brian) have ancestors from a number of European countries, specifically Wales, Ireland, and Germany. When asked my "ethnicity," I often give this multifaceted answer. Yet none of the cultural traditions of those countries are particularly meaningful to me in terms of my current identity. In high school I studied the German language as a way to "get in touch with my roots." When visiting England, I made a special trip to Wales just so I could say I had been there. I have yet to make it to Ireland.

If I were to live in Germany, based on my heritage I could claim German citizenship. However, until I learned the German language and culture, I have no doubt that I would be considered a foreigner. Even after learning German, I would certainly have an accent that would give me away. My children could learn to speak German like natives, and they would be given citizenship through my family, but since they have a mother who is originally from Asia, I doubt they would ever be considered "ethnically German."

My father, whose family history in the United States predates the Civil War, likes to call himself a "Native American." That doesn't seem quite the right ethnic label for people whose family originally emigrated from Europe. Yet claiming Irish, Welsh, or German as my ethnicity—without having the linguistic, cultural, or social knowledge to be accepted as a member of those communities—does not quite work either.

Sociologist Mary Waters describes how white Americans often choose ethnicities, picking from a number of European groups to which they are actually related or to which they just believe they are related. She notes that white Americans sometimes develop minor forms of attachment to their European ethnicities, as I did, and others develop strong ties to those places. Other white Americans affiliate most strongly with "American" (like my father), or with their racial identity of "white," abandoning their families' historic ties to Europe.[1]

If nothing else, my personal circumstances help me understand the complexity of racial, ethnic, and national labels in our country and around the world.

1. Mary Waters, *Ethnic Options: Choosing Identities in America* (Berkeley: University of California Press, 1990).

Among many people, the "ethnic" term for the group can be translated into English as simply "the people" or "humans." The Waorani people of Ecuador are known to many North Americans (particularly Christians) through the killings of five U.S. missionaries in 1954.[9] At the time, these people were called the Auca Indians, but *Auca* is a Quechua word meaning "enemy" or "savage." The name used by the people themselves came from their word for "human"—*Wao*. In other words, while those around this group called them "The Savages," they referred to themselves as "The Humans." Similarly, prior to the arrival of the Spanish, the Navajo did not call themselves Navajo but used the term *Diné*, meaning "human." Examples come from all over the world, suggesting that human beings have a deeply rooted, if not universal, propensity to create social boundaries, distinguishing "us" from "them."

What these examples also demonstrate, however, are the political dimensions of ethnicity. By naming the Waorani the "Auca," the Ecuadorian majority was able to justify oppressive policies and discrimination. Anthropologists note that ethnic identities always have political and economic dimensions, often facilitating the exclusion of some from land, resources, or opportunities that belong to "us." *Instrumentalism* (or *constructivism*) is the idea that ethnicity changes with people's interests and context. Instrumentalist scholars counter the view that ethnic identity formation is a product of a universal human impulse. Instead, they emphasize the ways in which ethnic identities are created, shaped, and mobilized in response to economic and political circumstances.

While they disagree about the cause of ethnic identities, both primordialist and instrumentalist views acknowledge that ethnic identities are expressed and maintained through linguistic, cultural, and social markers. These markers, such as language, food, and clothing characteristic of a group, often have a long history. Even where unique languages disappear or distinctive clothing or foods are forgotten, however, people develop ways to distinguish themselves. The English tried at various points to assimilate the Scottish, forcing them to give up their distinct identity and to submit to English law and culture. The English were successful in virtually eliminating the Scottish language (few modern Scots speak Gaelic except those who have studied it in school). Scottish identity was not so easily squashed, however. In the eighteenth century, politicians in Scotland, in the long tradition of resistance to English rule, promoted a distinctive type of clothing, the kilt. Prior to that point, the kilt was not widely worn by Scots living in the lowlands (that is,

9. The story of these men—Jim Elliot, Nate Saint, Ed McCully, Roger Youderian, and Pete Fleming—was told in a series of widely read *Life* magazine articles in the 1950s. Later Elisabeth Elliot (Jim Elliot's widow) wrote a bestselling book recounting the incident and the years that followed; see Elisabeth Elliot, *Through Gates of Splendor* (Wheaton: Tyndale House Publishers, 1981). The story is fictionalized in the film *End of the Spear* (Beverly Hills, CA: Twentieth Century Fox Home Entertainment, 2006).

the majority of Scottish people), and likely looked quite different when worn by highland Scots. Historian Hugh Trevor-Roper credits the invention of the kilt to Thomas Rawlinson, an Englishman working in an iron-smelting furnace, who found the traditional tunic of the highland people a "cumbersome, inconvenient habit" and had a tailor cut it down for ease of use. Today, the kilt is seen as an example of "historic" Scottish identity, not the invention of an English metalworker and a tool of Scottish politicians for protesting oppressive English laws. Regardless of its history, it has become an indispensable symbol of Scottish identity that shapes an ongoing sense of shared history and culture.[10]

In some societies, ethnicity is seen as fairly unimportant for social organization. In relatively homogeneous societies like Korea or Armenia, more important differences within society include class or religion. Also, in multicultural societies with a dominant majority, ethnicity does not play a significant role in the way those in the majority think about themselves. For example, many white U.S. Americans only consider their "ethnicity" in terms of a distant heritage, relevant on holidays or at family gatherings where key markers (foods, songs, clothing) are brought out in celebration. Instead of ethnicity, U.S. Americans in the racial majority are more likely to think in terms of nationality and citizenship as key categories of belonging.

In other countries and cultures, ethnic identity is critical. Ethnic identity can become dramatically more or less important over the course of a single generation. At the end of the twentieth century, bloody ethnic conflict broke out between Serbs, Croats, and Bosnians living in the former Yugoslavia. This represented a dramatic shift from how they had interacted just three decades earlier. For centuries, neighbors of various ethnicities had lived side by side, intermarried, and spoken the same language. When the central powers dissolved and national identity crumbled, ethnic identities became critical determinants of who would live in specific areas, who would control the government, and how resources would be distributed.

New ethnic categories may emerge as a response to discrimination or the need for representation. The ethnic categories used in the U.S. Census, Hispanic/Latino versus non-Hispanic/non-Latino, are not based on an obvious sense of shared history or identity. Peruvians, Puerto Ricans, and Guatemalans may all speak Spanish, but they have very different cultures and histories. In the United States, however, these disparate people often have similar experiences of exclusion and discrimination. They may discover common interests and political goals around such concerns as immigration law, education, and political representation. The label "Hispanic" therefore becomes a political resource as well as an ethnic category.

10. Hugh Trevor-Roper, *The Invention of Scotland: Myth and History* (New Haven: Yale University Press, 2008).

Is "American" an Ethnic Category?

Most people in the United States would likely argue that "American" is *not* an ethnicity. America, they would argue, is made up of many ethnic groups—Irish, Italian, Vietnamese, Puerto Rican—but anyone can "be American." It is part of the American legacy of immigration that we are a "melting pot" (or "quilt," or "salad bowl") of different ethnicities.

At the same time, unacknowledged markers of Americanness are defended in the ways Americans vote. Occasionally states or towns will pass "English Only" laws, prohibiting the use of languages other than English for government services. Although the United States does not have a national language, the use of English is often highlighted as an "American" attribute.

Christianity, particularly Protestantism, has often served as a marker of Americanness. In 1960, the first—and only—Roman Catholic president was elected (John Kennedy). In 2006, Minnesotans elected Representative Keith Ellison, the first Muslim to serve in Congress. There has never been an avowed atheist elected as president of the United States, and many people thought former Massachusetts Governor Mitt Romney's membership in the Mormon religion hurt him in his run for the U.S. presidency in 2008. It is hard to imagine a Buddhist or Hindu being elected president, regardless of how well qualified or capable. Other than Kennedy, only Protestants claiming membership in a Protestant denomination have been elected president.

The fact that Asian Americans and Hispanic Americans, who have lived in the United States as long as European Americans and African Americans, are only recently being elected to public office reflects the slowly changing definition of "American" from "white," to "white or black," to finally include other so-called racial groups.

Although belief in equal opportunity and individuality work against the idea of "American" as an ethnic identity, cultural markers still allow for an evaluation of who's in and who's out.

Just as racial categories became the basis for legal and everyday forms of discrimination, so too has ethnicity become a way to exclude some from access to resources or power. When new immigrant groups come to the United States, the established population of the country often stigmatizes the ethnic category of the newcomers. Although they would later benefit from their ability to move into the "white" racial category, Irish and Italians at the turn of the twentieth century experienced discrimination. Because previous European immigrants resented their arrival, they were denied housing, employment, and educational opportunities based on ethnicity. Today, Mexicans, Africans, and Central Americans often find themselves stigmatized due to accents or skin color. As a result, doctors, lawyers, and engineers from other countries may find themselves unable to get any but the most menial jobs after immigrating to the United States.

Class and Caste

Class (also called *social class*) is a cultural category describing how people are grouped according to their positions within the economy. Class systems are intrinsically hierarchical; membership in higher classes always provides privileged access to prestige, power, and wealth. Class systems may be more or less open, depending on the criteria by which a person is considered a member of a class. The United States is what anthropologists call an *open class system*, meaning it is possible for people to move from one class to another. U.S. Americans celebrate rags-to-riches stories on stage and screen, and use them to promote the belief that the class system is very flexible and opportunities are open to all. Many studies have demonstrated that while social mobility is possible, however, the vast majority of people live, marry, worship, and socialize throughout their lives with members of the class in which they were raised. This is due both to the ways in which wealth provides access to political and social prestige, as well as the cultural boundaries of class identity.

In societies in which class is particularly fixed, anthropologists use the term *caste*. A caste system assigns individuals to a position at birth, and mobility between castes is restricted. Such a system often prohibits people from marrying outside their caste and restricts caste members from working with, living near, or even touching members of other castes. The most well-known example of a caste system is in India, where caste membership is supported by Hinduism. Specifically, members of the highest caste, called Brahmins, are deemed superior while those at the bottom, the Dalits or "untouchables," are deemed almost less than human.[11] Traditionally, members of particular castes would be restricted to the jobs of their caste. As the Indian economy has changed rapidly in recent years, some of these economic distinctions have begun to change. Yet many people, based on their commitment to Hinduism and traditional Indian culture, maintain strong marriage and social preferences for those within their own caste or higher.

Culture and Class

Karl Marx (see chap. 11) made class the foundation of his social theory, arguing that differential access to economic resources was the most basic inequality in society. He argued that all the social and cultural differences between the classes—educational attainment, religious practices, crime rates, ways of looking at the world—were consequences of economic disparities created by capitalism. Although many people in the United States consider class to be almost entirely based on income, studies have demonstrated that how people speak often influences others' assumptions about their background, intelligence, and education. In the 1960s, linguist William Labov compared the speech of employees in three New York department stores—Saks, Macy's,

---

11. The Dalits are considered so impure that technically they are not part of the caste system at all; they are Hindus born without a caste. For this reason they can do things generally forbidden for Hindus, such as eating beef and touching dead animals. However, their "caste-lessness" effectively makes them the lowest category in the system, or the bottom caste.

and S. Klein (which has since closed)—catering to the upper, middle, and lower classes respectively. Measuring specific indicators, such as the pronunciation of the final "r" on the word "floor," he found disparities between the employees. Labov concluded that the upper-class stores only hired people with the "proper" accents for the image and clientele they sought.[12]

Many anthropologists have noted that in highly stratified societies, class identity is less about having money than it is about having the opportunity to learn the cultural norms that suggest membership in a particular social class. Classes are symbolically differentiated by patterns of speech (a country twang as opposed to the Scarlet O'Hara–like Southern drawl), tastes and preferences (the jazz club over country line dancing), and even religious affiliation. Even when a person does not have a high income, by exhibiting symbols of class affiliation, he or she has a better chance of networking toward access to money and power.

Sociologists study the degree of mobility in various societies, looking primarily at variables such as education, race, religion, sex, and income. Anthropologists add the element of culture, as well as the ways people learn to be part of a class. For example, while anyone can go to an art museum, many people do not know what to do there. They may wonder why a giant canvas covered in multicolored squares should be called art, or what makes a Renoir different from a van Gogh. Those who have learned what anthropologist Pierre Bourdieu called "the code" know why abstract art (that is to say, *some* abstract art) is hanging in the museum even though it seems any four-year-old could paint it. Moreover, they have learned how to stand, move through the museum, and mutter appreciative phrases at just the right time. Those who do not know these habits and codes often see it all as a matter of personal taste. They may leave the museum saying, "I'm just not into that fancy stuff." Bourdieu argued that rather than simply personal preference, those who enjoy art have learned to do so as part of their social class. The same is true, of course, for learning how to appreciate a NASCAR race or a country music concert, but those forms tend to be more open and can be learned in more informal and accessible settings (watching television) and do not require access to privileged places (e.g., elite schools or art studios). How to be a member of higher classes is learned and taught in institutional settings that are often restricted by income, reinforcing the boundaries of class.

Some societies, even though they are more equitable in resource distribution, may be considered less open because class mobility is limited. The United States, which is relatively open in terms of class mobility, is also far more *in*equitable in the distribution of resources than many other countries in which class mobility is strictly limited. For example, in 2001, the richest 20

12. William Labov, *Social Stratification of English in New York City* (Washington, DC: Center for Applied Linguistics, 1966).

percent of households in the United States held more than 40 percent of the wealth (the poorest 20 percent had less than 10 percent). In Japan, by contrast, the top 20 percent had less than 35 percent of the wealth.[13] Because the symbolic boundaries of class are relatively less rigid and more easily adopted in the United States, as opposed to Japan with its centuries-old traditions of nobility and royalty, the class system in the United States is considered more open in spite of greater inequalities of wealth.

Christians, Inequality, and Reconciliation

An anthropological understanding of social organization helps Christians to perceive the invisible structures that give form to our social lives and to make more informed decisions about how to be a blessing to others on both the individual level and the structural level. Racial categories, for example, were not created by God. When the apostle Paul writes that Christians should not "conform any longer to the pattern of this world" (Rom. 12:2), we can see the idea of racial categorization as one such pattern.[14] In Revelation, John describes "every nation, tribe, people and language" worshiping God before the throne (Rev. 7:9). Ethnic identity and ethnic diversity are part of God's good creation, though at the same time, sin damages ethnicity through hierarchy and violence.

In his vision of the new heaven and new earth, John writes of a place without suffering (Rev. 21:4), where nations are united in peace (Rev. 21:24), economic resources are available to all (Rev. 22:2), and everyone lives under the reign of God. Until that time, the Scriptures call on God's people to serve Christ by serving "the least of these," and to do what we can to redress oppression and injustice.

Christians have, of course, disagreed about what redemption may mean. Some have argued Jesus would have us overthrow the systems perpetuating inequality in society. Liberation theology emphasizes the role of the church in directly confronting the structural roots of inequality and oppression. Others, citing Paul's injunction for Christians to be subject to earthly rulers and Jesus's unwillingness to lead a revolution against the Romans, believe Christians should work within current systems for reform. Sometimes known as "incarnational" or "missional" theology, this approach emphasizes the need for wealthy or privileged Christians to identify with the poor and marginalized. Others, such as Mennonites and other Anabaptists, have traditionally encouraged Christians to develop separate social lives and structures, chal-

13. Data taken from The World Bank, *2001 World Development Indicators* (Washington, DC: The World Bank, 2001).

14. Jenell Williams Paris, "Race: Critical Thinking and Transformative Possibilities," in *This Side of Heaven*, 19–32.

lenging injustice by refusing to participate in social systems that support oppression.[15]

However we read the Scriptures, there is no doubt that the church has often been shamefully slow to challenge systems of inequality. In 1963, in response to a call from several white ministers to work only through legal means and abandon his protests, Martin Luther King Jr. wrote, in his famous "Letter from a Birmingham Jail":

> I have heard numerous southern religious leaders admonish their worshipers to comply with a desegregation decision because it is the law, but I have longed to hear white ministers declare: "Follow this decree because integration is morally right and because the Negro is your brother." In the midst of blatant injustices inflicted upon the Negro, I have watched white churchmen stand on the sideline and mouth pious irrelevancies and sanctimonious trivialities. In the midst of a mighty struggle to rid our nation of racial and economic injustice, I have heard many ministers say: "Those are social issues, with which the gospel has no real concern." And I have watched many churches commit themselves to a completely other-worldly religion which makes a strange, un-Biblical distinction between body and soul, between the sacred and the secular.[16]

Billy Graham, who integrated his crusades when many told him he should not, regretted that he did not address inequality in the United States sooner. When asked what he might have done different in his life, Graham replied, "I wish I had gotten more education. If I could have, I would have gotten a PhD in anthropology, to understand the race situation in this country better."[17] Both King and Graham saw that understanding and confronting the cultural and social dimensions of inequality are important for living out the second greatest commandment: to love our neighbor as ourselves.

Terms

achieved status: a status that a person chooses or becomes associated with due to behaviors or skills.

ascribed status: a status given to an individual through no choice or action of her or his own; it is a status granted by circumstances of birth.

15. For a comparative study of Christian approaches to social institutions, see Sandra Joireman, *Church, State, and Citizen: Christian Approaches to Political Engagement* (New York: Oxford University Press, 2009).

16. King's famous letter has been reprinted many times and may be found on many internet sites. One published source is Martin Luther King Jr., "Letter from a Birmingham Jail," *Philosophical Questions: East and West*, ed. Bina Gupta and Jitendra Nath Mohanty (Lanham, MD: Rowman & Littlefield, 2000), 274–87.

17. Graham as interviewed in *Parade*, October 20, 1996, 6.

caste: a tightly bounded social group based on family background. Caste systems assign individuals to a position at birth, and mobility between castes is restricted.

class (or *social class*): a cultural category describing how people are grouped according to their positions within the economy.

cultural capital: cultural knowledge, including linguistic skills.

ethnicity: a category based on the sense of group affiliation derived from a distinct heritage or worldview as a "people."

hypodescent: the belief that race is inherited from one's ancestors.

institution: a cluster of statuses organized around a common focus, such as education, law, or art.

instrumentalism (or *constructivism*): the idea that ethnicity changes with people's interests and context.

master status: the status that tends to be most important in shaping a person's life.

open class system: a class system in which it is possible for people to move from one class to another.

power: the ability to influence others.

prestige: the social affirmation and approval given to some members of society.

primordialism: the view that ethnic identity, like race, is a naturally occurring and immutable feature of human life.

race: a cultural category that divides the human race into subspecies based on supposed biological differences.

role: prescribes expected or required behaviors for those who occupy a particular status.

role conflict or *role strain*: the stress that occurs when the behavioral expectations from various roles come into play simultaneously.

social inequality: the differential access to economic resources, political power, or social prestige that results from social stratification.

social stratification: the organization of people into ranked groups, or hierarchies, based on particular characteristics.

social structure (also called *social organization* or *social order*): the ways people coordinate their lives in relation to one another at the level of society.

status: any position a person may occupy in the social structure.

wealth: economic status, or access to economic resources.

Devotion 1

Who Are We in Christ?

. . . for in Christ Jesus you are all children of God through faith. As many of you as were baptized into Christ have clothed yourselves with Christ. There is no longer Jew or Greek, there is no longer slave or free, there is no longer male and female; for all of you are one in Christ Jesus. And if you belong to Christ, then you are Abraham's offspring, heirs according to the promise. (Gal. 3:26–29 NRSV)

In this passage, Paul addresses three dimensions of social inequality: gender, ethnicity, and class. Paul encourages the Galatian believers to view themselves with a new perspective. Believers should not rely on the social hierarchies of their culture, which prioritized men over women, free persons over slaves, and (among some believers) Jews over Greeks. Instead, they should see themselves as Abraham's seed, all heirs to the promise given to Abraham. This passage doesn't speak directly to race, because race wasn't a concept in the culture at the time. Interestingly, however, the metaphor of Abraham's seed calls forth a consideration of genetics. In Christ, we are all part of the same family, so racial concerns about genetic purity are no longer valid.

This passage doesn't erase all distinction between men and women, slaves and free persons, or different cultures. That is as ridiculous as it is impossible, and would ignore the suffering of those in the lower ranks of each hierarchy. Instead, the new perspective empowers people to see each other for who they really are: children of God in the lineage of Abraham. This fresh view may encourage new forms of love and mission that would address the inequalities in society that demean those who deserve better because they are part of God's family.

Devotion 2

Real Worship

If you do away with the yoke of oppression, with the pointing finger and malicious talk, and if you spend yourselves in behalf of the hungry and satisfy the needs of the oppressed, then your light will rise in the darkness, and your night will become like the noonday. (Isa. 58:9–10)

In this passage, the prophet Isaiah addresses the Israelites harshly. The Israelites had been fasting—but also exploiting their workers. They had been praying—but continuing to quarrel and fight. With their words they said they were seeking God's will, but with their actions they showed that all they really wanted was to advance their own self-interest.

Isaiah encourages them to discover the deep meaning of fasting and praying. Real worship isn't just a day or an hour set aside for personal devotion. Real worship includes loosing the chains of injustice (v. 6), sharing food with the hungry (v. 7), providing shelter to the homeless (v. 7), and, at the very least, caring for those within your own family and religious group (v. 7). These are the worship practices that will bring true healing and blessing. They will infuse conventional worship practices, such as prayer and fasting, with real meaning.

5

Gender and Sexuality

After studying this chapter, you should be able to:

1. Describe how anthropologists define gender, sex, and sexuality.
2. Appreciate how anthropologists study gender variations, gender socialization, and sexuality.
3. Explain how sexuality and gender are embedded in systems of social inequality.
4. Understand how anthropological perspectives on gender and sexuality can be helpful for the church.

Introduction

In everyday conversation, sex and gender are often used interchangeably to refer to various aspects of maleness and femaleness. A woman may mean the same thing by describing a man as the "opposite sex" or the "male gender" or "masculine." Similarly, sexuality is often considered to be automatically, or naturally, linked to sex and gender. In this view, most people in a society are assumed to have a sex, a gender, and a sexuality that all fit together in a male way or in a female way.

These assumptions are being challenged today on a number of levels. In various cultural contexts, men and women are challenging the gender roles and expectations associated with their biological sex. Some work to change gender-related social inequalities. Sexual minorities are challenging their status as "minorities," arguing instead that links between gender and sexuality should be more flexible. Some challenge even the link between biological sex and social gender roles, with people born male living as women, and vice versa.

Sexuality and gender are some of the most challenging issues facing Christians today. Local churches and entire denominations are fraught with conflict over the proper role of women, the morality of homosexuality, same-sex marriage, and ordination of gay ministers. Many of these issues are at the forefront of anthropological research as well, as ethnographers describe how gender and sexuality are lived out in various cultures and theorize more generally about what gender and sexuality mean in the human experience.

In this chapter, we first describe how anthropologists study gender. Then we discuss anthropological perspectives on sexuality and sexual diversity. After exploring how social inequality and discrimination are often expressed in terms of gender and sexual differences, we offer some ways in which anthropology can benefit the church as Christians engage these topics.

Gender

For anthropologists, sex and gender are distinct concepts. *Sex* refers to biological maleness or femaleness, known as *sexual dimorphism*, usually given at birth. *Gender* describes what it means to be male or female in a particular culture. For example, gender statuses such as girl and boy, or man and woman, are English language categories that correlate gender with biological sex and make an age distinction between childhood and adulthood. In cultures around the world, gender finds a wide variety of expressions, with many gender statuses changing according to age (boy versus man), class (a "broad" versus a "lady"), marital status (Miss or Missus) and more. Sex, on the other hand, is typically fixed as male or female as given at birth. In the case of sex-change operations, an anthropologist may refer to a person as natally male (born male), but socially female, or vice versa.

It is an oversimplification to assume that gender is cultural and sex is biological because people invented gender distinctions and God created sexual differences. Sex and gender are both cultural insofar as humans create categories to organize the diversity of the natural world. Even the sex of a newborn is already influenced by culture; the uterine environment and even the condition of sperm and egg before conception were influenced by the parents' environment. Sex and gender are both part of creation as well, insofar as God created humans both with sexually differentiated bodies and the capacity to name and assign meaning to human biological traits.

Sex and gender are elemental for human social organization. If you walk toward the baby clothing section of a department store, you may notice the section divided in two. Even from a distance, it is easy to see that one part (usually larger) is dominated by pink and pastels. The smaller part is dominated by shades of blue and primary colors. Upon closer inspection, in addition to the different colors, particular motifs are reserved for one side or the other. On the pink side are flowers, harmless animals (e.g., herbivores such as bunnies and ponies), and symbols associated with love, such as hearts. On the blue side are forms of transportation (trucks, spaceships), sports, and carnivorous (or at least omnivorous) animals such as bears and tigers. From infancy, our society associates girls with love, gentleness, and beauty, and boys with risk taking, accomplishment, and industry.[1]

Gender is socially constructed; it does not flow automatically from biological sex. People need to know where to place another person in a social order, and gender is a basic element of that order. Parents are often concerned, for instance, that strangers correctly perceive their newborn as a boy or girl; they often choose symbolically colored clothing, blankets, strollers, and diaper bags to communicate that "it's a girl" or "it's a boy" to the public. Dressing an infant in gender-specific clothing makes the sex of the child visible while reinforcing meanings and significance of the sex difference. Sex and gender are expressed and reinforced in order for members of the society—from infants to adults—to internalize their culture's norms.

In the United States, gender statuses—boy, girl, man, or woman—are usually ascribed, based on biology. A *gender status* is a position a person can occupy in the social order that is directly related to maleness or femaleness. In most Western countries there are two dominant genders, reflecting sexual dimorphism. Each gender status is connected to a *gender role*, a set of expectations regarding proper behavior and appearance for a particular gender. Cultures may have periods of time in which gender roles are widely accepted by most people, and also have periods of change during which norms are renegotiated and redefined. Gender roles in the United States, for instance, have changed over the past century, particularly for women. Whereas it used to be unacceptable, even inconceivable, for a woman to wear pants in public, work in construction, or be a professional boxer, these are now unremarkable occurrences. At the same time, research on U.S. families shows that women continue to perform the vast majority of domestic labor (child care, laundry, cleaning), even when they have full-time work outside the home. Women have moved toward traditionally masculine domains much more than men have adopted traditionally feminine roles.

U.S. society is in an active time of negotiation and change with respect to gender roles, but these changes extend to gender statuses as well, and even

1. This is certainly true in U.S. department stores; throughout much of the world today, the pink/blue motif has been successfully marketed. Shoppers in many countries would find their own department stores selling similar goods.

Studying Men in Anthropological Perspective

The anthropology of gender isn't just about women. While the experiences and perspectives of men have been overrepresented in anthropology, most of the time they weren't analyzed in terms of their maleness. Men's experiences were simply taken as "human" experiences. It is important to analyze women's experiences as such, and the same is true for men.

What happens when men work in a feminized occupation? Sociologists Kevin Henson and Jackie Krasas Rogers did participant observation among male temporary clerical workers in the United States.[1] Temporary clerical workers are most often women, and the work environment is "feminized" in that it calls for caretaking behaviors, deference, and is low status because it has no upward mobility. How do men preserve or assert their masculinity in this context?

Henson and Rogers found that men's masculinity was challenged in that others perceived them as failures, not having secured a "real" job. Their heterosexuality was also called into question when temporary clerical work required caretaking behaviors or deference. Instead of redefining clerical work as masculine, most men reinforced the view that temporary clerical work is feminine. They distanced themselves from their job with cover stories that explained why they had this job, why they weren't professional losers or gay, and why they wouldn't be there long. Men also refused or resisted particularly deferential tasks, such as fetching coffee, tolerating supervisors' bad moods with a smile, or filling the office candy jar.

The ethnographers wondered whether male presence in a female-dominated industry might raise the status of the industry or change the nature of the work. What they found instead was that men preserved and defended their masculinity by reinforcing the feminine nature of the work. This is an example of how the anthropology of gender can bring insight to men's experiences as well as to women's.

1. Kevin Henson and Jackie Krasas Rogers, "Why Marcia You've Changed! Male Clerical Workers Doing Masculinity in a Feminized Occupation," *Gender and Society* 15, no. 2 (2001): 218–38.

sex. In academics, activism, and politics in particular, some believe the binary gender structure should be opened up to allow those born male or female to define and present themselves in myriad ways beyond the "girl or boy, woman or man" framework that currently exists. "Gender blenders" are individuals who blend existing gender categories or create something entirely new. Others, including some anthropologists, push for a new cultural configuration of even biological sex. A small percentage of people, referred to as *intersex*, are born with ambiguous genitals due to a variety of biological conditions. Some argue that these manifestations of biological sex should be considered normal, not an aberration of maleness or femaleness. In this view, sex as well as gender should be conceptualized as a spectrum of human diversity with all points on the spectrum given equal respect, not as a binary system that privileges some and portrays others as abnormal.

Many theologians and Christian laypersons as well see Genesis 1:27 as teaching that sex difference is part of the image of God in humanity. In Genesis 2, in which the man and woman meet each other, the man recognizes the biological differences between him and the woman while affirming their common humanity. Most Christians today agree that sexual dimorphism and a binary system of gender statuses correlate with God's creational intent.

Christians disagree, however, about gender roles. Even as Christians continue negotiating what biblical gender roles would mean in our culture, we need to be aware of secular arguments that push much further, deconstructing gender statuses and sex categories.

Gender variations

Christians have always accepted some degree of gender variation according to local cultural customs. For instance, in 1 Corinthians Paul described how particular gender roles symbolize authority and respect for God. Women should wear head coverings and have long hair, and men should not cover their heads while praying. Christians today still discuss what this passage means, and while some continue these practices literally, most Christians agree that these symbols reflected specific gender norms, even as the values to which they refer are timeless and universal. Men and women may symbolize authority and respect in various ways, and gendered presentation of the head is not a requirement for Christians in all cultures.

Some cultural understandings of gender, however, push beyond a two-gender system that reflects biological dimorphism. In the Philippines, for example, it is not uncommon to encounter a man—in the workplace, on public transportation, or even in church—dressed as a woman. These men are known as *bakla*, a gender status that involves a natal man dressed as a woman. *Bakla* is sometimes translated into English as "transvestite" or "cross-dresser," but that does not capture the *bakla*'s role in Philippine society. Men who dress as women in the United States or other Western countries generally do so secretly, in special clubs, or in urban places known for nonnormative behavior. *Bakla*, on the other hand, exist in many Philippine towns and cities, from the largest urban centers to the smallest rural villages. They dress as women all day, not just for contests, festivals, shows, or parties. Sometimes they are dressed in men's clothing but wear makeup, nail polish, and have long hair. Other times they may be seen on the bus wearing a velvet cocktail dress or demure pant suit with a stylish manicure and jewelry. Many, if not most, Filipino television shows feature a *bakla* character, typically a flamboyant, fast-talking, sarcastic jokester in a role meant for comic relief.

Bakla are understood to be involved in same-sex relationships, although there is a category of "gay man" in the Philippines that is not the same as *bakla*. Gay men are understood through the lens of traditional masculinity; gay identity is stigmatized, perhaps even more strongly than in the United States. At the same time, a young, unmarried man may have his first sexual experience with a *bakla*, and it would not necessarily mark him as "gay," or be considered deviant sexual behavior, so long as he goes on to marry and have relations with a woman.

Although media portrayals of a variety of gender statuses and sexualities are becoming more common in the United States, it is hard to imagine the same scenario in everyday life. Even as some distinctions between men's and women's behavior and dress have been minimized, for a man to go to work every day dressed as a woman would raise a few eyebrows in most U.S. towns. It cannot be argued that the difference between the two countries is primarily one of religion and morality. In terms of church attendance, the Philippines has a much higher percentage of Christians than the United States. Catholic and many Protestant churches in the Philippines, as in the United States, teach scriptural injunctions against homosexual behavior.[2] So why would people in the United States react negatively to this phenomenon while Filipinos seem to tolerate and even approve of it?[3]

The difference is in the social construction of gender in the two societies. Filipinos call the *bakla* a third gender. *Third gender* is a gender other than man or woman. Third genders are conceptualized differently in various cultures. Unlike in the United States, where a man dressing as a woman is seen to be mixing two distinct social statuses—a violation of the social order—the *bakla* is a separate status with a distinct place in the social structure. Historians and anthropologists trace the contemporary *bakla* back to pre-Christian religious practices in the Philippines. A *baybalan* was a natal man who dressed as a woman, or was born with ambiguous genitalia, and occupied a social status "betwixt and between" the two genders. This ancient social role was understood to offer specialized access to spiritual power that ordinary men and women did not have (see the discussion of liminality in chap. 9). Anthropologists have found many cultures where third (and even fourth, fifth, and more) genders exist along with men and women. Because there is no confusion or ambiguity with who or what they are, what looks like highly socially aberrant behavior from one perspective is understood as making perfect sense in another.

Anthropological research on gender

Gender is now considered such an important element of culture that any ethnographer should take it into consideration. In the early years of the discipline, however, most ethnographers were male, and they often developed

2. A 2001 study found Filipinos the most likely to call homosexual behavior "always wrong" in a survey of people in twenty-nine different nations. The United States was number twelve. Jonathan Kelly, "Attitudes towards Homosexuality in 29 Nations," *Australian Monitor* 4, no. 1 (2001):15–20.

3. This is not to argue that every person in the Philippines responds to *baklas* in the same way, nor that everyone in the United States would have the same opinion about the phenomenon. However, the ability of the *bakla* to maintain a public presence and be received very differently than he would in the United States reflects a widely shared distinction in the way Filipinos and Americans respond to the identity. Note, however, that there is another category of "homosexual" in the Philippines that includes women and men who fit the category of "gay" in the United States. This identity remains a highly stigmatized one in the Philippines.

A *bakla* in a civic parade.
Photo: Brian Howell

the strongest rapport with male informants in the culture they were studying. They often overgeneralized the male experience as the "human experience," or simply focused on male life to the exclusion of women's activities and perspectives.

Some anthropologists, even in the early twentieth century, worked to counter this bias. Anthropologist Margaret Mead's 1949 book, *Male and Female: A Study of the Sexes in a Changing World*, offered anthropological insight to American readers interested in creating change in their own society.[4] Mead studied numerous cultures in the Pacific, sometimes on her own and sometimes with a male research partner or partners who could establish a different kind of rapport with male informants. Based on her fieldwork, she argued that gender traits commonly taken as natural—such as affection for parenting, capacity for nurture, ambition, or styles of childhood play—are culturally produced; that is, in various cultures, supposedly gendered traits are sometimes held by women, sometimes by men, and sometimes by both genders.

Other anthropologists have restudied classic ethnographies, uncovering gender bias in their analysis. For example, early twentieth-century anthro-

4. Margaret Mead, *Male and Female: A Study of the Sexes in a Changing World* (New York: William Morrow & Co., 1949).

pologist Bronislaw Malinowski described the *kula ring* exchange system, a predictable pattern of exchange around the chain of Trobriand Islands.[5] Men in the Trobriand Islands exchange armbands and shell necklaces across islands. The items are not valuable in and of themselves, but the exchange solidifies relationships and strengthens the regional economy. Decades later, Annette Weiner traveled to the Trobriand Islands to study tourism but was surprised to see a complex system of exchange among women, involving banana leaf bunches and grass skirts, that Malinowski didn't document. Her ethnography, *Women of Value, Men of Renown: New Perspectives in Trobriand Exchange*, influenced anthropologists to consider not only what earlier ethnographers reported but what they failed to report.[6] It also emphasized the importance of women's work and women's perspectives.

Gender came to the forefront of anthropology when feminist anthropologists launched a major critique of the discipline in the 1970s and 1980s. They did gender-focused restudies (such as Weiner's), analyzed entire subdisciplines in light of gender, and wrote theory about sex and gender. Much of this work is still influential today.[7]

Gender socialization

Compared to those of other species, the physical differences between human males and females are quite small. Anyone who has seen bears is struck by the enormous difference between males and females; males are often twice the size of the females. Among some insects, birds, and fish, the males and females do not even look like the same species and have very different body shapes, colors, and sizes. In humans, men average just a few inches taller and perhaps 20 percent heavier than women. Through exercise and diet, individual women can become stronger than the average man. In other words, biologically speaking, human men and women are more alike than they are different.

Yet we often experience significant differences between men and women, such as in styles of communication or emotional responses and expressions. There is a great deal of research and debate about the relative importance of cultural versus biological origins of such traits, but the wide variety of

5. Bronislaw Malinowski, *Argonauts of the Western Pacific: An Account of Native Enterprise and Adventure in the Archipelagoes of Melanesian New Guinea* (New York: Routledge & Sons, 1922).

6. Annette Weiner, *Women of Value, Men of Renown: New Perspectives in Trobriand Exchange* (Austin: University of Texas Press, 1976).

7. Three important sources include: Micaela di Leonardo, ed., *Gender at the Crossroads of Knowledge: Feminist Anthropology in the Postmodern Era* (Berkeley: University of California Press, 1991); Rayna Reiter, ed., *Toward an Anthropology of Women* (New York: Monthly Review Press, 1975); Michelle Zimbalist Rosaldo and Louise Lamphere, eds., *Woman, Culture, and Society* (Stanford, CA: Stanford University Press, 1974).

behaviors, norms, and ideals associated with masculinity and femininity seen around the world makes it clear that culture is the stronger variable in the production and maintenance of gender differences. Humans everywhere are taught how to properly live as men and women (and other genders) in their own cultures. The process of learning how to act according to the gender norms of society is called *gender socialization.*

Anthropologists and other social scientists have studied the many ways adults socialize children, including the use of rituals, images in the media, mythology, and more. In every society, socialization begins with direct contact between caretakers (usually parents) and infants. Researchers in Europe conducted an experiment in which very young infants were dressed in gender-specific clothing. The gender-specific clothing (e.g., blue or pink blankets and hats) was assigned randomly, so it did not necessarily reflect the sex of the baby. The researchers observed adults interacting with the infants and found that the adults treated the babies differently, depending on the perception of sex. They were generally more verbal, used more eye contact and had closer facial proximity for those infants thought to be girls, while being more physical with the "boys." In the Western context, these responses should not be surprising, as girls and women are believed to be more emotional, verbal, and relational while boys and men are said to be physical and less attuned or interested in emotional connections. This test did not prove that behaviors associated with adult men and women are *only* the result of socialization, but it revealed the often unconscious and subtle ways adults communicate gender norms to children, virtually from birth.[8]

Young girls poised for their entrance to the annual "Little Miss Santa Fe" competition. Talent shows and beauty competitions for girls of all ages are extremely popular in the Philippines. *Baklas,* a third gender class in the Philippines, usually organize and run these pageants. A *bakla* is standing behind the girls on the far right.
Photo: Katrina Friesen

Gender ideals are often expressed in shared stories. In the United States, stories expressing ideals of masculinity involve men conquering the wilderness, including larger-than-life characters like Paul Bunyan. Living alone (except for his blue ox, Babe), Bunyan typified ideals of a solitary man known for strength and the ability to overcome nature. Other popular fictional characters such as the Lone Ranger, Superman, and Batman exemplify cultural themes of men as stoic, strong (physically and emotionally), and preferring to work alone. These popular characters are based on widely shared cultural

8. For a review of this study, as well as other similar work, see Marilyn Stern and Katherine Hildebrandt Karraker, "Sex Stereotyping of Infants: A Review of Sex Labeling Studies," in *Sex Roles* 20, no. 9–10 (1989): 501–22.

A young Mexican woman being presented at her quinceañera.

norms of masculine ideals.[9] Western folktales depicting women—Cinderella, Sleeping Beauty, Rapunzel—make physical beauty a key virtue and depict the key character's desires as being principally (or exclusively) for marriage and rescue.

As children grow, gender socialization continues. Ideals of womanhood or manhood are often expressed in rituals, particularly rites of passage in which a community marks a person's transition from childhood to adulthood (for more discussion of ritual structure, see chap. 9). The *quinceañera* is a ritual passage of a girl from childhood to adulthood that is popular in Mexico and other Latin American countries and in the United States. Traditionally, at age fifteen, a girl is considered a woman and therefore marriageable. The *quinceañera* is marked with many symbols of ideal womanhood as the girl is arrayed like a bride, symbolizing her beauty and purity. She may be escorted by a young man known as the *chambelán*, her father, or godfather, emphasizing her availability for marriage and the importance of male protection. In many ceremonies, especially in Mexico, there is a strong emphasis on the Virgen de Guadalupe, reinforcing the centrality of motherhood for women. The ritual

9. These characters are popular in many countries where they may or may not reinforce ideals of masculinity. Even in the United States, there are multiple narrative versions of masculinity; for example, some modern heroes like Spiderman are depicted as sensitive caretakers of women and children, as well as being a strong, solitary hero. All these sorts of characters and narratives work in concert with other forms of socialization. Simple exposure in another context would likely be insufficient to be considered socialization.

Chapter 5

Gender and Language

Linguist Deborah Tannen has brought her scholarly understandings of gender and communications to mass audiences with books such as the bestselling *You Just Don't Understand: Men and Women in Conversation*.[1] Tannen claims that when men and women speak to each other, it is a cross-cultural effort. Her "genderlects" theory explains how a woman and a man may walk away from a conversation with very different understandings of what happened. In her view, women are often more concerned with establishing human connection in conversation, whereas men are more concerned with establishing status. Because they are seeking different goals as they talk, men and women often misunderstand each other. Understanding these gendered tendencies is key in developing better strategies for harmonious conversation in the workplace, home, and other settings.

Tannen has been criticized by some anthropologists for overgeneralizing, and she has nuanced her work with the acknowledgment that men and women are different across cultures and across time and that individual men and women vary even within a society. Her recent work on mothers and daughters shows how age and family relationship can cause strife in communication even among members of the same gender.

On a research team with sociologist Ines Jindra and communications scholar Robert Woods, I (Jenell) have researched gender and language, using interviews and surveys to investigate how gender affects how Christians tell the stories of their conversions. We found that men more often describe religious conversion as an individual, heroic achievement in which the man is clever enough to realize his need for God. Women more often describe webs of relationships as instrumental in their conversions, and themselves as foolish people in need of God's rescue. Using the Sapir-Whorf hypothesis as a theoretical guide, we as the researchers raise questions of what conversion even is. If language influences our perceptions of reality, then maybe men and women don't just narrate conversion differently; they may even experience it differently.

1. Deborah Tannen, *You Just Don't Understand: Men and Women in Conversation* (New York: Morrow, 1990).

---

also emphasizes family unity, cultural continuity, and a variety of other culturally significant values, but gender ideals are very much on display.

Gender socialization occurs through the economic life of societies as well. Jean Kilbourne has surveyed text and images used in advertisements in magazines and other media targeted to Western audiences. She demonstrates that often women are depicted as objects of desire, youthful and attractive. At the same time, violence and dehumanization are glorified when photographs obscure women's faces, turn their gaze away from the camera, portray them as victims of violence, and eclipse their heads, faces, or other individualizing features. What this suggests, she argues, is a view of femininity that emphasizes physical attractiveness as a primary (or the primary) virtue of a woman, and an acceptable (even "beautiful") link between sex and violence in relationships between men and women.

I (Jenell) did similar research on Christian advertisements in which I looked at hundreds of Christian magazines, websites, college catalogs, and other commercial literature, coding the images for what they say about Christian ideals of masculinity and femininity. Unlike Kilbourne's study, which found images that are primarily designed to sexualize and objectify women, I found that Christian advertisements are likely to portray women as relational and emotional, happy in relationships with other people or lonely without them, and to use motifs of princesses, wives, and mothers. In this way, I observed, the Christian world communicates ideals of Christian womanhood.[10]

Men in Christian media, on the other hand, are far more often portrayed as solitary figures (in line with U.S. ideals of masculinity), often in images of strength, leadership, and individual dependence on God (as opposed to within a community of believers or a family). Men are associated with motifs of warriors and involved in active pursuits, such as athletics or organizational leadership. None of these images, for men or women, are necessarily negative, but the prevalence with which these images appear—and the relative rarity of images depicting women handling responsibility well, or men in nurturing relationships—reveals the process of cultural socialization by which members of each sex are being taught to conform to particular ideals.

Sexuality

Sexuality includes biological sex but also refers to sexual thoughts, feelings, and behaviors. Though some societies (including the contemporary U.S.) enculturate people to believe sexuality is just natural, anthropologists study the many ways in which human sexuality is shaped by cultural norms and values. While biologists, psychologists, therapists, and other professionals study human sexuality, anthropologists' contributions stem from anthropology's cross-cultural perspective.

Views of sexuality are changing in the United States and other Western countries. Only fifty years ago, standards of modesty led most people (particularly women) to choose clothing that downplayed their sexuality. Today, girls as young as six wear Halloween costumes of sexy kittens and seductive devils, complete with high heels and heavy makeup. In a lot of popular Western music today, female singers assert their right to be sexually aggressive and express sexual appetites that were reserved for men not many years ago.

Anthropology illuminates that not only do these expressions of female sexuality come from cultural changes, but the earlier views of male and female sexuality, in which only men were sexual aggressors and women constrained or controlled men's sexual urges, were equally products of culture. In many conservative Islamic countries, this understanding of male and female sexuality is expressed in cultural institutions such as *purdah*—the seclusion of

10. Jenell Williams Paris, "Gender Messages in Christian Media," conference talk available from Christians for Biblical Equality, www.cbeinternational.org.

women from public view—and restrictive clothing such as the *burqa*, a long garment covering every bit of a woman's body, including her eyes. In part, this expresses a cultural logic of male sexuality that says temptation is rooted in men's exposure to unrelated women and visual stimulation. Men's control over their own sexual desires requires that women be hidden from view.

In other cases, it is assumed that it is women's sexuality, not men's, that needs to be controlled. This is often the motive for a practice known as *female circumcision* or *Female Genital Mutilation* (FGM). FGM is practiced in many places throughout the world, but is most common among Islamic communities in northern and sub-Saharan Africa. FGM varies in the specifics, but it involves removal of part or all of a girl's genitalia and may involve the surgical closure of her vagina until she is married. In many cases, this practice is rooted in a belief that unless sexual activity is made less pleasurable for women, they will be unable to control their sexual desires, leading them to have sexual relations before marriage or to commit adultery after marriage.

Even physical responses to sexual stimuli are culturally conditioned. Most North American men would say that the sight of a group of topless women would be sexually stimulating. Yet in parts of rural Africa, women frequently remove their shirts to work in the fields, clean their homes, or perform other daily tasks that could involve making their clothes dirty. Men in the community, having been raised to view this behavior as normal, see this as no more sexually provocative than most North American men would find the sight of a woman mowing a lawn in an old T-shirt. Even the general assumption that men are sexually stimulated visually and women by words or affection doesn't stand up to cross-cultural investigation. This gendered generalization is often attributed to nature, but the example of the Wodaabe shows otherwise. The Wodaabe are nomadic cattle herders in Niger, Cameroon, Nigeria, and the Central African Republic. One of the important elements of their annual clan gatherings is making marriage arrangements. Young Wodaabe men dress with elaborate makeup, feathers, and other decorations and perform dances and songs to impress the marriageable women who will judge the men's appearance and skill. The male beauty ideal includes elaborate accessories, white eyes and teeth, and height. Women are socialized to appreciate male beauty, and men are socialized to dress and act in ways that will catch a woman's eye.

The evidence that sexual expression and desire are features of culture has made sexual diversity an important area for anthropological research. One important question for anthropologists beginning to study diversity in sexuality was, "Is homosexuality cross-culturally present?" Evidence of same-sex sexuality across world cultures, however, changed even the way the question is asked. Today, anthropologists argue that while same-sex sex happens in many (maybe most) cultures, homosexuality is rare. That is, while same-sex

sex is not uncommon, it is rare for people to create social identities centered on sexual feelings, such as heterosexual or homosexual.

Sociologist Stephen Murray cataloged descriptions of same-sex sexual behavior from ethnographies and developed four categories of same-sex sexuality. Though same-sex sex occurs in many cultures, there are only a few recurring ways in which it is patterned: age-structured, gender-structured, profession-based, and egalitarian. In age-structured same-sex relations, difference in age between partners is essential. This describes the dominant Roman same-sex practice of Jesus's day, in which Roman soldiers had relations with adolescent boys. Instead of making them effeminate, same-sex sex enculturated boys into warriorhood and masculinity. Gender-structured same-sex relations involve two people of the same sex adopting different gender roles in their relationship. The mid-twentieth-century female "butch-femme" relationship is an example of this. Profession-based same-sex relations usually involve entertainment, prostitution, or religious work. Old Testament scholars speculate about whether same-sex sex was part of religious rituals in the cultures surrounding the Hebrews. Egalitarian relations are same-sex relationships that occur between persons who are relatively equal in age and social status. Our society's same-sex relations generally fall into this category.

Understanding variations of gender and sexuality in anthropological perspective is important for Christians. This illuminates Bible study as Christians gain understanding of what same-sex sex meant to Old Testament Hebrews and surrounding cultures, or what role eunuchs played in the Roman Empire, or what cultural practices Romans 1 may have referred to in its original context.

Anthropologists today study sexuality as an important part of culture, documenting and theorizing about how culture shapes human sexuality. Anthropologists study many aspects of sexuality, such as the formation of sexual minority neighborhoods in cities, how kinship works for gay and lesbian individuals, and how the cultural idea of heterosexuality has developed over time.

Like gender, sexuality is a topic that has been important to some anthropologists since the discipline's inception. The *two-spirit* (also *berdache*), for example, was a social role documented in over a hundred Native American cultures, including Navajo, Zuni, Cheyenne, and Crow; the two-spirit person dressed as the other gender and performed the work of that gender or both genders. The two-spirit person often was seen as embodying both male and female essence and was gifted in healing or spiritual roles. The sexuality of a two-spirit person varied by culture; sometimes the person had sex with persons of the same sex, sometimes both sexes, and sometimes the opposite sex. Importantly, the term "berdache" is an anthropological term that is mostly rejected today because it is a colonial term borrowed from the French word

Christians Studying Sexual Diversity

One of my (Jenell's) graduate professors, William Leap, studied gay men's English, applying his linguistic theory and ethnographic background to gay men in the United States and South Africa.[1] He encouraged me to study a LGBTQ (Lesbian-Gay-Bisexual-Transgender-Queer) focused church (a Metropolitan Community Church) that was located in the African American neighborhood that was also the site of my doctoral research. A colleague, Rory Anderson, and I did an ethnographic study of how the spiritual values of these gay and lesbian Christians shaped their strategies for neighborhood development (purchasing and upgrading homes, relocating to the neighborhood, treatment of neighbors of other races and social classes, etc.).[2]

Rory and I were members of another local church, an African American Church of God (Anderson, IN) that was theologically opposed to homosexuality. Doing participant observation in an LGBTQ-dominant church was a challenge for us! We learned that LGBTQ Christians often felt marginalized in the Washington, D.C., LGBTQ social scene, because their religious values

made them more conservative in their socializing. The Metropolitan Community Church was, in part, a safe haven for LGBTQ people who had burned out on socializing, who were aging, or who had contracted AIDS. I interviewed one church member who was living with AIDS and who had altered his entire life in order to move to this neighborhood, invest in the church, and reach out to others with AIDS. And while the church and its members were contributing to rising real estate values that were pushing out some former low-income residents, they tried to address these problems by offering their building free of charge for neighbors' funerals and weddings and by being good neighbors in interpersonal ways.

As a lifelong conservative Christian, I had only learned about homosexuals as people to be judged. Not only do many conservative Christians judge homosexuals, we often judge each other on the basis of how quickly and severely we judge homosexuals. This fieldwork reminded me of the spiritual value of anthropology. Anthropological fieldwork requires cultural relativism—a suspension of one's own prejudgments for the sake of really understanding the perspective of the research informants. I was enriched by working to understand the culture of LGBTQ urban Christians from an insider's perspective.

1. William Leap, *Word's Out: Gay Men's English* (Minneapolis: University of Minnesota Press, 1996).
2. Jenell Williams Paris and Rory Anderson, "Faith-Based Queer Space in Washington, D.C.: The Metropolitan Community Church D.C. and Mount Vernon Square," *Gender, Place and Culture* 8, no. 2 (2001): 149–62.

---

for male prostitute. Native cultures had various terms for the two-spirit role, and today some Native people have reclaimed two-spirit as an indigenous social role.

Research on the berdache was an exception, however. For the most part, European and American anthropologists carried their own cultural values about sex into the field, treating it as a private, unmentionable area of life. Today, anthropologists who study sexual diversity try to glean meaning from euphemisms, footnotes, or brief mentions of sexual diversity in classic ethnographies as they prepare for their own fieldwork.

Based on his fieldwork among the Sambia, Gilbert Herdt has developed a theoretical perspective on sexuality that is widely used today.[11] *Sexual culture*

11. See Gilbert Herdt, *Sambia Sexual Culture: Essays from the Field* (Chicago: University of Chicago Press, 1999).

is the system of cultural meanings about sexuality and the social practices of sexuality. *Sexual identity* is an element of some sexual cultures, the intentional sense of having a sexual desire around which your social identity is built. North American concepts such as homosexual, heterosexual, gay, lesbian, and so forth are sexual identity categories that are very important to the society's sexual culture. Many cultures don't have sexual identities; people do not build social roles or identities around sexual desire. A *sexual life way* is a culturally constructed expression of sexuality and gender roles. Herdt encourages anthropologists to study individuals' sexualities in terms of their sexual culture and the sexual life ways present in that society.

Sex, Gender, and Inequality

Cultural configurations of sex and gender carry implications for access to economic and social resources. In some Islamic societies, for instance, men are portrayed as both sexually aggressive and sexually vulnerable, having less power than women to control their sexual impulses. Thus it is the responsibility of women to control male sexuality through the concealment of women's bodies. This ideology maintains social control over women, who are charged with responsibility both for male sexuality and for their own. Women may, and often do, interpret this notion of gendered sexuality as a kind of social prestige—their ability to keep men from seeing them affords women control over their own bodies and gives them "honor." That is, women may not experience the wearing of veils or heavy clothing as oppressive. At the same time, in terms of access to political or economic resources, this expression of gender and sexuality clearly limits the ability of women to participate in the public institutions in which political and economic power are exercised.

In the United States, the notion that women are more emotional, and thus less likely to use reason in decision making, has historically led to the marginalization of women in political and economic spheres. In Indonesia, it is thought that men are the more passionate and emotional gender.[12] Men, the thinking goes, are more likely to give in to their passions. They are more easily tempted by things like gambling, drinking, and sex. It makes good sense, then, for women to control family finances, trading, and other aspects of economic life. Men do have more control in much of the public sphere, including religion and politics, where values of "spiritual strength" and "social status" are considered important. But without the dominant stereotype of women as more emotional, Indonesians have elected a woman to be prime minister and

12. See Suzanne Brenner, "Why Women Rule the Roost: Rethinking Javanese Ideologies of Gender and Self Control," in *Bewitching Women, Pious Men: Gender and Body Politics in Southeast Asia,* ed. Aiwah Ong and Michael Peletz (Berkeley: University of California Press, 1995), 19–50.

generally accept women in high-ranking positions in the business and political world more readily than has happened in many Western countries.

Whatever biological differences exist between the sexes in terms of brain structures, hormones, strength, and flexibility, anthropological studies demonstrate the power of culture to interpret and express those differences as good, bad, important, or irrelevant. It is those interpretations that become the basis for excluding some from areas of social life and restricting access to resources.

Anthropological Contributions to the Church

Information about how other cultures configure sexuality and gender may be challenging for many Western Christians to hear, but it offers important insight into how God created the world and how human creativity shapes God's creation. Cross-cultural understanding about sexual diversity, for example, provides a mirror for us to see our own cultures. Instead of seeing our sexual culture as just normal, or natural, we can see how even our most deeply held assumptions about what it means to be men and women, and what it means to be sexual, are shaped by culture. As Christians, then, we may see that the call to holiness is for people in all cultures, including our own.

Cross-cultural understandings of Christian practices related to gender and sexuality are also very helpful. How have Christians of other times and places interacted with the sexual diversity and the gender roles in their societies? How have Christians taken action to reduce the social inequality and discrimination that harm people based on their sex, gender, or sexuality? How have Christians in other times and places negotiated foundational disagreements, as churches today are attempting to do, with issues such as church leadership and marriage rites? Ongoing dialogue with Christians across the world today, and Christians from the past who left writings behind, can benefit our attempts to pursue unity, holiness, purity, and justice in our own churches and traditions.

In terms of gender, it can be argued that gender is part of God's original creation. Note, however, that while gender status is described as part of the pre-fall creation, distinct gender roles are not described until after the fall, as part of what is often called the "curse" of Genesis 3. Some have taken this description of how the woman and the man, after the fall, will relate to one another as being normative: that is, how men and women *should* relate to each other. Whereas "traditional" views of women's and men's spheres in twentieth-century Western cultures have put women as wives and mothers and men as breadwinners, women in Scripture are commended for pursuing economic activity (Prov. 31), theological education (Luke 10:42), and exercising leadership skills (Judg. 4:4), as well as in roles as wives and mothers.

Likewise, men are encouraged to display humility in marriage (Eph. 5:33), and long-suffering patience (Hosea 3:1–3), in addition to more typically masculine roles of economic provision or political leadership. Both men and women are depicted as serving faithfully in a wide variety of roles. Regardless of how individual Christians interpret passages about men's and women's roles and status in the church, it is clear that there is to be no oppression or inequality in how Christians treat one another (Gal. 3:28; Col. 3:11).

Terms

bakla: a gender status in the Philippines that involves a natal man dressed as a woman.

baybalan: a natal man who dressed as a woman, or a man born with ambiguous genitals. This ancient social role in the Philippines was understood to result in specialized access to spiritual power.

burqa: a long garment covering every bit of a woman's body, including her eyes.

female circumcision (or *Female Genital Mutilation* [FGM]): a cultural practice that involves removal of part or all of a girl's genitalia and may involve the surgical closure of her vagina until she is married.

gender: what it means to be male or female in a particular culture.

gender role: a set of expectations regarding proper behavior and appearance for a particular gender.

gender socialization: the process of learning how to act according to the gender norms of a culture.

gender status: a position a person can occupy in the social order that is directly related to maleness or femaleness. Gender status is usually ascribed. English-language gender statuses are girl, boy, man, and woman.

intersex: people born with ambiguous genitals due to a variety of biological conditions.

kula ring: an exchange system around the chain of Trobriand Islands.

purdah: the seclusion of women from public view.

quinceañera: a popular Catholic tradition of Mexico involving a ritual passage of a girl from childhood to adulthood.

sex (or *sexual dimorphism*): biological maleness or femaleness, usually given at birth.

sexual culture: the system of cultural meanings about sexuality and the social practices of sexuality.

sexual identity: an element of some sexual cultures, the intentional sense of having a sexual desire around which your social identity is built.

sexual life way: a culturally constructed expression of sexuality and gender roles.

sexuality: includes biological sex, but also refers to human sexual thoughts, feelings, and behaviors.

third gender: a gender other than man or woman.

two-spirit (also *berdache*): a Native American social role in which a person dressed as the other gender and performed the work of the opposite gender or both genders.

Devotion 1

The Proverbs 31 Woman

Charm is deceptive, and beauty is fleeting; but a woman who fears the LORD is to be praised. Honor her for all that her hands have done, and let her works bring her praise at the city gate. (Prov. 31:30–31)

The activities of the Proverbs 31 woman exceed those prescribed by her gender socialization. She works in the domestic sphere, pleasing her children and her husband with her diligence and care. She wears beautiful clothes and earns her husband's trust. In addition to these domestic skills, she also works in the public sphere, calculating profits as she produces and sells merchandise. She buys real estate and works in agriculture and has admirable physical strength. Especially for cultures that prescribe a narrow social role for women, Proverbs 31 provides an example of femininity that includes a wide range of women's gifts and abilities. How do those in your Christian community tend to talk about the "Proverbs 31 woman?" What do they emphasize? Which aspects of her character or activities are most inspiring or thought provoking for you?

Devotion 2

Is It Well to Remain Unmarried?

To the unmarried and the widows I say that it is well for them to remain unmarried as I am. But if they are not practicing self-control, they should marry. For it is better to marry than to be aflame with passion. (1 Cor. 7:8–9 NRSV)

Marital status is often a contributor to social inequality in the church. In New Testament times, widows were vulnerable to poverty, and widows without sons even more so. For women, financial stability required being linked to a man in marriage. Today, in some parts of the world, being single makes a person more vulnerable to being pitied or excluded from certain activities (like family activities or married-only groups), and a single person may also be more vulnerable to poverty or neglect as they age. For many men and women, the nuclear family is important for financial stability. Paul encourages Christians to make the church into a community that truly supports all believers. Within the church, believers should provide social and material support to each other in such profound ways that though the widow and the single person lack spouses, they still have family. In this way, the church becomes a beacon to the society and a blessing to believers. How do you see the Church in your context serving as family for the widow, orphan, or unmarried? In what ways can we all be more faithful in supporting one another and exalting all members of the Body?

6

Production and Exchange

After studying this chapter, you should be able to:

1. Identify and describe the four modes of subsistence.
2. Distinguish between the three systems of exchange.
3. Compare and contrast substantivist and formalist economic theories.
4. Appreciate the variety of economic systems described in Scripture.

Introduction

Everyone eats and sleeps. Because all humans need food to eat and shelter for sleeping, all cultures provide ways to meet those needs. *Economic anthropology* is the study of how people meet needs through production, exchange, and consumption. Throughout time, adapting to historical and ecological conditions, people have employed their God-given creativity to develop an extraordinary variety of systems to organize the production, exchange, and consumption of items that meet human needs. Because economics is always linked to culture, anthropologists study economics in holistic perspective.

Anthropologists classify myriad economic systems with a few categories based on means of subsistence and type of exchange. In this chapter we first describe the four major categories of subsistence systems: foraging, horticulture, pastoralism, and agriculture. We then turn to systems of exchange and consumption, which explain how items procured or produced through subsistence strategies are distributed and used by people. Next, we describe how economic anthropologists build theory to analyze economic life more generally. We conclude with a discussion of how Scripture describes and evaluates economic systems.

Modes of Subsistence

In the early years of the discipline, anthropologists used unilinear cultural evolution theory to arrange subsistence strategies into a linear progression. This view assumed all societies start with simple forms and move on to more complex arrangements, and this trajectory implies general progress in human cultures over time. While it is true that humans began life on this planet using simple production technology, they had a deep and complex knowledge of the natural environment and well-developed exchange systems. Furthermore, there are examples of cultures moving from complex systems to simple ones, so there is not a single trajectory of progress when it comes to the economy. Nevertheless, the categories of economic organization help identify some important characteristics of economic life—in particular, how economic strategies are related to other features of culture and how economies reflect environmental adaptation.

Since everyone must eat, people everywhere have developed cooperative ways to provide for themselves and their groups. A *subsistence strategy* (or *mode of subsistence*) is a culturally created means of securing food. What humans eat always comes down to resources available in the environment, although that is not always limited to a local environment. Today many people have access to food from areas far from their homes and are not directly involved in the production of their own food. Trade technologies have allowed people to survive without close ties to their local environments. Historically, however, people were much more dependent on the immediate environment and made choices reflecting the local ecology.

Despite amazing variation, anthropologists classify nearly all cultures as being rooted in one of four modes of food production: foraging, horticulture, pastoralism, or agriculture. Even as they rely on this classification system for analysis and comparison, anthropologists are quick to acknowledge that diversity in subsistence practices in the real world can't be easily or neatly reduced to four categories. Nevertheless, identifying the distinctive features of each system continues to aid anthropologists in understanding historic and contemporary cultural variation.

Today, nearly everywhere, all four types are situated within a market capitalist economic context. Many people use strategic combinations of two, three, or all four modes of food production, negotiated within an overarching market context. Peasants who raise subsistence crops, for instance, may sell part of their harvest at market for cash. Suburbanites may access food primarily through cash exchanges at a grocery store, but may also garden, tend animals on a family farm, hunt, fish, or occasionally gather berries or edible plants. The strategic use of several modes of subsistence at the same time—what anthropologists call *articulation*—is a popular area for contemporary anthropological research.

Fig. 6.1 Modes of Subsistence

Subsistence System	Definition	Examples in This Chapter
Foraging	A subsistence strategy based on gathering plants that grow wild in the environment and hunting available animals	Intuit Ju/'hoansi Waorani
Horticulture	A subsistence strategy in which people cultivate varieties of wild or domesticated crops, primarily for their own use, using relatively little technology	Ikalahan Yąnomamö Kofyar
Pastoralism	A subsistence strategy based on the use of domesticated herd animals	Maasai Nuer Samburu
Agriculture	A subsistence strategy that requires constant and intensive use of permanent fields for plant cultivation	United States Latin American plantations Southeast Asian plantations

Foraging

Foraging (also called *hunting and gathering*) is a subsistence strategy based on gathering plants that grow wild in the environment and hunting available animals. In some cases, foraging might not seem like production at all. Walking through the forest, finding a fruit-bearing tree, picking the fruit, and eating it might strike contemporary urbanites as living in Eden, not producing. Most people who live in direct contact with the environment and employ relatively little technology in the acquisition of food actually work harder than simply picking low-hanging fruit, but gathering what grows wild in the environment is a form of production. It is also a key economic strategy of foragers. *Production* refers to any human action intended to convert resources in the environment into food. Berries growing on a bush are simply seed-carriers for the reproduction of the plant; they do not become "food" until they are identified as edible and taken off the bush. Identifying and picking the fruit, then, is an act of production.

From tropical forest people's invention and expert use of poison-tipped blow darts to desert-dwellers' ability to use virtually undetectable indicators in the environment to locate water-rich tubers, foragers rely on specially adapted technology and deep knowledge of the environment for their livelihood. Relying on intimate knowledge of the ecosystem, foragers may employ complex techniques in their food production. Some Inuit people living north of the Arctic Circle cut a small hole in the ice, where they place a feather behind a small windscreen. The hunters wait, sometimes many hours, until they see the feather move ever so slightly. This movement signals a seal coming to the surface, underneath the hole in the ice, in order to take a breath. The hunter thrusts a strong, barbed spear into the hole, killing the seal and immobilizing it until the hole in the ice can be expanded enough to bring the seal through.

Foraging has been a primary subsistence strategy throughout human history, with people relying on a consistent supply of plants and vegetation and occasional supplies of meat. Adam and Eve in the garden are portrayed as foragers; God gave them plants, trees, and fruit for food.[1] Likewise, around the world, most foragers rely primarily on vegetation. The Ju/'hoansi, for instance, historically lived as foragers in the southern African desert areas of Botswana, Namibia, and South Africa. Today, most Ju/'hoansi mix foraging, pastoralism, agriculture, and employment in cash economies. As foragers, Ju/'hoansi traditionally received 75 to 80 percent of their calories from vegetation such as Mongongo nuts, wild roots, and other edible plants. The animals in their environment were mostly either very large (such as giraffes) or very fast (rabbits, birds, antelope), so animals were not an easily accessible source of food. Animal protein was valued, and hunting parties spent time and energy pursuing it, but the bulk of the foraging diet was necessarily vegetarian.

A few foraging groups live in environments where animals are the only, or primary, source of food. Traditional Inuits of northern Alaska and Canada (sometimes called Eskimos) subsist on a diet composed almost entirely of animals such as seals, whales, and caribou. Native people of the Pacific Northwest used salmon and other regularly available animals as key sources of protein. Regardless of the specific ecological conditions in which foragers live, anthropologists have noted features of their social lives that are common.

First, these societies are relatively egalitarian, meaning that every adult man has roughly the same knowledge, skills, and status as every other man, and likewise for the adult women. When hunting is a male-dominated activity, every boy of the community is taught to hunt. Access to knowledge of hunting, along with most hunting resources (bows, stones, slings, nets, and so forth), is open to all, rather than the property of just a few. Likewise, all adult women learn and do the same things. Women may also do some hunting, as well as gather plants and roots or build shelters. Regardless of the

1. "Then God said, 'I give you every seed-bearing plant on the face of the whole earth and every tree that has fruit with seed in it. They will be yours for food. And to all the beasts of the earth and all the birds in the sky and all the creatures that move on the ground—everything that has the breath of life in it—I give every green plant for food.' And it was so" (Gen. 1:29–30).

work, all adult women would be expected to learn and do what other adult women do. While most foraging cultures have a sexual division of labor, assigning production tasks by sex, the intensity of the sexual division of labor varies across cultures. Some, such as the Waorani of Ecuador, have minimal distinctions between male and female work, and similar ideals for male and female behavior and temperament. On the whole, compared to other forms of production, foraging allows flexibility in the sexual division of labor, allowing women and men to work cooperatively together.

Egalitarianism is often supported by cultural norms that discourage individuals from thinking of themselves more highly than others. Anthropologist Richard Lee tells of giving a gift to a group of Ju/'hoansi people who had assisted him with his research.[2] Although he chose the largest ox he could find, an impressive animal with the prized fat and meat, when he presented the gift, people immediately ridiculed the animal as thin, measly, and worthless. Even while people were carving up the animal and distributing enormous quantities of meat, they continued to berate Lee for his "stingy" gift. Later, a Ju/'hoansi informant explained that such behavior was meant to keep anyone from getting an inflated sense of self. Insulting the contributions of individuals kept everyone on an even playing field and prevented some from lording their accomplishments over others.

Even a skilled hunter will not receive status or recognition for his skill. The owner of the slain animal is the person who made the first arrow that penetrated the animal's skin. Because Ju/'hoansi constantly make, share, and swap arrows, the skilled hunter can rarely claim ownership over the animal he killed. Ownership, achievement, and skill are diffused and shared across the community, which contributes to the overall success of their foraging subsistence strategy. Ju/'hoansi work and live together very closely and favor cultural norms that encourage harmony, cooperation, and survival.

Successful foraging requires a relatively low population density, sufficient land, and mobility. One inherent tension of a foraging lifestyle is that the food supply begins to diminish as soon as people begin collecting it. Foragers, then, are usually nomadic, moving in response to food and water supplies. Specific groups that wander together must remain small in size, as the need for trust and interdependence between group members is very high. Some anthropologists have argued that the upper limit on most foraging societies is about two hundred people, the point at which most environments reach their capacity to support the population and networks of relationships are difficult to maintain. Many groups maintain group size and reduce interpersonal conflict through *fissioning*, or splitting a group into numerous smaller groups that then move independently.

2. Richard Lee, "Eating Christmas in the Kalahari," *Natural History* 78, no. 10 (December 1969).

The Original Affluent Society?

People who rely on agriculture often view foragers with agricultural ethnocentrism: when viewed with the assumption that agriculture is a superior way to acquire food, foragers appear desperately poor and hungry. This ethnocentrism was prevalent even among anthropologists.

Since the mid-twentieth century, anthropologists such as Elizabeth Marshall Thomas, Helen Lee, Richard Lee, and Marshall Sahlins have worked to counter this ethnocentrism by studying foraging societies around the world, both as they exist at the time of fieldwork and in the past as evidenced by oral history and archaeology. Marshall Sahlins claimed, famously, that the foraging way of life represented the "original affluent society."[1] Foragers prize freedom and mobility, and their sparse possessions allow them to enjoy those values. Their sparse possessions and absence of storage also encourage interdependence and harmonious relationships free of status competition.

Sahlins posited that there are two ways to be wealthy: to have more, or to want less. People in market-based economies accumulate goods in order to satisfy their desire for wealth and live in a state of constant deprivation—either wanting more or worrying over the loss of what they have. Foragers want less, and therefore feel "wealthy."

Alastair Bland, an undergraduate anthropology major at the University of California–Santa Barbara, spent ten weeks living as an urban forager in Southern California.[2] He relied on nature and the generosity of his gardening friends to acquire figs, passion fruit, pears, persimmons, berries, scallops, sea urchins, lobster, and a wide variety of other foods. Nutritionally, he lived the good life, even gaining weight over the course of his experiment. He recorded, "I was made purely and solidly, through to the bone, down to my heart, of the best stuff on Earth." He struggled with loneliness, however, and came to a sharp awareness of how social humans are. "To be an individual hunter-gatherer in America is to lead a lonely life," he concluded. The wealth of the foraging lifestyle requires an adequate food supply, which he enjoyed, but also a web of interdependent relationships.

1. Marshall Sahlins, *Stone Age Economics* (Chicago: Aldine-Atherton, 1972).

2. Alastair Bland, "Going Wild in Urban America," *The Daily Gullet*, August 18, 2003, www.egullet.com.

Given sufficient conditions, foraging strategies are sustainable. Unfortunately, sufficient conditions are rarely accessible today due to agriculture, political expansions of modern nation-states, global population growth, and increased extraction of natural resources from land. Contemporary foraging societies have survived by living in environments unsuitable for agriculture—deserts, tropical rain forests, and arctic regions—but even these areas are becoming desirable for the extraction of timber, oil, minerals, or other natural resources. Foraging cultures have mostly vanished. Sometimes this is through *ethnocide*, the death of a culture when its members shift to a different way of life, even as the people group survives. Other times it is due to *genocide*, the systematic killing of most members of a culture.

Horticulture

Horticulture is a subsistence strategy in which people cultivate varieties of wild or domesticated crops using relatively little technology. This typically involves *subsistence farming*, growing food exclusively, or at least primarily, for consumption by one's own family or group. Like foraging, subsistence farming involves everyone in production, with a division of labor between sexes. But there is usually less flexibility between men's and women's roles than among foragers, and a larger community size due to a more settled lifestyle.

Some horticulturalists rely primarily on wild resources, cultivating slow-growing trees such as bananas, coconuts, or breadfruit. On the island of Papua, many people use the sago palm as their primary food source. Although they do not plant the trees, they care for them and may thin groves of trees to allow some to become large. Mature trees are cut down and the pith of trunks is scraped out to make a starchy flour used as a staple food. Others practice *extensive farming*, farming practices that involve putting relatively little energy into the land for the calories extracted (see fig. 6.2). Horticulturalists have domesticated various kinds of plants—grains, legumes such as beans or peanuts, squash, root crops, and so forth—that they cultivate from seeds in hand-cleared fields. Since virtually everyone in a horticultural society has a role in food production, it might seem that a society like the United States, where less than 2 percent of the population farms, is a much more efficient producer of food. Surprisingly, it takes a lot more energy (through fossil fuels, manufacturing, and chemical industries) to produce a calorie of food in the United States than in horticultural systems like those found in the traditional communities of the highland Philippines.

Ikalahan farmer Noemi Beilan, harvesting *lya* (ginger) at her family's swidden farm. Most of the ginger crop is used at home, but some of the ginger is sold at market for a small profit.
Photo: Katrina Friesen

Among the Ikalahan, an upland group in the high Gran Cordillera mountains of northern Luzon in the Philippines, each family traditionally maintains a garden that supplies most of their food.[3] Garden plots, which may be several kilometers from home, are cleared from the forest by cutting down trees and brush and conducting a controlled burn on the land. The plot cannot be too large or it will be impossible to manage, yet it must be large enough to supply sufficient food. Burning forest growth puts the nutrients of the vegetation,

3. The name of this group is somewhat controversial, with some speakers of the language using the term "Kalungoya" and others "Ikalahan." My (Brian's) research was in the town of Imugan, which is the center of the community typically using Ikalahan, hence the preference for that term. For an interesting anthropological study of the controversy about the name, see Babette Resurreccion, "The Social Construction of Ethnic Names," *in* C. J-H. Macdonald and G. M. Pesigan, eds., *Old Ties and New Solidarities: Studies on Philippines Communities* (Manila: Ateneo de Manila University Press, 2000), 41–52.

or *biomass*, back into the soil for use by the crops. The farmers then plant a variety of crops, such as the staple sweet potato called an *obi* (which grows low to the ground), corn, and beans (which can climb the corn). Farmers may include squash, ginger root, eggplant, and a number of other indigenous plants. Around the edges of the field, particularly on the low edge of the slope, the family grows Tiger Grass, a tall, broad-bladed grass that controls erosion and provides fibers for weaving brooms, baskets, and other household goods. By *multicropping*, or growing a number of plants in a single garden, the family can meet a variety of nutritional and domestic needs even as the variety of plants provides nutrients and support for one another.

This type of horticulture, which involves the clearing and burning of a section of forest for gardening, and after some time, moving on to a new forest space, is known as *swidden farming* (or *shifting cultivation* or *slash-and-burn*). It is highly efficient when considered from the perspective of energy-in versus energy-out. Initial phases, such as clearing the field, involve a considerable expenditure of human energy. Among the Ikalahan, this is generally done by men who will help neighbors and relatives for the few days of heavy labor. A field generally stays productive for three to five years, so no particular family undertakes this work very often. Putting nutrients into the soil is accomplished through the controlled burn, so much of the energy for future growth comes from the ecosystem itself; there is no need for manufactured fertilizers.

Planting, weeding, and harvesting crops also take labor power at particular times. Ikalahan women have traditionally been responsible for this work, often forming work parties of female friends and relatives who rotate among the fields, socializing and sharing expertise as they work. During times of crop growth, while waiting for foods to become ripe, there may be many days when no gardening is needed. Women traditionally work with textiles or basketry in those times. When women are in the fields, men are in the village, taking care of young children, socializing, and considering relationships with rival groups.[4]

When crops need to be harvested, a great deal of labor must be mobilized very quickly. This is particularly true for people who rely on grain crops such as barley or sorghum. Among the Kofyar, the horticultural group in the high plateau of Niger, West Africa, described in chapter 2, people host parties during which a family prepares vats of sorghum beer for the men who come from neighboring communities to help harvest. During those days, a great deal of energy goes into the production process.

Overall, however, swidden farming requires very little energy input for the calories that are produced. Most of the energy being extracted comes from the biomass itself. Technologically, horticulturalists may need little more than a

4. Lest this sound like an idyllic world, it is important to note that the men of the highland Cordillera traditionally planned raiding parties that would attack and kill members of rival groups.

digging stick, hoe, or other hand tool for breaking up the ground. The environment must provide the domesticable plants, predictable or accessible water, and suitable (arable) land. Horticulturalists may use some animal labor, although that often does not become helpful unless the community turns to agriculture (described below). Compared to the energy invested by most U.S. farmers through the use of fossil fuels, the building and support of technology, the use of irrigation, and the manufacture and distribution of fertilizers, pesticides, and herbicides, the horticulturalist can create calories much more efficiently.

Horticulture requires social organization and cultural norms that are either unnecessary or disadvantageous for foragers. Whereas foragers need to make resources available to everyone in the community, horticulturalists need *property rights*, a cultural understanding that some family or person has a right to the land and crops into which labor has been invested. That does not mean horticulturalists necessarily have property the way contemporary residents of the United States understand it. Many horticulturalists have *usufruct rights*, meaning that a plot of land "belongs" to the person or family using it. When they are done using it, their rights to the land end. "Using" the land may mean allowing a plot to lie fallow while wild plants regrow in preparation for later clearing, or it may mean only land on which crops are growing. Property rights may extend to trees, but not the land on which they grow. In other words, while the idea of private property is flexible, some form of it is necessary for horticulture to work.

Horticulturalists also have incentives to create settlements, though swidden agriculture usually involves a degree of mobility as groups relocate from garden to garden as soil regenerates. Unlike foragers who may need to stay mobile to access available food and water, horticulturalists invest energy in one place; thus they want to stay there and may aggressively defend their territories. The need to mobilize labor makes settled populations and larger families advantageous (see chap. 8). Horticulture may produce some surpluses, allowing for the development of specialists, people who are less involved in production and learn specialized skills. People may become religious specialists, artisans (weavers, basket makers, metallurgists), healers, herbalists, and warriors when they can be excused from production. Even those involved in production may develop skills of weaving, knitting, or metallurgy during times of waiting for crops to mature.

The potential for surplus and more control over production can also lead to differences in wealth and power. While the system and ecology will put some limits on inequalities, larger families who work hard and encounter favorable conditions can increase their production. With limited storage and increased consumption of the households, these families would not have substantially more resources than others, but their ability to produce more may bring prestige that can be used to influence social life or enjoy social rewards.

Like foragers, horticulturalists have not fared well in a globalized world. As culture contact and land pressures have intensified, many horticultural societies have ceased to exist as their members assimilated into agricultural states. Some remaining horticulturalists, such as the Yąnomamö of the Amazon rain forest straddling the Brazilian-Venezuelan border, are mobilizing to preserve their way of life. After years of new highways and increased settlement, many Yąnomami have died from violent conflicts with outsiders and from colds, influenza, and other newly introduced diseases. Those who remain have been pressured to assimilate into agricultural and urban ways of life, even with events as tragic as a massacre by gold miners who wanted to use Yąnomamö territory. Anthropologists, missionaries, Brazilians, and Yąnomami themselves worked to secure a small homeland, but that proved indefensible. Like that of many horticultural societies around the world, the survival of the remaining nine thousand Yąnomami in Brazil is in jeopardy.

Pastoralism

Pastoralism is a subsistence strategy based on the use of domesticated herd animals. Pastoralists use animals for a wide variety of purposes, such as transportation, trading, plowing, meat consumption, and dairy provision, and for making cultural artifacts from wool, hair, skin, bone, and horn. Animals used in pastoralism vary by culture and region. Herd animals, such as cattle in East Africa, sheep or goats in Central Asia, camels in North Africa, and llama and alpaca in South America, become centrally important for both the economic and social lives of pastoralists.

Just as horticulture requires particular ecological resources (predictable rainfall or other accessible water, domesticable plants, sufficient and fertile land) and social forms (private property, labor mobilization), pastoralists have particular needs as well. First, and perhaps most obvious, pastoralism requires a supply of domesticated or domesticable animals. East Africa and Central Asia provided many animals that could be herded, milked, and bred relatively easily, leading to a great deal of pastoralism in these areas that was later transported into Europe and East Asia. South America, on the other hand, provided wild ancestors of the llama and alpaca, which were well suited for cold mountainous regions but less successful in the hot lowland rain forests (meaning they could never be brought through Central America to the mountains of North America). North America, prior to the introduction of European horses and cattle, had no domesticated herd animals. Buffalo did not herd well and bears were hard to milk.

Pastoralism shapes culture in particular ways. For pastoralists in East Africa, for example, cattle represent wealth, prestige, and security. Cattle are used in marriage exchanges and to create links between families (see chap. 8). The Maasai use the milk and blood of cattle to provide protein crucial to

A young Samburu herdsman tends his family's cattle.
©iStockphoto.com/brittak

the human diet. The dung of animals is used for cooking fuel and building homes in places where wood is extremely scarce. Animal skins can be used for building homes, making clothing (where necessary), and containing water. Families must be large enough to care for the cattle but not so large as to deplete the resources provided by cattle.

Nomadic pastoralism is one form of pastoralism that involves moving animals in response to food and water supply. Nomadic pastoralists may move their whole community, or perhaps just their animals. In their effort to have access to sufficient water and grazing for animals, nomadic pastoralists may move hundreds of miles per year. Weather patterns and accessibility of grazing land in East Africa, for instance, prompted the development of nomadic pastoralism in that region. Cultures such as the Nuer of southern Sudan, the Maasai of Kenya and Tanzania, and the Samburu of Kenya and Somalia often range across several modern countries with herds of cattle.

Whereas the climate and geography of East and North Africa promote nomadic pastoralism, the environments of Europe, Central Asia, and South America require *transhumant pastoralism*, the practice of moving herds seasonally between high meadows in the summer and human settlements in the winter.[5] Transhumant pastoralists are likely to practice horticulture as well, since the annual return to the same lowlands makes the construction of settled communities with garden plots possible. Likewise, many horticul-

5. Some pastoralists, such as many depicted in the Old Testament, are seminomadic, meaning they have settlements or prefer grazing lands to which they periodically return; they do, however, take animals throughout a wide area during times of drought or in order to keep the animals from overgrazing the home fields.

turalists keep animals (such as pigs in Southeast Asia and the South Pacific) to provide protein and, as with pastoralists, to serve as a valuable trade item and source of prestige.

Like foragers and horticulturalists, pastoralists have not fared well under globalization. Pastoralists often have stronger loyalty to their tribe than to the state, and their nomadic lifestyle makes it difficult for states to assimilate or control them. (It is hard to tax people who are moving around!) Nonetheless, most pastoralists are finding their way of life impossible either by virtue of land restrictions, nation-state boundaries, involvement in national conflicts, or incorporation into wage labor. In East Africa, the Nuer maintained a pastoralist way of life into the twenty-first century, but they were recruited (often forcibly) into the Sudanese People's Liberation Army to fight in Sudan's civil war. The influx of weapons and cash has influenced their culture profoundly. Weapons are becoming more important than cattle as a source of prestige and wealth, and Nuer are even trading their cattle for weapons and ammunition supplies. Pastoralists may not survive the changes brought by globalization, and if they do, it will be with a new articulation of subsistence strategies and accompanying cultural forms.

Agriculture

Agriculture is a subsistence system that requires constant and intensive use of permanent fields for plant cultivation. By *intensive techniques*, anthropologists mean those techniques that directly replenish the nutrients in the soil, producing marginally higher crop yields. Techniques of intensification include the use of the plow, irrigation, fertilization, mechanization, and the application of greater human labor in increasingly specialized tasks. Increasing and maintaining the productive capacity of a given amount of land allows agricultural communities to be completely settled in one area for generations and thus to form permanent settlements.

Agriculturalists may be seen on a spectrum that spans from subsistence use of crops to market sale. Much of the time, at least a portion of the crop or sometimes the vast majority of it is sold at market. Agricultural systems support the specialization and stratification of society, whereby some become producers for many, allowing nonproducers to focus on other tasks. In agricultural societies, individuals no longer have roughly equal access to productive resources; because land is privately owned and may not be equally distributed, there is potential for extreme economic inequality.

Agriculture may also operate on extensive principles, such as the massive plantations of Latin America or Southeast Asia that use swidden techniques, but with much larger pieces of land for the purpose of *monocropping*. In addition to grains such as wheat, rice, corn, and barley, crops such as tea, coffee, sugar, tobacco, and cocoa have become primary products of agricultural systems in

Fig. 6.2 Extensive and Intensive Agriculture

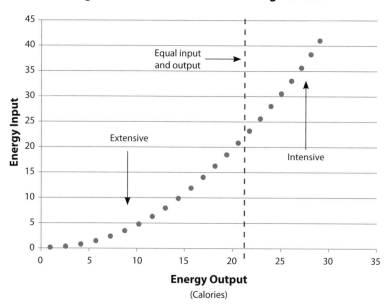

many parts of the world. These crops, which have little or no nutritional value, can be traded for valuable goods and cash. When combined with monocropping and conducted on a massive scale, this form of extensive cultivation is highly destructive to the environment. The process pulls massive amounts of energy out of the environment (through burning the biomass), puts tons of carbon into the air, and provides little incentive on the part of the agriculturalists to replenish the environmental resources destroyed as part of the process.

Just as horticulture and pastoralism require concepts of property rights and the ability to mobilize labor, agricultural systems also require social organization that allows for the mobilization of labor or other energy, often on a much larger scale. Today, this is largely accomplished through market systems, depersonalized and often decentralized systems of trade involving symbolic resources such as money. Centralized political systems regulate resource distribution and manage the depersonalized exchange of resources. These larger systems often remove any incentive for local populations to protect or preserve the ecological sustainability of their practices, as the wide circulation of money becomes the overriding incentive for cultivation (i.e., farmers are selling their produce for cash). Communities no longer require knowledge of other members or trust gained through face-to-face relationships. Even without the sorts of personal relationships of pastoral, horticultural, or foraging systems, however, individuals are interdependent as high degrees of specialization mean that each person is often incapable of providing for basic needs without the help of others.

Under globalization, agricultural systems have grown larger and provide most of the food to most of the people in the world today. As farm technology has developed, fewer people are needed in rural areas, producing a massive flow of urban migration. Cultures based on other subsistence strategies have died out or blended traditional subsistence practices with either agricultural work or wage labor in market economies.

Systems of Exchange

Subsistence systems are linked to *exchange systems*, social processes by which people give and receive goods and services. Anthropologists use three major categories to classify systems of exchange: reciprocity, redistribution, and markets.

Fig. 6.3 Exchange Systems

Reciprocity	Redistribution	Markets
• Generalized	• Taxation	• Buying and selling
• Balanced	• Potlatch	
• Negative		

Reciprocity

There are three forms of reciprocity: generalized, balanced, and negative. *Generalized reciprocity* refers to gift exchanges with no precise accounting of value and no precise expectation for type or time of return. It generally occurs between intimates or dependents. In foraging societies, people within the group all know each other well, so most exchange is generalized reciprocity in which each member of the group contributes as he or she is able. Those who do not pull their weight may be scolded or punished (or not), but it is an informal process that is not based on specific rules of how much each person should work or give. Distribution may be managed by kin relationships, indebtedness from past exchanges, or need. This generalized circulation of goods among members of a group helps to spread the risk of shortage and also creates bonds between the members of the group.

Generalized reciprocity was the primary mechanism of exchange for most of our human ancestors, but for those of us living under contemporary market systems, generalized reciprocity is reduced to the private sphere. In the United States, generalized reciprocity is practiced within small groups, particularly within families. It would be unusual, on someone's eighteenth birthday, for parents to present a young adult with a list of all the meals, laundry, toys, and other expenses involved in raising the child and demand repayment. Of course, many families have an expectation that each member will contribute to the family's well-being, but this is usually based on physical strength, age, and aptitude. There is no explicit or precise expectation for repayment of food consumed or services rendered. Likely, there is often a hope that children will respond to the care by being good members of the family (however that is defined). When children are grown, they may express gratitude by visiting, calling, or gift-giving. There may be some expectation that grown children will eventually provide financial, housing, or health care support for parents, though that is less common in some societies than in others. What family members do for one another is not "repayment," but rather part of the rhythm of relationships that create bonds of indebtedness, expectation, obligation, and trust.

Balanced reciprocity is a form of exchange in which roughly equivalent goods or services are exchanged immediately, or within a relatively short amount of time, with or without the use of money. In public markets around the world, this is a common form of exchange. People barter and swap eggs for carrots, cloth for firewood, and so on. Balanced reciprocity may or may not involve ongoing relationships between the partners.

Balanced reciprocity often involves more than just the satisfaction of immediate needs. As with generalized reciprocity, the expectation of balance can create important links of indebtedness. For most contemporary U.S. Americans, gift-giving follows a form of balanced reciprocity. For example, you may choose a gift for a friend based on your sense of closeness with him or her. If, after several birthdays or other occasions, that friend does not reciprocate at all, or gives gifts that are much less valuable (giving a card after receiving concert tickets), you may begin to question the relationship. We expect, informally, balanced exchange as a symbol of mutuality in the relationship. The "free gift" may seem to be an ultimate act of generosity or altruism, but balanced reciprocity suggests that accepting gifts incurs an obligation to reciprocate.

Reciprocity systems are not all about mutuality and strengthened relationships. *Negative reciprocity* involves exchanges in which one or both parties seek to receive more than they give. This may be as blatant as stealing, lying, or conning someone into an unequal exchange. In small-scale societies, negative reciprocity is less frequent, because the society requires positive, ongoing relationships. Even when practiced with strangers or enemies, negative reciprocity often creates conflict, but sometimes the short-term gain is considered worth the trouble. The used car salesperson might lie or apply pressure tactics to convince someone to pay more for a car than it's worth; if there are many potential car buyers out there, however, he or she might not be concerned about the negative reputation from a particular customer.[6]

6. Technically speaking, the sale of a car is not an example of reciprocity; it is a market exchange. However, the tradition of buying a car often involves trust and confidence on the part of the consumer and the price of the car is typically negotiated, at least partly, based on the

Redistribution

Redistribution is a system of exchange in which a centralized authority collects goods and services from a group of people and redistributes them. The most famous example was the *potlatch*, a ceremony of Pacific Northwest Native American groups (e.g., the Kwakiutl). Clan leaders would gather large amounts of valuable goods to give as gifts to rival leaders. Giving a large gift signaled the ability of a leader to mobilize resources, indicated the size of his clan (the leaders were always men), and placed the receiver in a subordinate position until the gift was repaid. In order for the receiver to shed the shame of having received an embarrassingly large gift, he would have to give an even *larger* gift, creating an ongoing process of exchange. The leader receiving the goods, which might include valuable commodities, animals, or even people, would distribute these among his clan.

In Melanesian societies, where gift-based redistributive economies used to be widespread, the leader (known as a Big Man, or, in rare cases, a Big Woman) would repay clan members who had given resources for earlier gifts distributed by that leader. As leaders accumulated resources for a gift, they gathered surpluses and redistributed them, making it impossible for one person or group to control so much that other groups were left wanting. The economic standing of community members, while temporarily unbalanced, would be leveled out over time.

In large-scale contemporary societies, taxation is the most prevalent form of redistribution. A political authority imposes a tax and then redistributes or spends the money in ways that, ideally, contribute to the common good. When a redistribution process reduces social inequality, it is called a *leveling mechanism*, though redistribution may also increase social inequality by rewarding those faithful to those in power.

Markets

A *market economy* is a system of exchange in which people exchange their labor (physical, mental, creative, etc.) for money, which is exchanged for goods and services. The value of goods and services is precisely accounted with money, and exchanges are typically precise and impersonal. Paying cash for an item at the store, for instance, is a precise exchange that results in no ongoing relationship between customer and cashier. Markets can exist within any system of subsistence, as they are designed to deal with the distribution and exchange of resources no matter how those resources have been produced. The image of a literal marketplace—a physical location where people come

---

testimony and skill of the car salesperson. In this way it is one of the few examples of a common situation that comes close to one of negative reciprocity in contemporary U.S. life.

Kinship as Economic Strategy

Carol Stack, a young white anthropologist, conducted fieldwork in a low-income African American urban setting in the Midwest, studying black urban families' survival strategies in the late 1960s and early 1970s. Her ethnography, *All Our Kin: Strategies for Survival in a Black Community,* described how people make it in a money-based market economy when they don't have very much money.[1]

Stack discovered complex networks of sharing and swapping between individuals and families. As exchange relationships became closer and more enmeshed, people extended their kinship networks. A neighbor could become an "aunt," a classmate a "cousin," and a fellow church member a "mom." These domestic networks solidified relationships of exchange that helped everyone access food, money, child care, shelter, and other necessities. Stack concluded that the urban poor become generous not out of altruism but necessity. "In times of need, the only predictable resources that can be drawn upon

are their own children and parents, and the fund of kin and friends obligated to them."

Nearly thirty years after Carol Stack's study, I (Jenell) began my fieldwork in a similar setting—an urban neighborhood of low-income African Americans—and saw that reciprocity-based survival strategies were still alive and well. Initially, I thought of myself as a "have" working and ministering among the "have-nots." I was a financially independent young adult working my way through graduate school, living on my own a thousand miles away from my family. I quickly learned that in the eyes of many of my African American neighbors, however, I was the one who was poor. I had no husband, and no parents, siblings, aunts, or cousins within range. I had no one to back me up when times were hard. In various difficult circumstances, I learned to lean on others and was grateful for neighbors who welcomed me into their lives as fictive kin. I received meals, information, companionship, prayer, and a variety of material goods, and then was obligated to give similar things in return—not with any precise accounting, but according to the rhythm of ongoing relationships of mutuality.

1. Carol Stack, *All Our Kin: Strategies for Survival in a Black Community* (New York: Harper & Row, 1974).

together to exchange goods—is a metaphor for the diffuse workings of the contemporary global economy.

Today, market economies are growing larger and more dominant, and reciprocity-based exchange systems that are vital for cultural survival are facing profound challenges. Most exchange throughout human history, however, has been much more personal. There was nothing like money to symbolize value. In foraging, horticultural, pastoral, and some agricultural societies today, while cash may be used in dealing with states or outside groups, people continue to exchange goods and services according to local norms of reciprocity.

Substantivist and Formalist Economic Theories

In comparing Western capitalism with other systems of exchange, anthropologists have debated whether or not humans everywhere use similar cultural logic to pursue their economic goals. *Formalist theory* argues that the logic people use to pursue economic goals is culturally universal and can be explained by universal economic models. *Substantivist theory* holds that economic behavior and motivations vary by culture.

Some early economic anthropologists, notably Melville Herskovits (1895–1963), argued that all people exhibit economic behavior based on concepts such as supply, demand, price, and money, even if the form of these things (say shells instead of coinage, or "price" determined by prestige as well as the perceived worth of the object), varies.[7] These anthropologists followed neoclassical economics and applied this formal theory of economics cross-culturally. Formalist theory studies exchanges in terms of the "price" of various objects, set by what others are willing to "pay." Formalists analyzed exchanges such as marriage, which in many societies includes the exchange of goods, in terms of the "scarcity" of items (such as marriageable women), and the "cost" of other goods (such as cattle), to see how a brideprice would be settled (see chap. 8 for a discussion of brideprice and marriage exchange).

Formalists did not view this work as ethnocentric because they believed economics was an objective, culture-neutral scientific discipline. Other anthropologists disagreed and argued that the formal theories of neoclassical economics—the logic of individual utility, price maximization, and supply and demand—were themselves culturally specific. The notion of people seeking individual utility, they argued, assumed a Western-bound notion of the self; that is, an egoist focused on individual desires. The rational thing, these substantivist theorists argued, may not be rational given different cultural assumptions about the nature of human existence and the purpose of life.

Substantivism grew out of the work of economist Karl Polanyi, who argued that any economy must meet the needs of its people by adapting to its context.[8] Thus anthropologists who are substantivists study economic behavior in the context of the beliefs and values of a culture. They see individual decision making as a product of cultural values rather than rational choice.

In advancing the substantivist view, anthropologist Marshall Sahlins held up formalist economic theories to a wide variety of ethnographic data, particularly from foraging societies. He argued, as we have seen, that where "affluence" in the Western world is achieved by increasing consumption (i.e., affluent people have the ability to amass and hoard resources), affluence may also be reached by decreasing desire. Time allocation studies, Sahlins noted, demonstrate that when unmolested by outside forces such as the state or settled societies, foragers spend by far the *least* number of hours each day "working" (i.e., in productive activities) while consuming a diet more balanced and higher in calories than most agriculturalists. In other words, foragers were simply not operating on a notion of scarcity in which supply and demand were stable

7. Melville Herskovits, *Man and His Works: The Science of Cultural Anthropology* (New York: Alfred A. Knopf, 1948).
8. Karl Polanyi, *The Great Transformation* (1944; repr., Boston: Beacon Press, 1957).

variables. Demand was a culturally constructed phenomenon worked out in terms of the foraging environment and society.

Contemporary economic anthropology continues to be divided into these two basic approaches, formalist and substantivist.

Economic Systems and the Bible

The books of the Bible were written in various economic contexts. Early in Genesis, before the fall, humans are depicted as having free access to everything in the garden. Although God gives the mandate to "care for" and "tend" the garden, production is described as the gathering (foraging) of products available in the garden (Gen. 1:26–30). The man and the woman are given the same task; thus there is no division of labor or inequality in access to resources. This description correlates with a foraging mode of production and a reciprocity-based system of exchange.

After the sin of humans, Adam was told to engage in horticulture or agriculture and was warned that it would be frequently frustrating and difficult. Correspondingly, Eve would suffer in her femininity, bearing children with pain and often experiencing disappointment in marriage. Genesis 3:14–19, often called "the curse," has been analyzed from many perspectives. Anthropology contributes a new layer of meaning, highlighting gender-based injustice: labor-related misery that men experience in some horticultural and most agricultural systems of production, and the kin-related inequality suffered by women once sexual divisions of labor are solidified in society.

Cain and Abel are described as practicing horticulture and pastoralism respectively (Gen. 4:1–16). Cain, the horticulturalist, brought "some of the fruits of the soil" to God, while Abel, the pastoralist, brought "fat portions from some of the firstborn of his flock" (Gen. 4:3–4). Abel's offering was accepted while Cain's was rejected. The point of the passage is not to prioritize pastoralism over horticulture but to comment on the state of the heart and the nature of sacrifice (Heb. 11:4). From an anthropological perspective, the passage also demonstrates how social conflicts, even violent ones, can emerge when different subsistence systems collide.

Pastoralism and horticulture are present throughout the Old Testament. There are examples of nomadic pastoralism (e.g., Abraham moving from Ur with his flocks), and transhumant pastoralism (Joseph and his brothers moving their father's herds to fields away from their home). Scholars of the Old Testament believe that for most of Israel's history, horticulture (subsistence farming) was the primary economic system.[9]

9. Charles Edward Carter and Carol L. Meyer, *Community, Identity and Ideology: Social Science Approaches to the Hebrew Bible* (Winona Lake, IN: Eisenbrauns, 1996), 11.

Agriculture, particularly among Israel's neighbors, is also described. The kingdom of Egypt, through the predictable flooding of the Nile and the early use of technology (metallurgy) in production, was able to create large food surpluses to support centralized government and relatively large cities. Archaeological evidence has revealed agricultural economies in the ancient Babylonian and Assyrian empires as well. The presence of large, grain-bearing grasses, predictable water, and fertile soils made the development of agriculture in these places the preferred system for those who wanted to consolidate political power.

Private property, or the concept of property rights, is certainly present in Scripture, though not until after the fall. In the depiction of a foraging economy in Genesis 1, there is human dominion over nature, but nothing that would correspond to property rights per se. Even with the development of property rights in ancient Israel, however, God made provision for land and other economic resources to remain fairly distributed throughout the nation of Israel. Through the program of Jubilee described in Leviticus 25—a redistribution every fifty years in which property was to be returned to the original owners—God provided a leveling mechanism that would reduce inequalities of wealth and guarantee basic resources for every member. Scholars debate whether Israel actually practiced the Jubilee, but its presence in the Law demonstrates the values of compassion and justice. Whether God's people are foragers, horticulturalists, pastoralists, or agriculturalists, they are to use resources for human survival and sharing, not for the aggrandizement of oneself or the advancement of their own group.

By the time of Jesus, most of Israel was living in the Roman Empire, which relied on a complex economic system involving long-distance trade, coinage, and taxation. Even though their economic world was not capitalist or global, and the scope of their agricultural pursuits was smaller, the New Testament context was most like our contemporary context, in that markets mediated exchange in an agriculture-based mode of subsistence. Jesus made a number of radical statements about how followers of God should value their material wealth and respond to social inequality. At the same time, Jesus didn't clearly endorse or condemn any particular subsistence or exchange system.

Some Christians of the early church lived, for some time, in an alternative economic arrangement in which they "had all things in common" (Acts 2:44); other Jewish and Christian sects withdrew from the market relations and economic life of the larger society (particularly the community at Qumran and early Christian monastic-type communities). At the end of the first century, however, most Christians were engaged in mainstream economic activities. The apostle Paul affirmed and encouraged them to continue such economic engagement when he wrote to the people that they should seek to "lead a quiet life," "work with [their] hands" (1 Thess. 4:11), and that "anyone unwilling to work should not eat" (2 Thess. 3:10 NRSV). He likewise told people that they should work in order to have something to share with those in need (Eph. 4:28). Many apostolic writers spoke strongly against allowing economic inequality to damage relationships among Christians (e.g., James 1:9–11; 1 Cor. 11:17–22).

In all this, what cannot be taken from Scripture is the idea that one subsistence system, or one system of exchange, is "biblical" or God's uniform will for all people in all times and places. Anthropologists view subsistence and exchange systems as adaptive; people create and shape systems that ensure human survival in accord with their ecological and historical environments. God calls people to be generous with one another and thankful for their provision no matter how they sustain themselves. God requires wise stewardship of material possessions because of people's tendency to develop emotional attachments and to place social significance on material wealth. From the beginning, God placed humanity in a symbolic relationship with the environment, declaring that it was more than simply a resource for human benefit but that it had a moral quality; it was pronounced "good." As Christians, we can value the vast cultural diversity of economies to the extent that they promote human survival and dignity, even as we examine all those systems—and our participation in them—for the ways in which they tolerate and even foster human deprivation.

Terms

agriculture: a subsistence system that requires constant and intensive use of permanent fields for plant cultivation.

articulation: the strategic use of several modes of subsistence at the same time.

balanced reciprocity: a form of exchange in which roughly equivalent goods or services are exchanged immediately, or within a relatively short amount of time, with or without the use of money.

biomass: all living things, plants and animals, contained in and supported by a particular area of land.

economic anthropology: the study of how people meet needs through production, exchange, and consumption.

ethnocide: the death of a culture when its members shift to a different way of life, even as the people group survives.

exchange systems: social processes by which people give and receive goods and services.

extensive farming: farming practices that involve putting relatively little energy into the land for the calories extracted.

fissioning: splitting a group into numerous smaller groups. A practice used by foragers to maintain group size and reduce interpersonal conflict.

foraging (or *hunting and gathering*): a subsistence strategy based on gathering plants that grow wild in the environment and hunting available animals.

formalist theory: an economic theory that teaches that the logic people use to pursue economic goals is culturally universal and can be explained by universal economic models.

generalized reciprocity: a form of exchange involving gift exchanges with no precise accounting of value and no precise expectation for type or time of return.

genocide: the systematic killing of most members of a culture.

horticulture: a subsistence strategy in which people cultivate varieties of wild or domesticated crops, primarily for their own use, using relatively little technology.

intensive farming: agricultural or horticultural techniques that directly replenish the nutrients in the soil, producing marginally higher crop yields.

leveling mechanism: a redistribution process that reduces social inequality.

market economy: a system of exchange in which people exchange their labor (physical, mental, creative, etc.) for money, which is exchanged for goods and services.

monocropping: growing one species of plant in a garden or field.

multicropping: growing several species of plants in a single garden.

negative reciprocity: a form of exchange in which one or both parties seek to receive more than they give.

nomadic pastoralism: a form of pastoralism that involves moving animals in response to food and water supply.

pastoralism: a subsistence strategy based on the use of domesticated herd animals.

potlatch: a form of redistribution and exchange traditionally practiced by Pacific Northwest Native American groups.

production: any human action intended to convert resources in the environment into food.

property rights: the cultural understanding that some family or person has a right to the land and crops into which labor has been invested.

redistribution: a system of exchange in which a centralized authority collects goods and services from a group of people and redistributes them.

subsistence farming: growing food exclusively, or at least primarily, for consumption by one's own family or group.

subsistence strategy (or *mode of subsistence*): a culturally created means of securing food.

substantivist theory: an economic theory that teaches that economic behavior and motivations vary by culture.

swidden farming (or *shifting cultivation*, or *slash-and-burn*): a form of horticulture involving the clearing and burning of a section of forest for cultivation, and after some time, moving on to a new forest space.

transhumant pastoralism: the practice of moving herds seasonally between
high meadows in the summer and human settlements in the winter.

usufruct rights: an understanding of property rights in which a plot of land
"belongs" to the person or family using it. When they are done using it,
their rights to the land end.

Devotion 1

True Wealth

As for those who in the present age are rich, command them not to be haughty,
or to set their hopes on the uncertainty of riches, but rather on God who richly
provides us with everything for our enjoyment. They are to do good, to be rich
in good works, generous, and ready to share, thus storing up for themselves
the treasure of a good foundation for the future, so that they may take hold of
the life that really is life. (1 Tim. 6:17–19 NRSV)

This passage takes on new meaning when read from a foraging point of
view. In foraging societies, people don't store up possessions and economic
inequality is minimal. For foragers, good works are a literal form of wealth.
Good works, generosity, and sharing are all foundational elements of generalized reciprocity. Giving and receiving solidify society-wide bonds of obligation
and generosity that extend for generations and across families. In this passage,
Paul reminds us of God's message in Genesis 1: God has provided humans
with everything they need. Reviving the economic strategies of sharing, generosity, and good works helps us rely less on hoarding wealth and more on
our relationships with others.

Devotion 2

Economic Dimensions of the Fall

To the woman he [God] said, "I will make your pains in childbearing very
severe; with pain you will give birth to children. Your desire will be for your
husband, and he will rule over you." To Adam he said, "Because you listened
to your wife and ate from the tree about which I commanded you, 'You must
not eat of it,' cursed is the ground because of you; through painful toil you will
eat of it all the days of your life. It will produce thorns and thistles for you, and
you will eat the plants of the field. By the sweat of your brow you will eat your
food until you return to the ground since from it you were taken; for dust you
are and to dust you will return." (Gen. 3:16–19)

This is a description of how life would be for Adam and Eve, and their descendants, because of their sin. It is a far cry from the material abundance and relational happiness of the garden. In today's world, these verses describe the experience of foragers, pastoralists, and horticulturalists who are forced—by virtue of land restrictions, political decisions, and economic necessity—to enter the globalized market economy.

Of course, foragers do not live a more sinless life than market industrialists, but in many cases, women who enjoyed relative equality and harmony with men are made subservient as men work in the productive sphere and women are isolated in the domestic sphere without the income-generating opportunities that build social status. Men who shared the work of subsistence with their wives and children are now forced to labor in agriculture or cash-based economies, hard work that too often results in poverty and hunger. Women and men experience sin and brokenness in gender-related ways, with particular pain for women in family life and particular pain for men in their work. "The curse" as recorded in Genesis 3 is, in part, a commentary on economic hardship and its implications for men, women, and families in a fallen world. In what ways do we see the effects of the fall in our own economic system? How can the church bring God's redemption to these systems and patterns of economic life?

7

Authority and Power

After studying this chapter, you should be able to:

1. Define political anthropology.
2. Define authority and power and distinguish between coercive, persuasive, and hegemonic power.
3. Understand how anthropologists model systems of political organization with the typology of bands, tribes, chiefdoms and kingdoms, and states.
4. Appreciate the variety of ways in which Christians may engage in politics.

Introduction

What does it mean to call something "political"? In contemporary U.S. news reports, public figures—often politicians themselves—complain that accusations of wrongdoing or questions about their integrity are "politically motivated." These same politicians accuse those opposing their legislation or reform efforts of "playing politics." In advocating for his or her point of view, a political leader such as a governor or a president may say, "Now is not the time for politics to interfere with the people's business." It may seem odd that politicians complain about politics, but in one respect this understanding of politics reflects a broader, anthropological use of the word.

In anthropological perspective, politics includes issues commonly studied by political scientists, including elections, governments, and international relations. Anthropologists see politics happening when lawmakers gather to pass legislation and also when politicians attempt to influence others with public commentary, backroom deals, and informal influence. Anthropologists often take the people's view, seeing the effects of official politics, as well as the processes of informal politics, from the vantage point of a local community. They study politics as part of culture, using a holistic, ethnographically grounded perspective.

Some political scientists and anthropologists use a simple but useful definition of politics: "Who gets what, when, and how." In other words, *politics* refers to the distribution, understanding, and use of power in social groups. Political anthropologists study politics in this sense, as well as the social organization of power and authority throughout time and around the world.

This chapter presents *political anthropology*: the study of power and authority and systems of organizing social life. First, we explain how anthropologists define and study power and authority. Then, we describe how anthropologists model systems of political organization with the typology of bands, tribes, chiefdoms and kingdoms, and states. We conclude with a discussion of Christians and politics.

Power and Culture

People exercise *power* when they influence or control the behavior of others. What makes it possible for one person to get what she wants while other people have little influence? Some individuals or groups have more authority than others; that is, people grant legitimacy to their words and actions. *Authority* is the right granted to exercise power. Attributes that make a person or institution persuasive, powerful, or authoritative reflect cultural understandings and social organization.

Fig. 7.1 Power and Culture

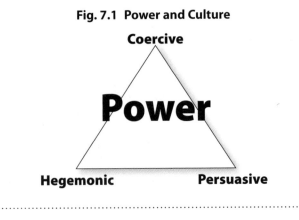

Power triangle diagram with "Coercive" at top vertex, "Hegemonic" at bottom left, and "Persuasive" at bottom right.

Power is an important theme in anthropology because power relations are present in all kinds of social interactions and cultural understandings. As described in chapter 4, power dynamics and inequality are fundamental to anthropological understandings of culture. Anthropological theories rely on three major categories of power: coercive, persuasive, and hegemonic.

Coercive power

Coercive power refers to the use of force, legitimate or illegitimate, by individuals or groups. A common understanding of coercion is a scenario in which an individual uses force illegitimately: a bully demands lunch money or a robber steals a wallet at gunpoint. These are examples of coercive power, but coercion occurs on a larger scale as well. One state sending its army to control the population of another state is a dramatic example of coercive power. These examples, insofar as they may be seen as wrong or are not approved by most people in the society, would be considered illegitimate, not having the support of cultural norms.

Coercive power may be legitimate. For example, throughout the world, parents and other adults force children to follow the adults' wishes. An adult may take a child's hand and lead her in a particular direction, or carry a child who is protesting. Few would call this an illegitimate use of power, since parents and other adults have responsibilities to keep children safe and to teach them how to function in society. Likewise, legitimate uses of coercive power exist at higher levels, such as a state forcing its citizens to pay taxes or obey traffic laws by imprisoning them or seizing their property if they do not. Warfare, one of the most extreme forms of coercive power, is sometimes seen by a citizenry as legitimate, depending on its aims and techniques. In systems in which those under the power of the state feel they have some say, people may accept coercive power as a trade-off in which they give control to the state in exchange for security, rule enforcement, and order.

Persuasive power

While coercive power is fairly easy to identify and seems pervasive and often dramatic, persuasive power is even more common and often more effective. In societies based on economic reciprocity, face-to-face relationships, and local autonomy, individuals are much more likely to use persuasive power to accomplish their goals. *Persuasive power* involves the use of words, relationships, and actions that influence others. Coercive power always brings the threat of retaliation and often disrupts relationships. Persuasive power, on the other hand, more often strengthens relationships.

For example, throughout Melanesia those who develop reputations for bringing people together in common cause become leaders. Often that cause is a large gift-giving ceremony in which a Big Man (or sometimes a Big Woman) convinces relatives to contribute to a gift to be given to a rival group.[1] Gathering pigs, shells, birds, foodstuff, and other valuable goods, the Big Man convinces his group to amass resources for the big gift. The gift links the two groups, because the rival group becomes indebted and obligated to respond with a gift of their own in the future. The extended family giving the gift is also brought together as they cooperate to pool their resources.[2] This process demands that leaders use persuasive power effectively. Not every individual will necessarily see that giving away their pigs, sweet potatoes, or sago palm flour will benefit either the individual or his or her immediate family. By employing rhetorical skill, promises of future benefit, and tactics of negotiation, some individuals in these groups emerge as particularly effective in convincing others to participate in these ceremonies. These leaders must be very careful that even as they are persuading others to follow, they are not perceived as pushing a selfish agenda or gaining advantage at others' expense. The ensuing personal reputation often translates into wider, or future, social power. Members of the community begin to seek out those individuals before making plans about where to live or where to plant a garden. In these communities, using coercive power may prove counterproductive. Even if a particular person has physical strength or can otherwise employ force to coerce others, that person must also have the voluntary support of friends or relatives. Otherwise, the leader may be toppled by others working together to resist.

Hegemonic power

The third type of power is complex, diffuse, and difficult to identify, yet hegemonic power is often the most powerful force for social control. Hegemony (he-jə'-mō-nē) means control or domination. A hegemony may be literal; for example, the control of the National Socialists (Nazis) in Germany in the 1930s could be described as a political and military hegemony. In anthropology, however, *hegemonic power* (or *hegemony*) refers to the dominance of ideas or culture, such that imbalances of power or other inequalities are maintained. This is a broad concept that includes political and military he-

1. For more on Big Men and Big Women on Papua and other Pacific islands, see Milan Stanek and Florence Weiss, "'Big Man' and 'Big Woman' in the Village—Elite in the Town: The Iatmul, Papua New Guinea," in *Common Worlds and Single Lives: Constituting Knowledge in Pacific Societies*, ed. Verna Keck (Gordonsville, VA: Palgrave Macmillan, 1998), 309–28.

2. Although there is a great deal of variation in the vast area known as Melanesia, common principles of persuasion and exchange can be found throughout these diverse communities. See John Barker, *Ancestral Lines: The Maisin of Papua New Guinea and the Fate of the Rainforest* (Peterborough, ON: University of Toronto Press, 2007), 152–69. See also Ann Chowning, "Leadership in Melanesia," *Journal of Pacific History* 14 (1979): 66–84.

gemonies such as the Nazis, and also hegemonic elements of culture such as dominant ideas or values.

For example, during the Middle Ages, approximately 600 to 1500 CE, hegemonic power helped stabilize European society and politics. European kings and queens had armies and other coercive means to control the population, but people rarely resisted monarchical control. Even the most inept rulers rarely faced uprisings or attempts by local people to challenge their rule. This was largely due to a widespread idea known as "the divine right of kings." The Catholic Church, using biblical passages about God's sovereignty over human governments, taught that God had established monarchs to rule and that to challenge them was to challenge God. In this way institutions such as the church, army, courts, and schools worked together to persuade people that, regardless of how cruel, capricious, or even insane a particular monarch might be, resistance would be wrong or even unthinkable. Hegemonies are not fixed, however; they change and even disappear over time. In the twentieth century, for example, the Roman Catholic Church in Poland was a major force for political resistance and governmental transformation from communist rule to a republic system.

To be successful, hegemonic power requires support from widely shared cultural beliefs. Supportive institutions embody and perpetuate the ideas and values supporting those in power. Discourses, or ways of speaking, connect these ideas to a vocabulary and set of concepts shared by members of the society. Italian political philosopher Antonio Gramsci (1891–1937) theorized about the social control of ideas as he sat in prison during the reign of fascist dictator Benito Mussolini.[3] Gramsci had been involved in workers' rights movements, organizing for now-common practices such as the forty-hour workweek, basic safety, and minimum pay. At the time, however, many people believed it was fate, or God's will, for some to be rich and most to be poor; working to change it was seen as a violation of the "natural order."

Gramsci argued that people had come to accept the ideas of the upper class (the bourgeoisie) as "natural," or "normal," not because this order was God-ordained, but because the ruling classes were controlling the values and thoughts of the masses. The bourgeoisie wanted all people, from the poor to the rich, to accept their place in society. In order to change society, Gramsci argued, it was necessary not just to change the government, but also the way people thought about government: what it should be and do, and how citizens should relate to the government. People needed to learn to expect government to serve the citizens, not just amass power to use in self-serving ways. In proposing new ways to think about society, Gramsci was involved in developing a *counterhegemony*, an ideology or movement that challenges a

---

3. Antonio Gramsci, *Selections from the Prison Notebooks*, ed. Quintin Hoare and Geoffrey Nowell-Smith (New York: International Publishers, 1971).

reigning hegemony. At times an alternative vision of society becomes a kind of hegemony of its own.

Eventually, many of Gramsci's ideas (and those of other like-minded thinkers) became widely accepted. Italian society changed, and people thought about the role of government, human rights, and political power in new ways. Gramsci's ideas about how power works, particularly in complex industrial societies, have become influential in many academic disciplines.

Power in action

In addition to defining and describing power, it is important to understand its dynamics. For analysis and theory-building, it is helpful to conceptualize coercive power, persuasive power, and hegemonic power as discrete phenomena. In practice, however, the three types of power are often in action simultaneously. Whether coercive or persuasive, power can be enacted formally or informally, through official organizations or by any individual or group. Hegemonic practices and beliefs that support the maintenance of existing power dynamics set a context for these formal and informal mechanisms.

Coercive and persuasive power are often mixed when certain individuals have a recognized right to accomplish something, but, in practice, need the willing cooperation of others. When individuals or groups without organizational power want to make change, they also rely on mixtures of coercive and persuasive power. When people want to change systems or cultures, they work at the level of ideas, expectations, and even religion; whether they are working through officially recognized roles or not, they are challenging a hegemony.

Power is often exerted through the use of social sanctions, which may be positive or negative, and formal or informal. *Social sanctions* are the responses, positive and negative, that people receive for their behavior. Some of these are *formal sanctions*, sanctions that are approved or delivered by institutions holding official power. Citizens of states are often aware of *formal negative sanctions,* fines or other punishments meted out for breaking official rules: drive too fast, get caught, and incur a fine. These are established sanctions meant to encourage particular behaviors. Organizations also establish *formal positive sanctions*, official rewards for socially desirable behavior. An example would be a prize for "good citizenship" in the community, being placed on the dean's list at a university, or receiving the Congressional Medal of Honor.

While formal sanctions have some effect, informal sanctions are generally far more pervasive and effective in everyday life. *Informal sanctions* are positive or negative actions or words intended to shape behavior. Informal sanctions are not approved or delivered by official organizations such as a government. As members of various groups—families, educational institutions, and churches—we are continually sanctioning other members of the group.

For example, in many undergraduate college settings, the resident advisor or assistant (RA) is a student given the responsibility of enforcing dorm rules. The RA uses persuasive power including verbal affirmations ("Great job!") or discouragements ("Knock it off, will ya?!"). The hegemonic context is one in which students are supposed to believe in following rules; the university stresses the importance of rule-keeping for personal character and later professional success (a reflection of the broader society's ideology of law and order).

Even in a residential setting like a dorm, overseen by peer leaders, coercive power is at play. Officially, the RA has the coercive power of the institution to enforce rules: students who break rules may be fined, placed on probation, or even expelled. This is the organizational use of coercive power through formal negative sanctions. In practice, however, most RAs do not want to simply act as police officers; they want to build community, offer wise counsel, help people with their problems, and enable the members of the dorm to get along well. These goals often involve convincing people that they should *want* to follow the rules for their own benefit and the benefit of others.

Members of the group can respond with their own mix of coercion and persuasion. On the dorm floor, there may be an official process for students to protest rules they feel to be unfair or consequences with which they disagree, such as appealing to the dean to force the RA to do something. If there are insufficient grievance policies, or if students feel their complaints were not handled well, they may use informal strategies. Students could turn to informal negative sanctions such as talking about the RA behind his or her back, deliberately leaving trash in common areas, boycotting floor events, or otherwise expressing their displeasure. When students talk positively about their RA, participate in dorm programs, or encourage others to follow rules, they are using informal positive sanctions (though they likely are not conscious or strategic about doing so).

The formal and informal strategies that students use on a dorm floor mirror ways in which people with little or no formal power assert agency. Labor contracts, such as those between labor unions and corporations, reflect a combination of coercive and organizational power. If the company fails to fulfill its contractual obligations, members of the union have the right to sue or strike, using the threat of monetary loss to force the company to comply. Most workers throughout the world, however, have no formal arrangements to protect them against abuses by employers or political leaders.

Political scientist and anthropologist James Scott studied Malaysian peasants and workers in other parts of the world and argued that Gramsci's theory overstated the effects of hegemony on people's consciousness.[4] He found that

4. James Scott, *Weapons of the Weak: Everyday Forms of Peasant Resistance* (New Haven: Yale University Press, 1985); James Scott, *Domination and the Arts of Resistance: The Hidden Transcript of Subordinate Groups* (New Haven: Yale University Press, 1990).

Informal Sanctions and Gossip

> For I am afraid that when I come I may not find you as I want you to be, and you may not find me as you want me to be. I fear that there may be quarreling, jealousy, outbursts of anger, factions, slander, gossip, arrogance and disorder. (2 Cor. 12:20)

The Bible condemns gossip as a sin. But what really is gossip? If I share a story about something funny—maybe a little embarrassing—my friend did, is that gossip? If I talk about something I personally witnessed, versus something I heard secondhand, is that gossip? Is gossip only talking about bad things? Untrue things?

Perhaps the better question to ask is why gossip is considered a sin. In the list above, many of Paul's concerns about the church in Corinth—quarreling, factions, disorder—are about social order and group cohesion. Gossip fits in this list because Paul recognizes gossip as a means of social control, a negative informal sanction used to control others' behavior.

When anthropological perspective aids biblical interpretation, it becomes clear that gossip is wrong for several reasons. The person spreading gossip may be poorly motivated, seeking to undermine the social standing, reputation, or even humanity of another member of their community. The person being gossiped about may feel hurt or angry. Gossip is wrong because it intentionally hurts another person and diminishes their place in the community.

Using informal sanctions is not sinful, in and of itself. Jesus spoke words of encouragement and rebuke to persuade people to live rightly. Paul encouraged the churches to exhort, rebuke, and correct other members of their community. Informal negative sanctions—which may include talking about other people—should correct a person's behavior or attitude and restore their place in the community. In contrast, gossip is destructive talk designed to demean another person and fracture the community.

In any community, each of us should examine our own behavior to see if we are exerting social control through informal sanctions in ways that restore individuals and edify communities, or if our words tear down, disrupt, and cause harm.

workers develop practices, beliefs, and ways of talking ("transcripts") that keep their sense of justice and their own best interests alive under repressive conditions. The "weapons of the weak" include practices such as working more slowly than usual, intentionally breaking machinery or equipment, underfilling bags of rice, or leaving some rice unharvested (which they might go back to get later and eat for themselves). In these ways, supposedly powerless people exert power in ways that enhance their own survival and also exert pressure on dominant people or organizations to change.

Political Organization

Power and authority are configured in a variety of ways as political systems that guide entire societies. Anthropologists model systems of political organization with the typology of bands, tribes, chiefdoms and kingdoms, and states. Developed by anthropologist Elman Service (1915–96), this typology highlights the correlations between economic strategy and political form (see

Fig. 7.2 Political Organizations

Political Organization	Size	Leadership	Social Organization	Division of Labor	Political Power	Level of Organization	Subsistence System	Conflict Resolution
Band	A few hundred.	Temporary and informal, decisions by consensus.	Egalitarian	Members are able to do the same task, but tasks may also be divided by gender.	Decentralized, informal, and based on charisma.	Local	Foraging	Informal sanctions, persuasive power.
Tribe	Several hundred to several million.	Informal election of elders based on unique qualities rather than family name or social status.	Strong kinship ties, age-set systems.	Commonly based on kinship, age, and gender.	Decentralized, based on kinship and charisma.	Local, but can create regional associations for temporary purposes.	May be associated with subsistence system.	Reliance on skilled negotiators and supernatural mechanisms of guilt determination. May use warfare rarely.
Chiefdom-Kingdom	Population becomes more highly concentrated.	Leadership that is an inheritable office. Not based on ability.	Hierarchical social statuses based on household, lineage, and clan. Also determined by relational distance from the chief or king.	More specialized. Food surpluses are redistributed using systems of tribute and taxation.	Centralized, inheritable.	Relatively permanent regional associations.	Pastoralism, horticulture, or agriculture.	More formal. Rules and punishments decided upon by ruler. War is waged more frequently and on a larger scale than tribes.
State	Highly concentrated. Today, some populations are over a billion.	Authority rests in institutions and offices.	Social status primarily based on economic status and ability.	Highly specialized.	Highly centralized, bureaucratic.	National and international associations.	Primarily agriculture.	Highly formal rules and sanctions decided upon by institutions and offices.

fig. 7.2).[5] Today, however, there are no bands, tribes, chiefdoms, or kingdoms that exist apart from the influence of states. In both politics and economics, anthropologists see societies blending political and subsistence strategies in adaptive ways. Nonetheless, Service's fourfold typology continues to be widely used as a general model of political organization.

Bands

The *band* is the most ancient political system, used by many of our human ancestors and still by some groups today. Bands typically consist of fewer than one hundred members, most of whom are related to one another through kinship. Band membership is flexible, and new members may be included and current members may leave with relative ease. Among the nomadic Ju/'hoansi people of the Kalahari desert areas of southern Africa, families generally consisting of a father, mother, and children stay with extended kin for as long as the gathering and hunting in the area can support everyone (see chap. 6 for a description of foraging). As resources diminish, seasons shift, or conflicts arise, the family may leave to find another cluster of extended kin with whom to live. Today, many Ju/'hoansi people have assimilated into Namibian or Botswanan society, some have blended their band organization with participation in the state, and a small number continue to live in the bush, fairly isolated from state politics.[6]

Leadership in band societies is usually temporary and informal. A person takes leadership in a particular situation because of the needs of the group or the person's gifts and abilities. A good hunter might take the lead with his hunting party, but when the group is choosing a place to live, they may ask a woman who is known for her ability to choose settlement sites that are safe from bad weather and predators. Because there are no formal offices for leadership, decisions are generally made by consensus. This does not necessarily mean that everyone has an equal ability to influence any particular decision. The use of persuasive power described above strongly influences whose opinions matter at any given time.

In bands, the egalitarianism seen in the division of labor extends to the realm of authority and decision making as well. Because almost every adult can do what every other adult of their same sex can do, there are few valid reasons for one person to exert power over another. Each member of the society is free to choose to go along with someone else's plans or not. Political organization never moves beyond the local level, since the ability to influence comes from face-to-face interactions. Band-level political organization works

5. Elman Service, *Primitive Social Organization: An Evolutionary Perspective*, 2nd ed. (1962; repr., New York: Random House, 1971).
6. Richard Lee, *The Dobe Ju/'hoansi* (Florence, KY: Wadsworth, 2003).

most easily with foraging societies because the subsistence system encourages direct and individual interaction with one another for survival.

Conflict resolution in band societies happens most frequently through informal sanctions such as talking, joking, mocking, or even shouting. Bands do not have militaries and rarely engage in warfare, although interpersonal and domestic violence varies across cultures. In the absence of centralized governments and military personnel and technology, band societies are highly effective at avoiding and resolving conflict by relying on communication and fissioning (splitting up a group when conflict arises) in the context of kin relationships.

Tribes

In popular usage, the term "tribe" usually evokes images of non-European, indigenous groups in Africa, North America, or the rain forests of South America.[7] Media may use "tribe" to refer to any language or ethnic group with a distinct identity, from groups of several hundred to several million. In terms of political organization, however, "tribe" has no specific racial, geographic or cultural connotation; its meaning is related to forms of leadership and association. Many groups that are called "tribes" in media accounts, or even by members themselves, do not fit the anthropological definition of a political tribe.

A *tribe* is a decentralized political system that may be associated with any economic form. Earlier in the twentieth century, tribes were more often associated with pastoralism and horticulture, but today, tribes rely on mixed subsistence strategies that blend pastoralism, horticulture, agriculture, and even some foraging. A number of tribes may be united as a society by culture, language, or heritage, such as the twelve tribes of Israel. Each tribe has its own leadership, usually based on personal ability; there is no central government to enforce decisions for the entire society. In the contemporary world, a tribe may function internally with decentralized political leadership, even as the entire tribe must contend with the centralized leadership of the state or states that control its territory.

The Ikalahan are an ethnolinguistic group organized as tribal communities in a traditional territorial homeland in the uplands of the northern Philippines.[8] The Ikalahan are organized into settlements, where each homestead is affiliated with a particular community. Around the Ikalahan territory are other tribal groups (such as the Ifugao, Ibaloi, Ilongot, and many others),

7. In many mainstream Western media reports, conflicts in Africa are often called "tribal" conflicts while civil unrest in Europe, such as in the former Yugoslavia, Chechnya, or the Basque country, are termed "ethnic" or "political" conflicts.

8. The Ikalahan are also known as the Kalungoya, which is sometimes combined as Kalungoya-Ikalahan.

each with their own language and identity. Each Ikalahan community has designated "elders," but this is not an elected position or formal office. Today there are government officials among the Ikalahan—as required by the Philippine state—but the communities continue to recognize their elders. One missionary-anthropologist who has lived in an Ikalahan community for more than fifty years described how someone becomes an elder.

> Being an elder means everyone waits. It's just that simple! You don't start talking unless all the elders come, so people will say, "We have to wait for Manong Rosario," or someone will say, "We cannot start yet. Manang is not here yet!" So you might not even know you are an elder until you see that people wait for you to come before they start talking about anything.[9]

For the Ikalahan, like many other traditional tribal communities, leadership adheres to particular people based on unique qualities, rather than in an office, family name, or automatic social standing. Being an Ikalahan elder, whether man or woman, generally means that people see that you are a good parent, that your fields are well kept, that you do not drink too much, and, these days, that you are a sincere Christian. Of course, members may disagree about who satisfies these criteria, and conflict may ensue as members debate who should be considered an elder and who should not. The Ikalahan will say, however, that it is generally pretty obvious who has earned the right to be heard and who has not.

In this way, many tribes have leadership structures similar to those in bands. However, whereas bands are entirely local, tribes can create regional associations for temporary purposes. Often in response to external threats, several local communities can come together to associate outside the local place in order to defend themselves, wage war, or engage in economic exchange or religious ceremonies.

As with the local community, regional groups are often organized by kinship. Someone in one community can identify a friend or potential ally by finding the kinship relationship. For example, my brother's wife's sister's uncle's wife's nephew can introduce me in a community where I may not know anyone personally, but by establishing the kinship connection, we can consider working together in a particular task. In addition, tribes may use *age-set* systems, social groups consisting of people of the same sex and similar age that link members of different communities as allies and friends. Among a number of pastoralists of East Africa such as the Maasai and Nandi, age-sets may be formed through rituals whereby the young men become a set

---

9. Delbert Rice, interview by Brian Howell, July 28, 1990. The Ilokano terms *manong* and *manang* can be translated "older brother" and "older sister" respectively. They are markers of relative age and respect.

and enter a warrior phase. From that moment on, the men are linked to one another, even as they are dispersed in various communities. They can rely on members of their age-set and coordinate with them for the good of their separate communities.

Conflict resolution within tribes is mostly informal, handled through talking, joking, and other forms of interpersonal interactions. But because people are bound to the tribe of their family, they are less likely to move away in order to avoid or reduce conflict, as in a band. This necessitates some formal mechanisms for conflict resolution, such as skilled mediators, judges, and courts. During their tribal period, Israelites relied on judges to resolve disputes, using techniques such as the ordeal described in Numbers 5. In a bitter water ordeal, a woman accused of infidelity would drink bitter water; if she was sickened, she was believed to be guilty, but if she was unaffected, she was innocent. Such conflict resolution mechanisms seem odd to most contemporary readers of Scripture, many of whom rely on legal conflict resolution typical of state

---

The Twelve Tribes of Israel Become a Kingdom

Judges 19–21 tells a grisly tale. The tribes of Israel shared a common culture, language, and religion, but they had no centralized political system. A man from one tribe, a Levite, had a second wife (or concubine) who ran away from him. He followed her to her father's house and reclaimed her. As he traveled back home, they spent the night in Gibeah, a region occupied by Benjaminites, fellow tribesmen to the Levite.

The men of Gibeah (not Benjaminites) demanded sex with the Levite. In a display of perverse hospitality, the host offered his own daughter and the Levite's concubine to the violent crowd. The men of Gibeah refused the offer, so the Levite pushed his wife out the door as a way of protecting himself. The men raped and killed her.

When the Levite returned home with his deceased wife, he cut her into twelve pieces and sent the pieces throughout the territory of the Israelites, one to each tribe. Her body became a means of mass communication that brought together a dispersed tribal society for the temporary purpose of waging war. Most of the tribes of Israel agreed to work together in warfare, but the Benjaminites sided with the people of Gibeah. In response, the Israelites waged war against their own, defeating the tribe of Benjamin, but eventually restoring it to the tribal collective.

Judges 19 begins with the phrase, "In those days, when there was no king in Israel." The book of Judges ends with a similar phrase: "In those days there was no king in Israel; all the people did what was right in their own eyes" (Judg. 21:25). The story is a cautionary tale of the interpersonal violence, mayhem, and war that can happen in tribal society. A wife was lost, which threatened family and lineage stability, and an entire group (the Benjaminites) was nearly lost, which threatened tribal solidarity and strength.

This story does not condemn tribal political organization wholesale; tribal organization is effective and sustainable. Rather, it was a specific story told by and for the Israelites as they were coming to terms with massive changes in their economic and political lives. By highlighting terror, destruction, and intertribal warfare, Judges 19–21 served as a legitimating narrative for Israel's shift from a tribal political system to a kingdom.

---

societies. But for tribes, reliance upon skilled negotiators and supernatural mechanisms of guilt determination work well. At times tribes also turn to warfare. Warfare involves a massive commitment to organize various tribes together in common cause and to likely lose members of the population, however, so it is not an option used lightly.

Chiefdoms and kingdoms

Like the term "tribe," "chief" is often misunderstood. The stereotype of the chief often conjures Hollywood images of Native Americans with eagle feather headdresses or rotund African leaders surrounded by servants. Although chiefdoms have existed among some indigenous North Americans and in sub-Saharan Africa, chiefs and kings take a variety of forms across cultures.

In anthropological terms, *chiefdom* or *kingdom* refers to a system of political organization involving an inheritable office, often passed through a family line, in which power adheres to the occupant of the office rather than being a product of his or her individual gifts, abilities, or qualities. This represents a centralization of political power that allows for relatively permanent regional associations.

The chiefdoms of Polynesia have been long studied by anthropologists. Raymond Firth's fieldwork in Tikopia, a three-square-mile island in Melanesia (though it is classified as a Polynesian island), is an early example. In the 1920s, there were about 1,200 people living on Tikopia, and though Europeans had explored the island, most Tikopians had very limited contact with the outside world. Island chiefs in Tikopia were seen as religious leaders who were descendants of important ancestral deities. Chiefs had broad religious, economic, political, and interpersonal authority. All the people of the island were organized into hierarchical social statuses based on household, lineage, and clan. The island had a very strong, interlinked social organization and a hierarchical, hereditary political system based on chiefs.[10]

Anthropologists debate the features that distinguish chiefdoms from other forms of centralization such as kingdoms and states.[11] Organizationally speaking, there is almost total overlap between chiefdoms and kingdoms, essentially different names for the same thing.[12] In both systems a family or individual

10. Raymond Firth, *We the Tikopia: A Sociological Study of Kinship in Primitive Polynesia*, 2nd ed. (1936; repr., New York: Barnes & Noble, 1975).
11. Peter Skalnik, "Chiefdoms and Kingdoms in Africa: Why They Are Neither States Nor Empires," www.uneca.org/itca/governance/documents/chiefdomsandkingdoms.pdf.
12. As with the terms "tribe" versus "ethnic group," the distinction of *chief* and *king* resides in the desire of the speaker to suggest something more or less "civilized" or familiar than in a particular distinction of political organization.

is vested with authority. The personal power and status of all members of the society are understood in terms of relational distance from this person. The sister of the king, for instance, would have more power than the cousin, great-aunt, or mother's sister's husband's niece. The office remains the locus of authority even if the individual is not particularly capable; the office passes, according to some system of inheritance, to a designee when the person holding the position dies or abdicates.

In the contemporary world, chiefdoms have largely given way to other forms of political organization, but kingdoms still exist, at least in name. In Britain, for instance, a monarchy continues that is based on authority vested in a lineage. The United Kingdom is a state, however, with a political system that blends the kingdom and the state. The constitutional monarchy relies on leadership from the monarch (as head of state) with the prime minister (as head of government). Around the world, kingdoms continue to be important political units, but like tribes and bands, they must accommodate the overarching power of the state.

Chiefdoms/kingdoms have the ability to consolidate control through coercive measures that bands and tribes do not. Like modern states, the chiefdom/kingdom system allows for higher population concentrations as the division of labor becomes more specialized. Segments of the population work to provide food surpluses that are redistributed through systems of tribute or taxation to the population working in other capacities. The centralization of political power allows for the formation of alliances and militaries that support the coordination of large populations into a specialized and generally highly stratified economy.

People living under chiefdoms and kingdoms continue to resolve interpersonal conflicts by using informal sanctions, but overall, conflict resolution becomes more formalized than in bands or tribes. Rules developed and delivered by chiefs or kings regulate interactions between groups of higher and lower status, serving to reinforce social stratification. When rules are breached, leaders are able to inflict punishment or encourage reconciliation, but the imposition of sanctions is largely dependent on the ruler rather than a body of law to which the ruler is also subject. The use of coercive force for control within society is common in kingdoms/chiefdoms. External conflicts also escalate as chiefdoms and kingdoms wage wars at higher frequency and in larger scale than tribes or bands.

States

The *state* is a highly centralized form of political organization in which authority rests in institutions and offices. Although individuals may be elected to these offices or appointed on the basis of their personal qualities, the underlying ideology of the state asserts that the office itself, rather than the individual who happens to occupy it at any given moment, is the real locus of power. In democratic systems, such as the United States, the explicit ideological position (often expressed in a constitution) is that individual members of the society agree to yield their own power to those who hold these offices, trusting the person in office, and the office itself, to represent their interests. When individuals leave office, they no longer have power; it passes to the person who takes the office next. The state may or may not have such democratic ideals, however. In many examples around the world, a state form of organization does not reflect the desires of the majority of the people nor protect their interests. Centralized forms of government sometimes result in a small group holding power over the majority (*oligarchy*).

The dividing line between the chiefdom/kingdom and the state is less about structure and more about ideology and culture. The chief/king requires cultural legitimacy rooted in the being of the individual, to some extent. For example, the kingdoms of medieval Europe used the idea of "blood" to determine who was eligible to rule. It was for this reason that some royal families of Europe violated incest rules—even those formally decreed by the church—because to marry someone too far removed from the family would have meant the dilution of "royal blood." Many chiefdoms and kingdoms throughout the world have operated on similar principles, limiting political authority to particular families.

States, on the other hand, grew out of new ideologies of human rights. In Europe, these changing ideas have been linked to the Protestant Reformation, during which members of the Roman Catholic Church, such as Martin Luther, began to question the legitimacy of the church regulating access to the Bible, knowledge of God, and even salvation. The work of Protestant reformers, and Catholic reformers who stayed within the Catholic Church, carried implications for the relationship of common people to institutions of all kinds, including political ones. In this way, Europeans began to imagine that rather than being bound to cruel and unjust rulers by the supposed will of God, they might challenge those rulers by finding in the Scriptures principles that made the rule of some illegitimate.

This shift in thinking brought about profound changes in the way millions of Europeans imagined their relationship to political power. Over several hundred years, through events such as the Hundred Years' War (a bloody conflict waged by Christian reformers), the signing of the Peace of Westphalia to end that war (a collection of treaties establishing territorial boundaries of citizenship for the first time), and the American and French Revolutions (wars in which citizens challenged their rulers), Europeans came to new understandings of political organization. Similar changes took place among populations in other parts of the world, although in many cases, European colonialism suddenly and forcibly brought political change.

John Calvin's Theology of Politics

John Calvin, along with other reformers of the Roman Catholic Church, encouraged Christians to read the Bible for themselves and taught that every member of the church has spiritual authority to learn and teach about God. This religious teaching carried tremendous political implications. For example, it confronted the view that average citizens had no right to question their rulers. If everyone could seek the will of God directly by reading the Scriptures for themselves then everyone had the ability, and perhaps even the responsibility, to interact directly with their political systems.

King James I of England declared that, as king, he was not accountable to the laws of parliament, an act which led to a bloody civil war. In response, Samuel Rutherford, a student of Calvin's teachings, wrote a book denying the absolute authority of the monarch. Finding support in biblical passages such as Deuteronomy 17, he asserted that law reflected the perfect will of God as seen in Scripture. Therefore, even the king must be subject to law. Rutherford's view, *Lex Rex* ("The Law is King"), refuted the widely held position of *Rex Lex*, "The King is the Law."

This was a radical shift in Europe. Later secular philosophers such as John Locke and Thomas Paine developed the idea of limited government that provided intellectual support for the constitutions of many nations, including the Constitution of the United States.[1]

1. For one of the most frequently cited versions of this argument, see Michael Walzer, *The Revolution of the Saints: A Study on the Origins of Radical Politics* (Cambridge, MA: Harvard University Press, 1965).

Today there are many examples around the world in which the cultural logic of the state has become intertwined with chiefdoms or kingdoms or even tribal forms of organization. Among the old monarchies of Europe, the monarch has largely become a ceremonial position stripped of any formal political authority. In other places, however, monarchs or chiefs maintain a great deal of real political authority. In the kingdom of Bhutan, the king works with a parliament but retains official authority to dismiss those leaders and act on his own.

In many countries where a state system was imposed by a colonial power, the official governmental system is a modern state even as many people at the local level continue to operate according to persuasive leadership in a tribal system, an inheritable system of chiefs, or even the consensus and context-dependent leadership of band systems. In Ecuador, some Amazonian bands live fairly isolated from contact with the state. Nonetheless, they are still Ecuadorian citizens, even if they don't think of themselves as such. Bands such as the Cofán and the Waorani have been drawn into interactions with the state because of oil development in the Amazonian rain forest. Having negotiated the right to live in ancestral lands, the Waorani people saw oil drilling as an incursion into their territory, but the Ecuadorian state asserted that the indigenous people had only surface rights to the land; the state had legal right to subsurface resources such as oil and could grant legal access for development to oil companies without Waorani consent. The Waorani had to quickly learn to mobilize with other affected groups in their region and throughout the world. They began working the political system as Ecuadorian citizens. They continue to adapt politically, retaining elements of band organization when possible and incorporating elements of state organization as necessary.[13]

There is no such thing as a society without a political system. Even the most informal and flexible systems are based on shared cultural understandings and forms of social life that are systematic. Anthropologists also agree that there is no system in which people cannot abuse one another, misuse power and authority, or otherwise act in selfish and cruel ways. Across cultures and throughout time, people recognize and negotiate legitimate and illegitimate forms of power.

Christians and Politics

Just as Scripture reflects a variety of economic systems, so too are the pages of the Bible filled with various political forms. The nomadic pastoralist families of Abraham's day were tribes. They later developed into a kingdom that relied on both pastoralism and agriculture (see 1 Sam. 9). In the New Testament, the Roman Empire (an empire is a type of state) was the political context for Jesus's ministry and the development of the early church. Does the Bible tell us which of these political systems, or perhaps another, is God's plan for humanity?

The New Testament teachings of Jesus and Paul focus more on encouraging believers to take a variety of stances toward existing political structures. They do not argue for a single political system that is ideal for all times and places. Jesus taught his followers to "give back to Caesar what is Caesar's and to God what is God's," suggesting that his followers can live in the state system of the Roman Empire even as they serve God (Mark 12:17). Christians have used this teaching to support the notion of Christians holding political office, contributing positively to a good political cause, or merely tolerating an existing political structure. Jesus, in his overturning of the tables in the temple and his own childhood refugee status (his parents escaped political oppression by fleeing to Egypt), also demonstrated the importance of challenging unjust religious and political leadership. Believers have relied on these stories to justify Christian involvement in political protest and even subversive activity for the cause of justice. Paul tells the early Christians that they should live according to the laws of their society. Although he encourages believers to avoid some parts of the legal system (1 Cor. 6:1), he also argues that believers can and should be subject to the laws and systems in which they live (Rom. 13:1–6). At the same time, Paul's teachings about the equal value of men and women, slaves and free persons, and Jews and Gentiles (Gal. 3:28) have inspired believers to challenge political systems that discriminate on the basis of gender, ethnicity, or race.

13. For more on Waorani culture, see Clayton Robarchek and Carole Robarchek, *Waorani: The Contexts of Violence and War* (Belmont, CA: Wadsworth Group, 2002).

There is nothing to suggest that one form of political organization is inherently more "advanced" or more suited to following Christ than another. The fact that terms such as "tribe" and "chiefdom" have come to carry the connotations of savage barbarians living in the bush, rather than complex and highly adapted systems of governance well suited for local communities, reflects ethnocentrism in language that has adapted to a state form of organization. The Bible is a valuable resource that can challenge this ethnocentrism because it records stories and teachings that come from tribe, kingdom, and state contexts.

Within all forms of political organization—bands, tribes, chiefdoms/kingdoms, and states—Christians may develop ways to engage political power that flow from their faith. The church is always a community set apart, yet it only exists in particular political and cultural contexts. Christians should not deny the place of power and politics in human life. Instead, we should think deeply about how Christians should engage, use, and understand power to encourage a vibrant life in Christ for believers and to contribute to the common good for all.

Terms

age-set: a social group consisting of people of the same sex and similar age.

authority: the right granted to exercise power.

band: the most ancient political system, in which power and authority are organized in informal, decentralized ways.

chiefdom or *kingdom*: a system of political organization involving an inheritable office, often passed through a family line, in which power adheres to the occupant of the office rather than being a product of his or her individual gifts, abilities, or qualities.

coercive power: the use of force, legitimate or illegitimate, whether by individuals or groups.

counterhegemony: an ideology or movement that challenges a reigning hegemony.

formal negative sanctions: fines or other punishments meted out for breaking official rules.

formal positive sanctions: official rewards for socially desirable behavior.

formal sanctions: social sanctions that are approved or delivered by institutions holding official power.

hegemonic power (or *hegemony*): the dominance of ideas or culture, such that imbalances of power or other inequalities are maintained.

informal sanctions: positive or negative actions or words intended to shape behavior. Informal sanctions are not approved or delivered by official organizations such as a government.

oligarchy: within a centralized form of government, a small group holding power over the majority.

persuasive power: the use of words, relationships, and actions that influence others.

politics: the distribution, understanding, and use of power in social groups.

political anthropology: the study of power and authority and systems of organizing social life.

power: influence or control over the behavior of others.

social sanctions: the responses, positive and negative, that people receive for their behavior.

state: a highly centralized form of political organization in which authority rests in institutions and offices.

tribe: a decentralized political system usually associated with horticultural and pastoral modes of subsistence.

Devotion 1

Jesus's Power and Authority

Then he went down to Capernaum, a town in Galilee, and on the Sabbath began to teach the people. They were amazed at his teaching, because his words had authority. In the synagogue there was a man possessed by a demon, an evil spirit. He cried out at the top of his voice, "Go Away! What do you want with us, Jesus of Nazareth? Have you come to destroy us? I know who you are—the Holy One of God!" "Be quiet!" Jesus said sternly. "Come out of him!" Then the demon threw the man down before them all and came out without injuring him. All the people were amazed and said to each other, "What words these are! With authority and power he gives orders to evil spirits and they come out!" And the news about him spread throughout the surrounding area. (Luke 4:31–37)

At the beginning of this passage, Jesus amazed people by teaching with authority. Authority is the right granted to exercise power, and in Jesus's day, Jews recognized the authority of certain religious officials who were trained and seated in official roles. Jesus spoke as if people ought to recognize and accept his power, though he didn't have an official religious role.

When Jesus cast out the demon, he was continuing to claim authority and escalate its meaning by displaying power in action. Power is the ability to influence others, and Jesus demonstrated his ability to influence even demons in the supernatural realm. People were amazed because Jesus's words and actions disrupted their sense of what was expected. Jesus came to teach and cast out demons, but he also came to change culture. Through the incarnation, Jesus lived within a local culture, but he was strategic about disrupting fundamental elements of culture like power and authority. He was showing people how to include God—the true God—in their understandings and in their daily lives.

We all have realms of life in which we have influence and power. How can we seek to include God in the exercise of those areas in which we find ourselves wielding power?

Devotion 2

Legitimate and Illegitimate Power

When the righteous triumph, there is great glory; but when the wicked prevail, people go into hiding. (Prov. 28:12 NRSV)

Throughout the Psalms and Proverbs and other prophetic writings from the time when Israel used a kingdom form of political organization, biblical writings reflect a strong concern for legitimacy in power. Scripture references to God as "King" often highlight God's legitimate use of power, thus encouraging earthly kings to exercise power and authority in righteous ways.

This proverb celebrates the potential for justice in political systems; when a righteous person takes leadership, people take heart. It also acknowledges the potential for illegitimate uses of power when a wicked person gains power. This passage does not provide positive sanction for whoever is in governmental leadership; instead, it acknowledges the profound consequences for people when leaders use power in ways that are legitimate or illegitimate.

The meaning of this proverb comes into view when Israel's political organization is taken into consideration. A follower of God in a band would not have written this proverb. Bands don't have seats of power and don't have mechanisms by which one person can wield significant power over others. If illegitimate power plays are attempted, others refuse to follow along, move away, or use mockery, gossip, or conversation to get the person back in line. Likewise in a tribal society, this proverb wouldn't carry as much weight because tribal organization was local, not regional or kingdomwide. And if the writer of this proverb had lived in a state society, he might have encouraged citizens to work together to influence leadership through the political process, not go into hiding. In a kingdom such as Israel, the masses were influenced by the king or queen's decisions, even though they had no direct voice in the political process. When a leader was good, the people were grateful. When a leader was bad, people had little recourse but avoidance and hiding.

The principle of the proverb—that legitimate power is better than illegitimate power—can be applied in any political system, and an understanding of the proverb's context helps readers draw appropriate points of application.

8

Kinship and Marriage

After studying this chapter, you should be able to:

1. Articulate the importance of kinship and marriage in social organization.
2. Compare and contrast the various descent systems.
3. Understand anthropological approaches to the study of marriage.
4. Describe the variety of family systems present in the Bible.

Introduction

In the Philippines, most families have several children, and birth order is considered an important aspect of a person's identity. A question that is rather complicated in English—"Where do you fall in the birth order of your siblings?"—can be asked very simply in Tagalog—"*Pang-ilan ka?*" The frequency and ease with which this question is asked in the Philippines reflects the importance of sibling relationships in personal identity. In Korea, along with many other countries, family name (or "last name" in English) is the first part of a person's name. "Lee Chun Kee" refers to a person who was named "Chun Kee" by his parents but whose family name is "Lee." Placing the family name before the given name emphasizes the importance of family identity. Among the Yoruba of West Africa, along with many other groups, referring to older relatives as "the mother of so-and-so" rather than using an individual name (a practice known as *teknonymy*) (tek-non'-u-mē) is a sign of respect. This can also be a mechanism for enveloping others into a kin system, for example, referring to a beloved woman as "mother of so-and-so" even though she is not actually the mother of so-and-so. Family is important in every culture, but family relationships relate to personal identity and to social organization in various ways throughout the world.

Anthropologists study many dimensions of family life, including how people define family relationships, how they practice marriage, where they live, how family relationships shape (or don't shape) social organization, and how people pass on culture through families. Kinship studies analyze the structure, process, and meaning of family relationships. In this chapter we define kinship and then consider the two major areas of kinship study: descent and marriage. We conclude with a discussion of family forms found in biblical cultures.

Kinship

Kinship refers to the ways in which people selectively interpret the common human experiences of reproduction and nurturance. Humans everywhere make more humans and every society has systems for answering the big questions of kinship: Who should marry whom? To whom do these children belong? Who is responsible for the care of these children? Where should wives, husbands, boy children, and girl children live? The answers allow people to organize themselves into groups and know who to trust, who to help, and who might be a threat. Kinship rules govern, among other things, inheritance of political position and property, ritual and religious responsibilities, marriage, territorial distribution, dispute resolution, and landownership.

Kinship is the basis of band and tribal societies. In societies in which most members do the same work and have roughly the same social status, people are known primarily by kinship relations. A person has status, reputation, honor, and even selfhood by virtue of who they are related to. Kinship identity carries through all aspects of life, not just family life. A person's kin identity is salient in religion, economics, and politics.

In contrast, in highly stratified societies with a complex division of labor and multiple political institutions, a person's kinship role is just one identity (though it is often a very important one); the person may also carry religious, professional, political, and leisure identities. These identities don't cohere into a single social role. People experience distress when roles collide, such as when family responsibilities interfere with a professional role or a religious identity causes family conflict. Some people even reject their given kinship identity, living without significant ties to their families of origin.

Whether of European, African, Latin, Asian, or Native ancestry, most North Americans have roots in places where kinship powerfully influences identity. But in this highly mobile society, economic opportunity is often enhanced by a person's willingness to relocate. Though some families prize physical proximity and may arrange their lives to stay close together, the majority of families set up separate households of parents and children—the nuclear family—and move this relatively small group in response to educational and economic opportunity. They may maintain important ties to family who live far away—new immigrants, for instance, often share resources with relatives still in their place of origin—but the household itself is composed of a fairly small group of people. Similar to foragers in this respect, most contemporary U.S. Americans require mobility for economic advantage and emphasize the nuclear family as the primary kin group comprising a household.

In addition to having a smaller vision of family than many other groups, North Americans are more likely to emphasize individual identity over family identity. When asked for an introduction, a North American will likely begin with his personal ("first") name, describe personal qualities (what he enjoys doing, where he works), and later describe his family. "Family" may include those who share his household, parents and siblings, a spouse and/or children, and perhaps a dog or cat. North Americans are unlikely to talk about grandparents, cousins, aunts, and uncles when introducing themselves, unless those individuals live with them or someone asks specifically. Many North Americans distinguish immediate family from extended family in terms of reciprocity obligations and emotional ties.

Descent

Descent is a social rule that assigns identity to a person based on her or his ancestry. Descent systems vary widely across cultures but may be organized into two main types: unilineal descent and cognatic descent. There are three types of unilineal descent systems: matrilineal, patrilineal, and dual. Cognatic descent reckons identity through both maternal and paternal ancestors in two primary ways: bilateral and ambilineal. There is tremendous variation in how particular systems are understood and practiced around the world, and many more divisions within anthropological analysis, but these form the two basic branches of kinship analysis in anthropology.

Unilineal descent systems

Unilineal descent traces relatedness exclusively or predominantly through one parent. Most unilineal societies are *patrilineal*, in which descent is traced through the male line. Though it is giving way to other practices, European

Americans retain a vestige of this system through the tradition of a woman taking her husband's family name upon marriage and giving the father's family name to children. The U.S. kinship system is no longer truly unilineal, however. Because we consider a person equally related to her mother's and father's families, this is better classified as cognatic descent (described below).

Fig. 8.1 Descent Systems

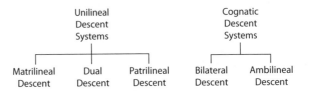

Most unilineal systems clearly mark distinctions between lineages in their kinship terminology. For example, in the Korean language, the father's father (FF) is your *halapeci*, while your father's mother (FM) is your *halmeci*. To refer to the *mother's* father (MF) or the *mother's* mother (MM), the terms are different (*oy-halapeci* and *oy-halmeci*, respectively). *Oy* is a term meaning "outside." In other words, grandparents on the mother's side are the "outside grandmother/father."[1] Relatives who are called the same thing in English—both the FF and MF are "grandfathers"—are named and understood as differently related in Korea.

Old Testament Hebrew culture provides a good example of a patrilineal kinship system. The Semitic cultures of the Middle East (Hebrews, Arabs, Kurds, and others) have long traced lineage through male ancestors. The Hebrews of the Old Testament believed in *monogenesis*, the idea that only one parent (the father) creates life. The metaphor for reproduction, still used in English, is the "seed and the soil." In other words, the man is thought to plant his "seed" (sperm) in the "soil" (womb) of the woman, where the seed grows into a child. Like a literal seed which contains everything necessary to create a new plant, the "seed" of the man was thought to simply need a place to grow in order for reproduction to occur. This cultural logic inspired Sarah to encourage her husband, Abraham, to "plant his seed" in her maidservant Hagar to produce his heir. In the logic of monogenesis, the child comes wholly from the father; the mother does not contribute anything to the physical being of the child any more than the soil would influence what kind of tree grows from a particular seed (see also Genesis 30). Therefore Ishmael, Hagar's son, received God's blessing along with Isaac, Sarah's son,

1. Jae Jung Song, *The Korean Language: Structure, Use and Context* (New York: Routledge, 2005), 12.

Fig. 8.2 Patrilineal Descent

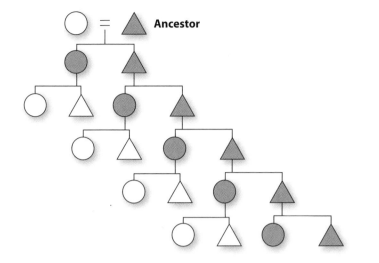

Ancestor

○ female
△ male
= marriage
⌐ line of descent
■ members of patriline/matriline
□ not members of patriline/matriline

because both were sons of Abraham. In patrilineal systems such as this one, children are *more* related to their fathers than to their mothers. Although a few women are mentioned in the important lineages of the Bible (e.g., Ruth, Rahab), it is because of what they did to preserve the line, not because they are considered true members of the line.

Patrilineality is not the same as *patriarchy*, or social rule by men. In patrilineal societies men typically have more social and political power than women, but lineage and sociopolitical authority are not necessarily related.

The second major unilineal system is *matrilineal descent*, in which descent is traced through the female line. In these families, names and inheritance are passed through the mother. Though less common than patrilineality, matrilineality is found throughout the world, from West Africa to Southeast Asia to indigenous North America.

In many matrilineal cultures, even though the family is named for the mother's relatives and inheritance is passed from mothers to daughters, the primary authority in a family rests with a male relative. The state of Mizoram, in northeast India, is the traditional home of several matrilineal groups, including the Garo. Among the Garo, the youngest daughter inherits family property. She is expected to live in the family home and care for her parents as they age. Upon marriage, her husband moves into the home and works alongside his wife caring for her parents, working the land, and raising children. The practice of a newly married couple living with or near the bride's family is known as *uxorilocal* (you-shor-uh-lo'-cal) *residence.*[2] In the case of

2. Whether matrilineal or patrilineal, family residence patterns (a family lives near or with the wife's kin, or the husband's, or some other pattern) support the lineage system.

Fig. 8.3 Matrilineal Descent

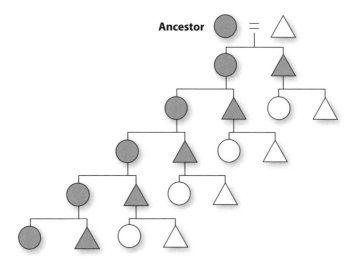

family disputes or even child discipline, the person most likely to be called on to exercise authority is the mother's older brother, the maternal uncle. The father is primarily a nurturing presence for his children. Although individual Garo fathers have different styles, when it comes to the discipline of children, the Garo equivalent of "Just wait until your father gets home!" is "Just wait until I call your uncle to come over!"

Just as patrilineal kinship does not necessarily link to patriarchy, neither does matrilineal kinship necessarily correlate with *matriarchy*, or social rule by women. Matrilineal kinship systems typically support women in more prominent social roles in religion, politics, and economics than patrilineal ones, but anthropologists have never encountered a contemporary society in which women exercise the kind of control men exercise in some highly patriarchal (and often patrilineal) cultures.[3]

The third type of unilineal kinship system is *dual descent*. This uncommon system traces descent through both the mother and father's lines. In the case of the Yakö of Nigeria, the two lines involve different rules of inheritance. Movable property, such as cattle or personal possessions, is passed through the mother's line. Fixed property (i.e., land) is inherited through the father's line. Instead of thinking of themselves as having two "sides" of one family, members of this group think of themselves as belonging to two different families. Out of more than 175 unilineal cultures documented by anthropologist

3. Some archaeologists argue that ancient societies of Eastern Europe and the Near East may have had goddess religions in which childbirth, lactation, and menstruation were considered sacred; this suggests that women may have had a great deal of religious and, perhaps, political power.

George Murdock in 1949, only eighteen (10 percent) were organized with dual descent.[4] Because there are two lines, dual descent may not seem unilineal, but anthropologists categorize dual descent this way because dual descent systems combine the rules for patrilineal descent and the rules for matrilineal descent without joining the matrilineage and the patrilineage together, as cognatic descent systems do.

Cognatic descent systems

Cognatic (also called *nonunilineal*) *descent* reckons identity through both maternal and paternal ancestors. There are two major types of cognatic descent systems: bilateral and ambilineal.

Most North Americans believe in cognatic descent and rely on the rules of *bilateral descent*. In the logic of this system, kinship is understood to exist equally through both the mother's and father's lines. An individual in the United States, for example, is related to an ever-widening group of people on both sides of the family. Bilateral kinship terms differentiate people based on gender (aunt versus uncle) or generation (great-grandmother versus grandmother), but generally do not distinguish between the mother's and father's kindred. People distinguish between mother's and father's kin in their interpersonal relationships, of course, but this distinction is not important enough to encode in kinship terminology.

Descent rules help explain recent trends in name changes at marriage. Some North Americans continue the tradition of a wife giving up her family name and assuming her husband's surname. Some wives retain their family names, so husband and wife have different last names. Some wives hyphenate their family name with their husband's name, and the husband may or may not hyphenate. Still other couples create new last names for both husband and wife. In all these variations, however, descent rules remain firm. In fact, because bilateral kinship systems engender a sense of identity linked to both mother and father, this widens the pool of possible marital names; the couple could symbolize their union with the male name, the female name, or a new name that embraces both sides or neither side. The tradition of taking the male name is a patrilineal idea that is not necessary for kinship stability in a bilateral kinship system.

The second form of cognatic descent is ambilineal. In *ambilineal descent* systems, individuals choose a lineage upon reaching adulthood (often marked by marriage). The individual may choose the lineage of his or her mother or father or the maternal or paternal line of his or her spouse. Ambilineal systems, then, look like unilineal systems because they trace ancestry through one line, but this system is considered cognatic because the lineages

4. See George Peter Murdock, *Social Structure* (New York: Macmillan, 1949).

Fig. 8.4 Ego (Self)-Centric Bilateral Descent System

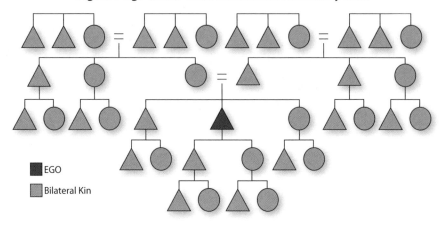

■ EGO

■ Bilateral Kin

are open for the choosing. Based upon considerations such as property, kin relationships, and personal ties, the individual may decide to live with his father's or mother's group after marriage, or may simply take the name of the group desired for affiliation. In either case, children are seen as related to both parents equally and therefore are able to choose a lineage when they reach adulthood.

Functions of descent systems

Kinship connects with many other areas of life. Three of the most important are inheritance, territory, and conflict resolution. Inheritance rules are often a function of kinship. In the Western tradition, patrilineality shaped practices such as the oldest son inheriting family property upon the death of his parents, or the oldest son being the heir of a royal dynasty. Biblical accounts reflect the same concerns, for example in the story of Jacob and Esau, twins who were destined to follow a strict rule of *primogeniture*, or priority of the firstborn. In collusion with his mother, Jacob (the second-born twin) convinced Esau to renounce his birthright and also tricked their father into passing the inheritance to him, the younger twin. Jacob's trick was an offense against his brother, and by violating the rule of primogeniture, was also a transgression of the kinship system that organized their family life. Seen in another light, however, Jacob and his mother were working to preserve their patrilineal lineage. By marrying Canaanite women, Esau had violated the Hebrew preference for cousin marriage, a preference that strengthened the patrilineage by marrying within it. When Jacob received his father's blessing, he made a point of promising to marry within the patrilineal kin group (see Gen. 27:1–28:9).

Kinship also organizes the distribution of territory. The clans of Jacob's lineage were given specific territorial claims based on ancestry from one

U.S. Kinship Terms

In the U.S. kinship system, most people can explain the relationship of "aunt," or "cousin," but what about a "second-cousin, once removed," or "great-grandniece"? U.S. kinship terminology is more complex than many people realize, as many terms have fallen into disuse. As U.S. society has become more mobile, families are smaller, and have become more geographically dispersed, and fewer families maintain links beyond parents, grandparents, aunts/uncles, and first cousins. This system strikes many around the world as almost absurdly simple. However, while most people in the United States may not *know* the kinship terms available, genealogists and interested laypersons can learn surprisingly complex ways of reckoning descent.

For instance, most people know that the first cousin is the child of a parent's sibling. The second cousin is any child of a parent's cousin. In other words, the linking relative is two steps away. (Another way to say it is that a second cousin is the child of a grandparent's sibling's child.) If two people share a great-grandparent, they may be third cousins, but only if they are of the same generation. If they are different generations, then we add the description "once (twice, thrice, etc.) removed." My grandmother's first cousin is also my first cousin, but because my grandmother is two generations removed from me, I call her cousin my "first cousin, twice removed." That cousin, incidentally, would call me the same thing. It doesn't matter which way the generations go; to be of different generations is to be "removed."

Within the direct lineage on both sides of the kindred, we add prefixes "grand" and "great-grand" to refer to generations above us and below us. Thus relatives within a direct lineage on either the mother's or father's side can be "great-grand-aunts" or "great-grand-nephews," but within the wider kindred, we turn to various uses of the term "cousin."

Most people do not use these arcane terms in their daily lives. People think of themselves as related to a nuclear family and an extended family composed of select members and do not spend much time reckoning descent beyond that. Defining people as kin broadens webs of reciprocity and indebtedness, and our society's valuing of individuality and mobility encourages us to keep our kinship groups small.

The complexity of our kinship system is valuable, however, for researching genealogy. Professor Henry Louis Gates Jr. researched Oprah Winfrey's genealogy and used complex kinship concepts to trace her lineage; he also offered advice to African Americans who wish to trace their kinship back as far as American slavery and even back to Africa. He is using kinship as a way of talking about what it means to be "American," using the genealogies of many different individuals to tell the stories of how various groups came to the United States.[1]

1. Henry Louis Gates Jr., *Finding Oprah's Roots: Finding Your Own* (New York: Crown Publishers, 2007).

---

of Jacob's twelve sons, as described in the book of Joshua. The book of Judges describes how the leaders of various factions within the lineage, known as *segments*, engaged in warfare with Canaanites or even other Hebrew lineages for possession of territory. Leadership of those territories was also assigned and legitimated through kinship. Even today, from the highlands of Papua New Guinea to the plains of East Africa, clan affiliation determines territory.

In addition to inheritance and territory distribution, kinship helps regulate social conflict. Knowing that someone is related means that although two people may not know each other personally, there is someone connecting them whom they *do* know. Where there is no kinship connection, or the kinship is weaker or more distant, there is less trust and a greater possibility of conflict or disregard.

Unilineal descent systems seem generally better suited to influence a wide variety of social behavior. In addition to inheritance, territorial distribution, and conflict avoidance or resolution, kinship may also be a significant factor in landownership, political representation, and ritual observance (as in the case of the Levites described in Num. 3 and 4). Cognatic structures often serve fewer roles in society, since their more diffuse organization influences political and economic spheres minimally.[5] One part of life shaped profoundly by both systems, however, is marriage.

Marriage

If we ask students in our classes to imagine who their parents would pick as spouses for them, they may name criteria important for both parents and themselves (attractiveness, compatibility, common religion). Students sometimes note that their parents take other concerns more seriously than they do (earning potential, reproductive potential, or the character of the prospective spouse's parents). Mostly, students make it very clear that they wouldn't want this scenario to happen. Romantic ideals of finding a "soul mate," "Mr./Ms. Right," or "the One" animate Western movies and popular music. One of the most influential works of Western literature is Shakespeare's *Romeo and Juliet*. The story of young lovers who defy the wishes of their families and ultimately give their lives for true love captures the Western imagination and resonates with a deeply held cultural value: true love conquers all.

For many people, however, the notion of pursuing marriage primarily for personal motives represents a neglect of family—the height of selfishness, irresponsibility, and immaturity. For most of human history and today in many cultures, marriage is primarily a social, economic, and political connection between two families rather than the free choice of two individuals. While Western marriage priorities such as companionship, love, and sexual fulfillment are part of ideal marriages everywhere, other cultures would add economic security, continuation of a lineage by producing heirs, and political alliances to the highest priorities and purposes of marriage.

Marriage is a publicly recognized social or legal union that creates a socially sanctioned context for sexual intimacy, establishes (in whole or in part) the parentage of children, and creates kinship. Marriage produces relatives; *affinal* (a-fi'-nul) *kin* are relatives created through marriage ("affinal" is related

---

5. Descent rules and structures have enormous variety and complexity. An excellent resource for understanding the technical categories and analysis of kinship can be found at "Kinship and Social Organization: An Interactive Tutorial," Department of Anthropology, University of Manitoba, www.umanitoba.ca/faculties/arts/anthropology/kintitle.html.

to the word "affinity," meaning attraction). Birth too creates relatives, and people related by birth are called *consanguinial* (kon-sang-gwin'-ee-uhl) *kin* (consanguinity means "of the blood"). Marriage is important for both the partners in the marriage and their families. The quality of consanguinial bonds are affected for better or for worse when a family member links with another family through affinity. For this reason, parents and even the wider community are often intimately involved in selecting marriage partners for young people. Many societies have specific rules about who should marry whom and how the choice should be made.

Anthropologists have found that every society has *incest taboos*, prohibitions against marriage or sex between two categories of related persons. The incest taboo that appears universal is a prohibition on parents marrying their own children, siblings with each other, and grandparents with grandchildren. Beyond that, however, rules for marriage avoidance and marriage preference vary a great deal.

Because the marriage of two individuals creates bonds between two families, many families would prefer to promote marriage between people who are *already* related. In many places there are preferences for a person to marry a child of one of their parent's siblings. *Cross-cousin marriage*, a preference for marriage between cross cousins, means a man should marry his mother's brother's daughter or his father's sister's daughter. The "cross" refers to the opposite-sex sibling of the person's parent. *Parallel-cousin marriage*, a preference for marriage between parallel cousins, directs a man to marry his mother's sister's daughter or his father's brother's daughter. "Parallel" refers to the parent's same-sex sibling. Cousin preference seems to be rooted, in part, in the desire to have stronger relationships within the family or to keep inheritance within a clan.

Scripture contains numerous examples of cousin marriage in which parents work with their siblings or other relatives to find good matches for their children. Seeking marriage partners within the family assures there will already be a level of trust and familiarity among the families, hopefully making life easier for the young couple. Jacob, for instance, was the son of Isaac and Rebekah. Isaac instructed Jacob to marry the daughter of Rebekah's brother, Jacob's cross-cousin. Jacob eventually married two sisters, Rachel and Leah, both his cross-cousins, due to his uncle's trickery. In this case, marrying within the family made life more difficult for Jacob because he had to provide fourteen years of brideservice (described later in this chapter)instead of seven, but it also contributed to his personal wealth. Additionally, the practice ensured patterns of descent and inheritance that were desirable to the broader kin group.

U.S. society bolsters its avoidance of cousin marriage with beliefs about birth defects and images such as the southern hillbilly who marries a cousin

Fig. 8.5 Cousin Marriage

Cross Cousin Marriage

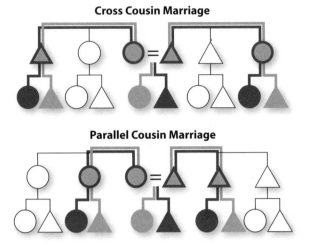

preferred marriage partners

Parallel Cousin Marriage

and produces children with feeble minds and bad teeth. In fact, there is no evidence that, within large clans, cousin marriage poses genetic problems.[6] And, to further challenge the hillbilly stereotype, the U.S. southern states have the strictest laws regarding marriage, following the rules of Leviticus 18. First-cousin marriage is legal, however, in most northern and western U.S. states. Though they would be considered respectable in many world cultures, cousin couples in U.S. society face stereotyping and discrimination.

Marriage and economic exchange

The seriousness with which families take the marriage of their children also promotes the use of marriage exchange. *Marriage exchange* involves exchanges of material resources between families before, at, or after the wedding. The three major types of marriage exchange are brideservice, bridewealth, and dowry. *Brideservice* requires the groom to work for the bride's kin for a certain period of time before or after marriage. *Bridewealth* (also called *brideprice*) is an amount of money, possessions, or property given by the groom and his kin to the wife and her kin before, at, or after the wedding. The word "brideprice" carries the connotation that the groom is purchasing the wife, which is not what the practice really means. "Bridewealth" is a synonym that highlights the value of the bride. Losing the bride represents a loss of wealth to her family; that is, the service, employment, companionship, offspring, and other resources she could have given to her consanguinial kin will now

6. The only genetic concern within families is the possibility that recessive conditions would appear more frequently. Enlarging the genetic pool would make those conditions less likely to manifest. Families without such recessive conditions, however, would be *less* likely to see such conditions in their children through cousin marriage.

go to her affinal kin. An exchange of wealth between families recognizes the value of the bride to both sets of kin.

Genesis 29 describes the brideservice transaction between Jacob and his uncle Laban. They agreed that in exchange for working for Laban, Jacob could marry Laban's daughter Rachel at the end of seven years. This arrangement would solidify trust and relationship between Jacob and Laban and would also give financial gain to Laban in exchange for the loss of a daughter and the companionship and household labor she represented. When Rachel married Jacob she would leave Laban's patriline and join the patriline of Jacob (Gen. 29:19). Her children would belong to Jacob and his ancestors, not to her and her ancestors. Of course, in this case Laban used another marriage preference—that the older daughter marry before the younger—to insist that Jacob work *another* seven years to marry Rachel (Gen. 29:26).

In other cases, families use bridewealth, or an exchange of goods, to mark a marriage. These exchanges may be largely symbolic, or they may involve substantial goods. Anthropologist and former missionary Jon Arensen uses the example of the nomadic Murle people to illustrate bridewealth. The Murle are pastoralists whose traditional lands range across southeastern Sudan. As with all pastoralists, the labor of the family is critical to maintain the herd that provides almost all the family's resources. Cattle are wealth and crucial to survival. When it is time for a family to arrange the marriage of a son, they seek out a family with a marriageable daughter and begin to negotiate with her parents over an appropriate bridewealth, which for the Murle always means a number of cattle given in exchange for the marriage. To Westerners, this often appears as buying a wife (and equating women with cows), but the Murle do not think of it this way. They recognize that in this marriage the families will be united, and the cattle represent something tangible to mark the connection.

The Murle word for relatives, *atiinok*, comes from the word for cattle, *tiin*. To be related means "to have cattle between us."[7] This occurs when, upon marriage, the groom's family sends the agreed-upon number of cattle to the bride's family. While this may seem like a great deal for the bride's parents, they do not simply keep the new cattle. Twenty years earlier, when the father of the bride got married, he had to go to his relatives and borrow cattle from a number of different families for his own bridewealth. These families remember the debt and once the marriage of the man's daughter is complete, they come back to get the cattle they loaned to him twenty years earlier. Now, the dozen or so families who loaned the young groom his bride-wealth are connected to the dozen families who collect on the twenty-year-

7. For further analysis of Murle language and social categories, see Jonathan E Arensen, *Mice are Men: Language and Society among the Murle of Sudan*, International Museum of Cultures Publication 27 (Dallas: International Museum of Cultures, 1992), xvii, 362.

The Kinsman Redeemer

U.S. weddings frequently reference the story of Ruth as a story of ultimate love and devotion. While it is that, it is not love between a man and a woman but rather the love of Ruth for her mother-in-law, Naomi, and devotion to her dead husband.

Ruth, a Moabite, married Mahlon, coming into the patriline of Elimelech, husband of Naomi. When Mahlon died without providing heirs, it left the already-widowed Naomi destitute and vulnerable in a male-dominated society. Neither Ruth nor Naomi had a male relative linking them to the wider patriline. Rather than accepting Naomi's offer to leave the family and return to her parents (essentially restarting her life), Ruth elected to honor her connection to her dead husband and his family, meaning her mother-in-law, Naomi.

This decision left her extremely vulnerable in a patrilineal culture, in which only the birth of sons guaranteed the continuation of the family and only sons would inherit land. Women without male relatives had, essentially, no legitimate claim to economic resources.

When Ruth and Naomi returned to the land of Judah, they found that they did have a connection to Elimelech's family, though it appeared to be a weak one. When Naomi learned that Boaz, Elimelech's relative (i.e., in the patriline) lived in Judah, she knew he *should* serve as the "kinsman redeemer," marrying and impregnating Ruth so that she would have a child who was part of the lineage, reconnecting Ruth, Naomi, and even Ruth's dead husband, Mahlon, back to the lineage. She would be brought back in from outside the family.

After a period of testing, Naomi believed Boaz to be honorable and likely to do the right thing. She sent Ruth to him at night, so that, if he were an honorable man, he would impregnate her and "redeem" her back into the family. Boaz was willing, and praised Ruth for not "running after younger men," since Boaz, as a wealthy man, was certainly quite old. What made him the right choice for Ruth was not principally his physical attractiveness or personal wealth, but that he was a link to the lineage.

In the end, Boaz told Ruth that there was a man more closely related than he—meaning the closer relative should take Ruth, provide her with children, and bring her into his household. The risk to that man (and Boaz for that matter) was that were Ruth to have male children, those children would inherit part of whatever he owned. This meant his current children would receive less, in addition to adding to his economic responsibilities to care for Ruth, her mother-in-law, and all children Ruth may bear. That man ended up passing on his responsibility to Boaz, who did the right thing by taking Ruth as one of his wives and caring for her and Naomi.

What Scripture notes as most important in Ruth's story is her righteousness in making sure the line of Jacob continued. It was that line, of course, that led to King David and eventually to Jesus. It was the faithfulness of Ruth, and a few other women who took extraordinary measures to overcome circumstances or the sin of male relatives, that is singled out for mention in the genealogy of Jesus (Matt. 1:1–17).

old debt with the bride's father. Divorce becomes difficult when it involves giving back twenty cattle that, in the subsequent years, have been herded hundreds of miles, died, been eaten, or perhaps exchanged again in another marriage. Bridewealth becomes a significant social institution encouraging the stability of marriage and family, creating links between multiple segments of various clans.

An opposite form of exchange is the *dowry*, the practice of a bride's family providing resources, wealth, or gifts to the groom and his family upon marriage. This has been common in many parts of India, Europe, and other strongly patrilineal societies in which people understand the groom to be taking over the care of the bride from the bride's father. For the husband taking on the cost of caring for the wife, the dowry is meant to symbolize the gratitude of the bride's family while also providing material resources to the newly married couple. Sometimes the dowry remains the bride's property as a kind of insurance against divorce or abandonment, particularly when the dowry consists of items such as gold jewelry or household goods associated with women's work (e.g., kitchenware). This sort of dowry is common in many Middle Eastern societies.

Although Western conceptions of marriage as the free choice of two individuals have made marriage exchange largely a thing of the past, there are remnants of the practice. A man is expected to buy an expensive item (i.e., the ring) in exchange for a woman's agreement to marry him. As in other places, in the United States there are circulated "rules" about how expensive it should be. (Two months' salary has been the tradition passed on from the DeBeers diamond monopoly.) The dowry survives through the tradition of the bride's family (traditionally her father) paying for the wedding expenses. With the average U.S. wedding costing many thousands of dollars, this can represent a significant dowry.

Plural marriage

Plural marriage, or *polygamy*, is a form of marriage in which one person is married to two or more other persons. The two major types of plural marriage are *polygyny* and *polyandry*. *Polygyny* (puh-lij'-uh-nee) is the marriage of one man to two or more wives. *Polyandry* is the marriage of one woman to two or more husbands. Marriage exchange is one of the reasons that plural marriage often represents wealth or brings prestige. If marriage requires bridewealth, only men of considerable means can afford more than one marriage. Additional wives and children provide more labor, however, which should allow the man to regain what had been given in brideprice.

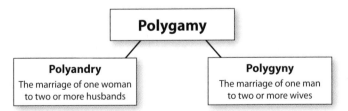

Polygyny is the most common form of plural marriage. It allows a man to develop alliances with multiple families through his wives and affinal relatives. King Solomon's three hundred wives, recorded in Scripture, were entirely about the alliances such marriages created. It's possible that an important ruler like Solomon wouldn't even know all of his wives, nor would they necessarily be grown women. Some neighboring rulers may have married their young (even infant) daughters to a powerful king such as Solomon simply to be able to claim him as a relative. This extreme form of polygyny emphasizes the economic and political benefits of marriage. Most polygynous marriages in the world are between a man and two or three wives, and each relationship carries a degree of intimacy and companionship.

The other form of plural marriage, polyandry, involves one wife with multiple husbands, and is relatively rare. The most well-known manifestation of the system occurs in the high Himalayas of Tibet and Nepal. Here several men, usually brothers, share one wife. Frequently the oldest brother will marry and his younger brothers will live with him and his wife. When those younger brothers are old enough, they will marry the wife. One theory as to why this form of marriage developed in this part of the world concerns the need to keep the small amount of arable land within families as well as to keep the population density low. Men travel extensively in their subsistence work as well, so husbands essentially rotate through the home, some being home and some traveling at any given time.

Family in the Bible

When it comes to kinship, the stakes are high. For their very survival, societies must have functional marriages and families. Kinship patterns are a fundamental part of enculturation; people are socialized to believe that their ways of marrying, raising children, charting ancestry, and relating with kin are good. This easily becomes ethnocentrism: the belief that one's own culture is superior and the norm against which all other ways of life are measured. Judgments about family are some of the most common stereotypes and insults that people turn to when encountering cultural difference. "*They* don't raise their children well." "*Their* marriages aren't as stable as ours." "*They* don't love their children as much as we do." For Christians, the temptation to use religion to bolster ethnocentrism is often present. It's all too easy to assume that God's sense of good and normal is the same as ours.

It is tempting, for example, for Christians in the United States to think that a bilateral kinship structure emphasizing the nuclear family represents God's intent for all families everywhere. While it is true that the Genesis account declares monogamy as God's creational intent for marriage, it would be a stretch to suggest that God prefers *neolocal residence* (the practice of a newly married couple living separate from both partners' parents), or that the nuclear family pattern common in contemporary industrial societies is more biblical than unilineal family compounds of many children, their spouses and children, grandparents, and others living together.

Using Scripture to promote one particular view of kinship is difficult. Patri-lineality and even patriarchy are dominant among the societies represented in Scripture, and polygyny is common. Scripture never explicitly condemns polygyny, and God is even compared to a polygynous man with Jerusalem and Samaria as his two wives (Ezek. 23). Paul writes that male leaders in the church should be the "husband of one wife," but he does not explicitly extend this to all Christians (Titus 1:6). Biblical writings refer to family forms famil-iar to their original audiences, using stories and metaphors of brideservice, cousin marriage, polygyny, and patrilineality. Drawing applications from these contexts for another time and place is a complex cross-cultural task.

Family forms are adaptive; people innovate marriage practices, child-rearing strategies, and household arrangements that suit their geography, political conditions, and social organization. The family forms of God's people shifted as Israel lived as a tribe, then a kingdom, then a diaspora, and then a minority group within an empire. Kinship system seems less important in Scripture than the behavior of and relationships between kin. In 1 Timothy 5:8, Paul instructs those in the church to care for their relatives, "especially [their] own household." The New International Version uses the term "immediate fam-ily" instead of "household," but in Paul's day, most households consisted of older members (grandparents, aunts, uncles) and many younger ones (nieces, daughters-in-law), in addition to just the nuclear family. Additionally, there is nothing in Scripture commanding that descent be reckoned through the male line or that unilineal kinship (or cognatic forms) have divine favor.

It appears that Scripture emphasizes kinship behavior as more important than kinship rules or structure. The metaphor of family is used to describe, first, the nation of Israel, and then the Jesus followers of the New Testament era. This is meant to illustrate the closeness of the bonds within those groups and the mutual responsibility of the members. The relationship of Jesus and the church is compared to a marriage, as a model of oneness. God is called "Our Father" and compared to earthly fathers and mothers in order for God's people to understand God as the source of life. The use of "brothers and sisters" in the church is meant to convey the significance of relationships between believers and something of the behavior that is to govern those rela-tionships. This emphasis on behaviors conveys important ethical and moral principles but does not answer questions about specific forms, roles, or the way Christians should think about kinship in society at large. Christians in various times and places disagree about important elements of kinship—for instance, gender roles in marriage or government marriage laws.

Despite these differences, a general principle is clear: Scripture teaches love, mutual concern, and sacrificial love as the norm for Christians in marriage and family life. The bonds between Christians should be like those of family. In the church we have eternal bonds of commitment that are not based on our own choices and preferences but on God's work placing us in the family.

Anthropologists call this *fictive kinship*, that is, kinship relationships that are real but not based on marriage or descent. This is more than a mere illustration; Paul teaches that when we become Christians we *become* members of a family in a very real way (Heb. 2:11; Gal. 6:10). Those of us living in Western societies where kinship has lost much of its importance in shaping behavior and identity may have much to learn from Christians in places where kinship relations maintain a powerful, organizing role in daily life.

Terms

affinal kin (a-fi′-nul): relatives created through marriage.

ambilineal descent: a type of cognatic descent system in which individuals choose a lineage upon adulthood (often marked by marriage).

bilateral descent: a type of cognatic descent system that traces relatedness equally through both the mother's and father's lines.

brideservice: a duty of the groom to work for the bride's kin for a certain period of time before or after marriage.

bridewealth (also called *brideprice*): an amount of money, possessions, or property given by the groom and his kin to the wife and her kin before, at, or after the wedding.

cognatic (also called *nonunilineal*) *descent*: a system of descent that reckons identity through both maternal and paternal ancestors.

consanguinial kin (kon-sang-gwin′-ee-uhl): relatives related by birth.

cross-cousin marriage: a preference for marriage between cross cousins. A cross cousin is the child of one's mother's brother or father's sister.

descent: a social rule that assigns identity to a person based on her or his ancestry.

dowry: the practice of a bride's family providing resources, wealth, or gifts to the groom and his family upon marriage.

dual descent: a form of unilineal descent in which descent is traced through both the mother's and father's lines. The person belongs to two separate families.

fictive kinship: kinship relationships that are real but not based on marriage or descent.

incest taboo: prohibition against marriage or sex between two categories of related persons.

kinship: the ways in which people selectively interpret the common human experiences of reproduction and nurturance.

marriage: a publicly recognized social or legal union that creates a socially sanctioned context for sexual intimacy, establishes (in whole or in part) the parentage of children, and creates kinship.

marriage exchange: the practice of exchanging material resources between families before, at, or after a wedding.

matriarchy: social rule by women.

matrilineal descent: a form of unilineal descent in which descent is traced through the female line.

monogenesis: the idea that only one parent (usually the father) creates life.

neolocal residence: the practice of a newly married couple living separate from both partners' parents.

parallel-cousin marriage: a preference for marriage between parallel cousins. A parallel cousin is the child of one's parent's same-sex sibling (mother's sister's child or father's brother's child).

patriarchy: social rule by men.

patrilineal descent: a form of unilineal descent in which descent is traced through the male line.

polyandry: the marriage of one woman to two or more husbands.

polygamy (also called *plural marriage*): a form of marriage in which one person is married to two or more other persons.

polygyny (puh-lij'-uh-nee): the marriage of one man to two or more wives.

primogeniture: priority of the firstborn.

segment: a faction within a lineage.

teknonymy (tek-non'-u-mē): the practice of referring to adults with children as the mother/father of the child in place of the parent's given name.

unilineal descent: a descent system that traces relatedness exclusively or predominantly through one parent.

uxorilocal residence (you-shor-uh-lo'-cal): the practice of a newly married couple living with or near the bride's family.

Devotion 1

Adoption into God's Family

Blessed be the God and Father of our Lord Jesus Christ, who has blessed us in Christ with every spiritual blessing in the heavenly places, just as he chose us in Christ before the foundation of the world to be holy and blameless before him in love. He destined us for adoption as his children through Jesus Christ, according to the good pleasure of his will, to the praise of his glorious grace that he freely bestowed on us in the Beloved. (Eph. 1:3–6 NRSV)

Paul begins his letter to the Ephesians with a family metaphor. He says that God is our Father who chose to adopt us as children in God's family. Ephesians 1 goes on to describe how the adopted children now qualify for inheritance: the inheritance of redemption.

The original recipients of this letter would have appreciated the significance of adoption into a powerful man's family. God, the Father, is willing to fully accept newcomers, not just as charity cases or outsiders, but as full family members who will become heirs to the father's wealth (in this case, spiritual wealth). The implications for life in the church are immense: believers should treat each other as siblings, with all the rights, obligations, respect, and concern that they show their consanguinial siblings. And they should establish their own identities in terms of their patriline that stems from God the Father.

How does the idea of adoption into God's family affect our relationship with God? With other members of the church? How should it?

Devotion 2

The Patrilineal Descent of Jesus

An account of the genealogy of Jesus the Messiah, the son of David, the son of Abraham. Abraham was the father of Isaac, and Isaac the father of Jacob, and Jacob the father of Judah and his brothers, and Judah the father of Perez and Zerah by Tamar, and Perez the father of Hezron, and Hezron the father of Aram, and Aram the father of Aminadab, and Aminadab the father of Nahshon, and Nahshon the father of Salmon, and Salmon the father of Boaz by Rahab, and Boaz the father of Obed by Ruth, and Obed the father of Jesse, and Jesse the father of King David. (Matt. 1:1–6 NRSV)

When an American Christian hears the beginning of the book of Matthew, the likely response is a yawn. We'd rather skip to the exciting part, later in chapter 1, when Jesus is born. Jews and Jewish Christians in Matthew's original context, however, would sit up on the edge of their seats when they heard the beginning of a genealogy and say, "Tell us more!" This passage goes on for seventeen verses, detailing the genealogy of Jesus from his father Joseph back through King David to Abraham.

Understanding the genealogy and its powerful message requires an understanding of patrilineal descent. For Jews at that time, identity was reckoned through patrilineal descent, so establishing Jesus's identity as the fulfillment of the promise to Abraham required a linkage of Jesus to Abraham. The genealogy meets these cultural expectations, but it upsets them as well. The genealogy includes several women, asserting their importance in the history that leads up to Jesus even though their inclusion wouldn't be strictly necessary in a patrilineal genealogy. And though Jesus is linked to Abraham through Joseph, he wasn't born of Joseph's seed. Jesus is the one promised through this lineage, but he cannot be said to belong to the lineage alone.

His true paternal ancestor is God the Father, which extends the promise to all people.

In U.S. society, in which people use cognatic descent to establish identity, people are interested in both Jesus's mother and father. We can appreciate the importance of the promise extending through Abraham and David, but a genealogy of many, many generations of male ancestors is not the way we begin an exciting story. Reading the genealogy of Matthew 1 with an understanding of the kinship structures of Jews and Jewish Christians in the original context illuminates the incarnation: God becoming fully human, coming to live in culture.

Religion and Ritual

After studying this chapter, you should be able to:

1. Define religion, ritual, and myth and explain their social functions.
2. Describe the history of anthropological studies of religion.
3. Understand Clifford Geertz's definition of religion as a cultural system.
4. Explain the relevance of anthropological study of religion to Christian life.

Introduction

A popular Christian bumper sticker reads, "Christianity is not a Religion; it's a Relationship." This phrase is often used to emphasize that being a Christian is not about merely following rules or believing doctrines but knowing God in personal and intimate ways. It's true that Christianity is a relationship, but is it really *not* a religion? That depends, of course, on what is meant by "religion."

Christian believers sometimes find the study of religion strange because they are used to approaching religion as a way of life rather than as a social phenomenon. In this chapter we highlight ways in which the study of religion can be helpful for Christians and describe how Christian anthropologists study religion as a cultural system even while they practice religion as a way of life.

In this chapter we describe how anthropologists study religion. First, we define religion and then describe how anthropologists study it. Next, we describe the social functions of religion. Then, we discuss religion as a cultural system. Finally, we explain how the scientific study of religion can be helpful to Christian believers and to the church.

Studying Religion

Defining religion is difficult. Many definitions refer to the so-called supernatural or spirit world, calling religion "a worldview in which people personify cosmic forces and devise ways to deal with them in ways that resemble the way they deal with powerful people in their society."[1] But this approach neglects significant systems, beliefs, and behaviors that ought to be included in the category "religion." Take, for example, Buddhism. Although many people who call themselves Buddhists believe in a spirit world of ancestors or local spiritual beings, the teachings of the Buddha center on the belief of *anatma* ("non-being"). To achieve enlightenment is to realize that nothing exists—not humans, not spirits, not a god or gods—and join the universe in nothingness. Buddhism would not be considered a religion in a definition concerning the relation of humans to supernatural beings.[2] Atheism provides another example. Many people see atheists as practicing their own "religion" of *non*religion. Atheists such as Richard Dawkins, who has written fiery polemics against religious belief generally and Christianity in particular, seem to have a strong "faith" in their beliefs, even if those beliefs are about the absence of a supreme being.[3]

Additionally, some anthropologists studying the indigenous religious traditions of bands and tribes have argued that to say these cultures "believe in spirits" is to impose a Western conceptual framework on irreducibly different understandings of the world. A good definition of religion needs to encompass Buddhism, atheism, local indigenous religions, and monotheistic religions like Christianity, Judaism, and Islam.

No anthropological definitions of religion are without controversy, but Clifford Geertz's approach continues to be widely used. In an essay entitled "Religion as a Cultural System," Geertz proposed a definition that would encompass many different religious systems and a variety of perspectives in studying them. He called *religion*:

1. Robert Lavenda and Emily Schultz, *Core Concepts in Anthropology* (New York: McGraw-Hill Higher Education, 2003), 68.
2. See Walpola Rahula, *What the Buddha Taught* (1959; repr., New York: Grove Press, Inc., 1974).
3. See Richard Dawkins's website at www.richarddawkins.net.

A system of symbols which acts to establish powerful, pervasive and long-lasting moods and motivations in men [and women] by formulating conceptions of a general order of existence and clothing these conceptions with such an aura of factuality that the moods and motivations seem uniquely realistic.[4]

Divine beings can't be observed, and anthropologists can't do fieldwork in the supernatural realm; Geertz's definition directs the fieldworker's gaze to the social dimensions of religious practices while connecting practice to beliefs about the nature of the universe. Accordingly, this definition begins with the symbolic dimensions of religion rather than emphasizing political, economic, and material dimensions of religiously motivated behaviors. Anthropologists do study all these dimensions of religion (see, e.g., the discussion of religion and hegemonic power in chap. 7), but Geertz's definition is one that takes religion as something to be studied as part of culture, not just a feature of material or political life.

The benefits of this approach are, first, that it is broadly inclusive even of traditions such as Buddhism and atheism, because it is based on any conception of how the world is thought to be organized, not about spiritual beings per se. Second, it highlights the cultural dimensions of religion, the "conception of a general order of existence," and how that is reflected in a specific "system of symbols" of a particular religious context.

Anthropological definitions of religion may make some Christians uncomfortable. Including our own religion in a general definition that encompasses all religions may make it seem that our belief in Jesus Christ is being evaluated as no different than belief in Allah, Shiva, or the ancestors. Shouldn't we keep Christianity separate, if we believe it is true? Geertz's definition, however, along with other good definitions of religion, does not make claims about whether or not something is true. Geertz uses terms such as "*seem uniquely realistic*" and "*system of symbols,*" which make religion accessible for anthropological study. A researcher may study participants' perceptions and beliefs, the symbols used in a religion, and how various religions are like and unlike one another. The question of whether one religion is true is an extremely important one, but it is not one that can be answered through ethnographic fieldwork.

Anthropology offers an important perspective on one part of religion, the cultural part. In this way, Christians can subject our religion to scientific scrutiny without compromising the strength of our belief that Christianity is true. For a Christian, it is important to recognize that Geertz's definition does not suggest anything is *not* true. It does ask us to set that question aside for a moment, however, when we look at religious systems anthropologically.

4. Clifford Geertz, *The Interpretation of Cultures* (New York: Basic Books, 1973), 90; inclusive language added.

Using anthropology to study our own religion as a human system can have positive effects on our understanding of God and ourselves. First, we can learn to see that our symbols work in similar ways to other people's symbols. Human beings everywhere, made in the image of God, use material and linguistic symbols to understand the world. Even if those symbols represent something that is not ultimately true, the use of the symbols is common to all people.

Second, the study of religion can help us perceive and critique how Christian symbols intersect with other parts of social and cultural life. Some symbols (types of music, ways of dressing, eating, or relating) are deeply meaningful in one community or context and meaningless or even offensive in others. Understanding how religious symbols interrelate with economics, politics, and kinship can help Christians understand their own religious practice and more graciously approach Christians of other societies who practice the faith differently.

Third, an anthropological approach to Christianity can help us understand how symbols and practices change over time and across cultures. A form of religious dance that may be considered Spirit-filled in one locality may be seen as immodest in another. Within a single society, change over time presents similar challenges. In U.S. churches that are intergenerational, older people may interpret loud, fast music using drums and guitars as "worldly" and inappropriate for worship, while younger people may view organ music or hymns as an irrelevant tradition embraced by those who do not care about evangelism among contemporary non-Christians. Analysis of culture change and an understanding of how religious symbols are related to the broader culture can bring better understandings of various perspectives within the church.

Finally, the anthropological view will help us to understand how all religions reflect a common humanity. Scripture teaches that people everywhere once sought God, although because of sin, they often employed means that drew them away from God (Rom. 1). At the same time, the apostle Paul demonstrated how non-Christian religions can serve as guideposts for people everywhere to come to an understanding of God (Acts 17). We need not categorically reject anthropological understandings of religion because they do not speak to the question of truth. Instead, we can use these humanistic views to help us better understand our created nature and ways in which our culture(s) both enhance and inhibit our understandings of God.

Religion, Magic, and Witchcraft

Magic, witchcraft, and sorcery are related to religion but, within anthropology, are distinct categories. In practice, all three categories often overlap with religion, and with each other. In many circumstances the common use

A Christian Anthropologist Studies Islam

Miriam Adeney is an anthropologist and missiologist who teaches global and urban ministry at Seattle Pacific University; she also teaches at Regent College and Fuller Theological Seminary. She encourages Christians to be both biblically grounded and culturally aware as they develop strategies for short-term mission, global mission, international development, and women's leadership.

For her book, *Daughters of Islam: Building Bridges with Muslim Women*, Adeney interviewed Muslim women from eight countries across the Muslim world including Arab, Iranian, Indonesian, and African regions.[1] Her anthropological perspective reveals how women of Muslim backgrounds are very different, though they share a common religion. Adeney describes how Islam influences life for nomadic women,

educated professionals, political activists, and religious fundamentalists. Some women are sequestered, while others are more independent and active in public life. Some women critique the veil for repressing women, while others retain it as a symbol of modesty and even empowerment. Islam is a single religion, but it is lived out in very different cultural contexts.

The goal of *Daughters of Islam* is to help Christians understand what Muslims are really like and the variety of ways in which Muslims discover Christian faith. Adeney describes how Muslim women come to Christ, their motivations for religious change, and what they find appealing about Christianity. Adeney relies on both her missiological and anthropological training to offer advice for effective ministry to women of Muslim background. Building bridges with Muslims involves more than an understanding of Christian doctrine; an understanding of culture is equally vital.

1. Miriam Adeney, *Daughters of Islam: Building Bridges with Muslim Women* (Downers Grove, IL: InterVarsity, 2002).

of terms such as "witch," "witch doctor," or magic are used to denigrate someone else's religion as irrational "superstition." Some anthropologists may avoid these terms to prevent such prejudice, but the terms remain important in anthropological research.

Magic refers to ritual practices that are believed to have effects on particular situations. These results cannot be scientifically verified and are not directly related to the ritual. For example, a specific phrase uttered at the right time by the right person may be thought to ensure healing, or a set of gestures performed correctly may be done to guarantee success in a risky endeavor. Magic is like religion in that it addresses human insecurities and fears and it involves the invisible realm of life. Magic is often an element of religion, even though it is typically unrecognized as such. Religious people sometimes believe, for instance, that praying in a particular way, or at a certain time, or with a certain posture, will increase the odds of securing the outcome they desire. Using ritual to manipulate a certain outcome is still magic, even when it is practiced by religious people. Magic is unlike religion in that it is limited to specific events and outcomes, it doesn't involve a full lifestyle of devotion, and it has a much smaller corporate component.

Witchcraft is evil done by a person without her or his awareness. Unbeknownst to him or her, the person possesses a witchcraft "essence" that can be triggered without the person's knowledge. Harm that occurs to someone in the group may be attributed to the witch, which may serve as a plausible explanation when all normal causes for a problem have been exhausted. Political scientist Adam Ashforth describes a current resurgence in witch beliefs in South Africa. In the face of uncertainty and tragedy, even Christians often accuse a person in the community (often a marginal person such as a child or a widow) of causing the problem through witchcraft. Every year thousands of people around the world are killed by community members who have identified them as witches.[5]

Sorcery, on the other hand, is evil done by a person who intended for it to happen. A sorcerer has access to spiritual power and is able to activate the power to harm others. Witchcraft and sorcery are like religion because they help address otherwise unexplainable human suffering, and they provide an account of how the supernatural and natural worlds intersect. They are unlike religion, however, in that they involve less extensive ritual, less complex theologies, and few (if any) corporate practices.

Today, groups such as Wiccans and other neo-pagans identify themselves as witches and do incorporate extensive ritual, theology, and corporate practices. This is a new and different form of witchcraft that anthropologists study as phenomena separate from the labeling of an individual as a "witch" as an explanation for misfortune.[6]

Early Anthropological Approaches to Religion

This chapter focuses on religion as a cultural system, which is the primary approach taken by contemporary anthropologists. But first, we will review earlier approaches to the study of religion, beginning with unilinear evolution and then functionalism. While no longer used extensively, earlier perspectives offer important insights and remind anthropologists of how the field has developed over time.

Religion was an important area of interest for early anthropologists, many of whom hadn't traveled to the cultures they studied and who instead relied on reports from colonial travelers and missionaries. Using the unilinear evolutionary approach popular in his time (see chap. 2), Edward Tylor (1832–1917) saw change in religious systems as providing a prototype for cultural change generally. He believed that the "earliest" or most "primitive" form of religion was animism. *Animism*, from the Latin word for "soul" or "life," is the idea that souls or spirits exist not only in humans but also in plants, animals,

5. Adam Ashforth, *Witchcraft, Violence, and Democracy in South Africa* (Chicago: University of Chicago Press, 2005). For a Christian anthropologist's perspective on witchcraft, see Robert J. Priest, "Witches and the Problem of Evil," *Books & Culture* (November/December 2009), 30–32.

6. See, for example, Tanya Luhrmann, *Persuasions of the Witch's Craft: Ritual Magic in Contemporary England* (Cambridge, MA: Harvard University Press, 1989).

elements of nature, or even all of creation. In this view, the world is seen as "animated" by spirits that reside in everyday objects. George Lucas's *Star Wars* films portrayed animism through the idea of "the Force": an impersonal power with a light side and a dark side that some gifted people learn to control, understand, or use in various circumstances. Animistic cultures still exist today but are more often referred to as "indigenous religions" or by people's own name for their religion.

A well-known ethnographic example of a traditional religion often classified as animism comes from the South Pacific where a number of groups (Tongans, Samoans, and others) traditionally believe in *mana*, a spiritual force that imbues all living things. This force can be disturbed (to negative consequences) if people do things they should not do. Thus the community enforces *tapu*, prohibitions against those things that disturb the *mana*. The English word *taboo* is related to *tapu*. A *taboo* is a behavior, artifact, or symbol that must be avoided in order to evade harm. Around the world today, many people continue to believe in taboos, based on the idea that strong negative emotion or behavior will cause an animistic force to be activated or disturbed.

Like magic, taboo can be part of Christian religious practice. In my (Jenell's) upbringing, for example, I was warned against allowing a Bible to touch the ground. The belief was that the Bible carried a special spiritual essence, and it would be harmful to disrespect that essence by allowing a sacred religious object (the Bible) to touch the ground. Likewise, in my (Brian's) United Methodist church, I was taught that only ordained clergy were allowed to distribute the communion elements. Although the history and theology of this teaching is complex, for many members of my church, keeping the Lord's Table pure simply meant keeping a taboo against non-clergy distributing the elements.

In keeping with the theory of unilinear cultural evolution, Tylor believed all cultures progress through a common trajectory, so in his view, animism would eventually be replaced by *polytheism*, belief in many gods/goddesses. Hinduism is often seen as the largest modern example of polytheism. Hinduism is actually the name given by the British to the many different forms of religious practice on the Indian subcontinent. These systems often have local shrines or temples for the gods or goddesses who are thought to dwell in that community. Many Indian religious teachers deny that Hinduism is polytheistic, however. They assert that although many names are used—Shiva, Vishnu, Ganesh, and more—these are not different beings, but different manifestations of one being.

Whether or not Hinduism may be correctly called polytheistic in Tylor's use of that term, there are many examples of communities in which a pantheon, or collection of gods and goddesses, are thought to rule the spiritual world. In many ancient religions, including those of the Babylonians, Canaanites, Greeks, and others living around the ancient Hebrews, people believed in

Image of Hindu deity "Ganesh" from temple in Tulsa, Oklahoma. Ganesh is the remover of obstacles. One explanation of the icon's imagery from an informant is that the image symbolizes some qualities that should be desired by humanity. The depiction of large ears is to show us to "listen"; a small mouth is to show us "to talk less"; a large body over the mouse depicts the ego or selfish desires being crushed.

Photo: Tony Kail

groups of divine beings, each of whom had personalities, interests, and concerns that sometimes affected human life.

Tylor thought these polytheistic religions would eventually give way to *monotheism*, belief in one god, as found in Islam, Judaism, and Christianity. In Tylor's view, however, this was not the "highest" stage of religious evolution. Monotheism, he argued, would be supplanted by science (i.e., *atheism*), in which people held purely naturalistic explanations of the world.

Today, anthropologists see monotheism, along with various forms of polytheism and animism, thriving in the age of science. Religious beliefs and practices continue to help people make sense of the world. The work of early anthropologists is useful insofar as it documents religious practices and beliefs that have disappeared or changed. The theory of unilinear cultural evolution, however, is not only incorrect but also ethnocentric because it assumes all cultures of the world will follow a single path of "progress" that leads toward the philosophy and lifestyle of the European scientists who authored the theory.

Functions of Religion

As anthropologists saw the limitations of unilinear cultural evolution theory, they moved toward functionalist theory, which shaped the subsequent study of religion. Functionalists saw culture as a system of interlocking parts and asked how each part functioned to contribute to the stability and growth of the whole, or meet individual social, psychological and material needs. In terms of religion, then, anthropologists weren't asking whether or not a religion was really true; they were studying how religious beliefs and practices worked to stabilize or improve the culture as a whole.

In the early twentieth century, as fieldwork was becoming a required element of anthropological research, Bronislaw Malinowski traveled to Melanesia to study the Trobriand Islanders.[7] He noticed that when people went fishing in the lagoon, they just put their nets in the water and fished. Children, men, and women all felt free to use the boats and nets, fishing alone or in groups, sometimes from the shore or from a boat. Fishing in the lagoon was casual and didn't involve hard and fast rules. Fishing in the open ocean, however, was another story. Before fishing parties went beyond the protection of the lagoon and reefs, people would gather for special rituals, incantations, and prayers. Fishing expeditions beyond the reef were, Malinowski said, "encrusted with magic." Lagoon fishers and ocean fishers were, in one sense, doing the same work, but only trips to the ocean seemed to have religious significance.

Working from his functionalist perspective (see chap. 11), Malinowski argued that the rituals and requirements around fishing beyond the reefs were a way for the community to deal with anxiety caused by this dangerous activity. Unlike fishing in the relatively safe lagoon, going into the ocean was dangerous and unpredictable, and people sometimes drowned or were injured. The use of religious rituals, Malinowski observed, brought a sense of security and predictability to an otherwise insecure event.

Anthropologists studying the rituals of baseball have noted something similar.[8] Those in predictable positions who have more control over their success (fielders, catchers) have few rituals around their play. Those whose success is dependent on variables outside their control (batters and pitchers) often have numerous rituals (tapping the bat three times or eating pancakes before every game), taboos (not shaving during a good streak or not allowing others to touch their favorite bat), and lucky charms or *fetishes* (items thought to carry spiritual power, such as a rabbit's foot or a "lucky person" in the stands).

Cultural materialism is a theoretical approach that emphasizes ways in which humans adapt to the material conditions in which they live; it interprets religious behavior and beliefs in these terms. Like functionalism, it considers

7. Bronislaw Malinowski, *Argonauts of the Western Pacific: An Account of Native Enterprise and Adventure in the Archipelagoes of Melanesian New Guinea* (New York: Routledge & Sons, 1922).

8. George Gmelch, "Baseball Magic," in *Conformity and Conflict: Readings in Cultural Anthropology*, 13th ed., ed. James Spradley and David W. McCurdy (Upper Saddle River, NJ: Allyn & Bacon, 2008), 322–32.

Batters are often known for practicing elaborate forms of magic, including taboos, rituals, and fetishes.
Ken Durden/Bigstock.com

how parts of culture relate to the whole, but cultural materialism focuses on environmental adaptation as the force that motivates culture change. Marvin Harris (1927–2001) used cultural materialism to explain why millions of people in India consider the cow to be sacred, so it cannot be killed and eaten even in times of severe food shortage.[9] To many outsiders, this seemed an example of "irrational" religious behavior in which people held beliefs destructive to their very lives.

Harris pointed out that when the part (the belief that cows are sacred) is viewed in light of the whole (the entire culture and history of India), there were very good reasons for *not* killing cows, even when people were starving. In the agricultural economy of India, the cows serve a number of crucial purposes. First, they power agriculture by plowing. Their dung becomes fertilizer for the crops. Moreover, dung is used as a cooking fuel that burns longer and at lower temperatures than other fuels (e.g., wood), making it easier for those responsible for cooking to be involved in other productive activities at the same time. The disposal of dead cows is carried out by the low-caste members of society, who are also able to eat the meat, providing

9. Marvin Harris, *Cultural Materialism: The Struggle for a Science of Culture* (New York: Random House, 1979).

them with valuable protein. In short, Harris argued, if people were to kill and eat their cows to address food needs in the short run, it would jeopardize the entire society over the long run. Religion that promotes and explains the sacredness of cows, he contended, is a rational adaptation meant to

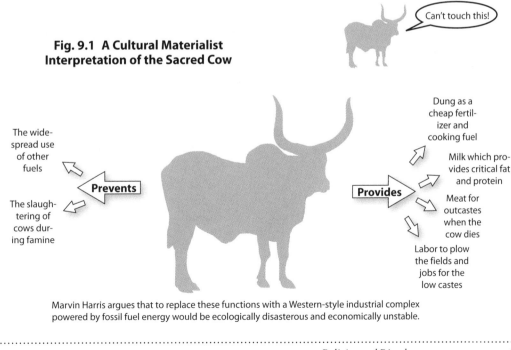

Fig. 9.1 A Cultural Materialist Interpretation of the Sacred Cow

Can't touch this!

Prevents

The widespread use of other fuels

The slaughtering of cows during famine

Provides

Dung as a cheap fertilizer and cooking fuel

Milk which provides critical fat and protein

Meat for outcastes when the cow dies

Labor to plow the fields and jobs for the low castes

Marvin Harris argues that to replace these functions with a Western-style industrial complex powered by fossil fuel energy would be ecologically disasterous and economically unstable.

preserve the population of cattle through difficult economic times. Although many anthropologists have criticized this view as reductionistic and perhaps simplistic (ignoring social inequalities, historical events, and other issues), Harris convincingly demonstrated that so-called irrational religion, when viewed in the ecological and economic context in which it exists, is not so irrational after all.

Religion as a Cultural System

In a time when many scholars viewed religion as irrational or even delusional, functionalist and materialist theories highlighted religion as a creative, adaptive, and important part of culture. These perspectives were reductionistic, however, insofar as they viewed religion as merely an effect of other parts of culture (in the Trobriand Island example, religion was interpreted as a response to insecurity and fear, and in the India example, it was said to be caused by food insecurity). When he mounted the argument that religion should be viewed as a cultural system, Clifford Geertz did not deny that religion has functional consequences or that it may develop and change in response to material conditions. He encouraged anthropologists to study religion as a thing in itself, however, rather than just the result of other causes.

When religion is viewed as a cultural system, anthropologists focus on how people use religion to make sense of life, the universe, and everything. In this section, we consider several of the most important dimensions of religion as a cultural system: symbols, ritual, and myth.

Symbols

In communicating the unseen world of doctrine, spirits, beliefs, or philosophies, religions use important symbols to focus people's attention or to create feelings and associations. A *symbol* is an object, sound, action, or idea to which people assign arbitrary meaning; that is, there is no necessary relationship between the symbol and its meaning. Christians have a broad repertoire of symbols such as the cross, fish, and dove. But symbols are much more pervasive than these obvious examples. For example, in many Protestant churches, the congregation sits in rows facing the front, where the pulpit or podium sits in the center of a (usually) raised dais or stage. In a Roman Catholic Church, the speaker's podium is off to the side, while the altar sits in the center. The physical arrangement of the church is a symbol that communicates the Protestant emphasis on the preaching of the Word. In liturgical traditions such as Roman Catholicism, Anglicanism, and Lutheranism (the latter two are Protestant), the central altar symbolizes the centrality of the Eucharist in the worship service.

The arrangement of people, leaders, and other elements are all part of the symbolism of Christianity as in other religions.
©iStockphoto.com/ Franky DeMeyer

Dress, music, architecture, preferred versions of the Bible, and myriad other symbols make up the symbolic system of Christianity. Symbols take on meanings in religious contexts that are linked to related meanings in secular contexts. Consider the issue of what to wear to church. Many U.S. Americans who wear business attire to work every day may feel these are "secular" clothes (this idea is strongly associated with European Americans, but people from other groups may agree). Wearing these clothes to church may make church seem like a continuation of the workweek, rather than a special time. Thus, some white-collar workers find themselves drawn to the casual services of contemporary megachurches, or informal congregations in which the pastor goes by her or his first name and everyone wears casual clothing. In this way, their church clothes symbolize the way church is a break from the workweek.

In many African American congregations, wearing casual clothes to church is offensive. Instead, people dress in their finest clothes, even in elaborate and showy fashions. This tradition developed among a group of people who, for many generations, was largely prevented from entering the ranks of professional work. Here, work in factories or on farms meant that putting on the "Sunday best" marked a very different moment from daily life. It made church a special place to wear distinctive, generally more expensive clothing. It is important to recognize how religious symbols express the wider world of economic and social life.

Symbols are also important because they affirm what people believe to be true about the world. A symbolic system evokes moods and motivations that allow for an expression of, and understanding of, a particular conception of a general order of existence. These understandings distinguish religious from non-religious parts of life. For instance, two people may each decide to give money to a charity. The action is identical. However, the first may do so because he believes it will impress his friends or because he feels guilty about having passed a person begging on the street the other day. The second person believes God commands us to give money to the poor. She believes when Jesus says he will separate the sheep from the goats, sending away those who ignored the needs of the poor on this earth, he will really judge believers for how they treat poor people. In other words, for the second giver, her understanding of the world goes beyond herself and what she thinks or feels to what Geertz profoundly calls the "really real." She believes God's creation and Jesus's teachings are really real. For the first giver, his motivations were just about his perceptions and feelings—what anyone would agree is real. The two givers have radically different views—one religious, the other not religious—of what the act of giving means and how it relates to the way the universe works.

The concept of the "really real" requires an understanding of things not seen, so Geertz notes that people become convinced of the reality of unseen things that are "clothed with an aura of factuality."[10] People believe in unseen realities, Geertz would say, because of what they think about things they *can* see. In other words, people use visible and tangible objects and actions to help create a plausible interpretation of the invisible, intangible realm. People organize the symbols of their religion and employ them in particular ways to evoke strong feelings, interpretations of reality, and a sense of the truth behind the objects or actions involved. In anthropological terms, this is known as ritual.

Ritual

A *ritual* (also called a *rite*) is any patterned, repeated, predictable action. Secular rituals include a high school graduation ceremony, a family dinner, or singing the national anthem before a sporting event. We might also put forms of greeting in the category of ritual. For example, consider how two friends typically greet each other in the United States:

"Hey, how's it going?"
"Good. How're you?"
"Good. So what's up?"
"Not much. What's up wi'you?"

These are questions, but not in the usual sense. What does "it" refer to? And why is "it" going somewhere? Why do we feel compelled to respond with

---

10. This does not mean the "really real" concerns spirituality, necessarily. It can also mean a conviction that "things not seen" do not exist.

"good" or "fine" even if we're not good or fine? Although this may seem to represent a lack of sincerity, this exchange is not primarily meant to elicit information about how someone feels at that moment or what sorts of things he or she is involved in. This is a ritualized greeting through which two people communicate, "I know you. You are a friend and/or acquaintance. We are not yet prepared to have a conversation until we acknowledge our relationship." The ritual form allows both people to get through the interaction quickly, communicating their desire to maintain a relationship even if the exchange goes no further than a brief greeting.

For many U.S. Christians, particularly nonliturgical Protestants, the word "ritual" is often preceded by the adjective "empty." As part of a tradition that protested against the over-institutionalization of religion, Protestants—evangelicals in particular—have historically been opposed to anything that would seem to be mere form over deeper concerns of sincerity, authenticity, and an individual relationship with God. But even a nonliturgical worship service is a ritual. Members of nonliturgical churches anticipate particular elements (three songs, repeated four times each, last time a capella), a given length (perhaps one and a half hours for most white evangelical churches in the United States), and a familiar aesthetic style of sermon and music. If any of those elements are changed, people notice, and may object, because it disrupts the ritualized form with which they are familiar.

Rituals, whether secular or religious, are performed to emphasize some fact, desire, or belief; to transform or influence the feelings or beliefs of those participating; or to give meaning to social relationships. Anthropologists often put the variety of rituals into categories based on the purposes and motivations people have in performing them. Three significant categories of rituals are rites of intensification, rites of affliction, and rites of passage.

Fig. 9.2 Types of Ritual

Ritual
- Rites of affliction
- Rites of intensification
- Rites of passage (life-cycle rituals)

RITES OF INTENSIFICATION

Rites of intensification are rituals in which elements of society, belief, values, or behaviors are made more dramatic, intense, or real than in normal life. A high school pep rally is an example of a nonreligious rite of intensification. Symbols of the school are displayed, a sports team runs out to the sounds of the fight song blasted by the band, and cheerleaders whip the crowd into a frenzy of school spirit with chants and dances. These rituals make people feel something more intensely than they normally do in daily life.

Christian worship may be understood as a rite of intensification as well. This may be an uncomfortable thought, because many Christians are taught that true worship is not of this world; it is a transcendent experience that lifts us beyond the physical world. It may seem false or manipulative to acknowledge that we use symbols or movement to create a mood or make something "seem uniquely realistic." But when Christians select a musical style, choose appropriate dress, decide between the use of written or extemporaneous prayers, inspire (or deter) clapping hands or raising arms, we are making culture; that is, we are choosing and shaping symbols to help participants feel close to God or understand God better.

Throughout the Scriptures, God's people are given specific actions, objects, and words to use in understanding and worshiping God. The Lord's Prayer and the Last Supper are two examples of Jesus teaching his disciples to practice rituals of intensification. While believers do not set aside their beliefs in the midst of everyday life, our ability to feel the reality of those beliefs is often influenced by the physical environment (and bodily physical condition) in which we find ourselves. Rituals of intensification help reconnect ordinary life with religious belief.

Consider marriage as an analogy. A husband and wife, though very much in love, may not feel the full force of that love in the midst of mundane life. It's hard to be overwhelmed with the beauty of your beloved when the dog has just made a mess in the living room, the kids can't find their shoes, and you are already ten minutes late for work. In order to counteract the stultifying effects of daily responsibility, some couples set aside special times to engage in rites of intensification. Using culturally appropriate forms (in the United States, these could include soft lighting, romantic music, a fine meal, and attractive clothing), the couple creates a time set apart in which they can experience emotions that, while true every day, are not felt in their full force at all times. The use of symbols in this set-apart venue creates moods and motivations that make love feel more real. In the same way, Christian worship draws on meaningful symbols to create a ritual space in which the commitments worshipers profess as part of their lives all the time can be *felt* more keenly and acutely. That these feelings are temporary and induced by material objects within a created ritual space does not negate the reality of the beliefs or that which is believed in.

RITES OF AFFLICTION

Rites of affliction are rituals directed at alleviating suffering or resolving a problem. A common Hollywood version of a rite of affliction may star a mystical-looking person (in Hollywood films, mysticism is often symbolized with old women or characters stereotyped as "primitive," such as Africans, "gypsies," or Native Americans) who casts a curse or goes through a scripted ritual to make someone fall in love, bring fortune, or restore peace between the living and the dead. In many societies, rituals for the growth and protection of crops, physical healing, or the maintenance of good social relationships are so much a part of life that people do not consider them "religion." The rituals would be called "farming," "medicine," or just normal family life. Among the Ifugao of the Philippines, with the planting of rice, people sacrifice a chicken or pig and pour the blood over the *bulol*, a carved wooden statue representing the god of the harvest. The sacrifice, as well as sharing the meat in the community, dancing, and praying are rituals that address the risk of crop failure. These rituals, considered a normal part of farming, are thought to protect the crop from pests, bad weather, or disease.

God's people have always engaged in rites of affliction, using physical objects and ritualized practices to address human problems. Jesus reinterpreted familiar rituals of Jewish life (most notably baptism) to emphasize the reality of God's work in removing sin and reconciling relationships. Other biblical rites of affliction involve the transference of affliction from one place to another (such as the scapegoat of Lev. 16:21), the substitutionary death of one being for another, or sacrificial offerings made as a payment on behalf of the one afflicted. The book of James commands Christians to engage a rite of affliction, calling the elders to pray over the sick and anoint them with oil (James 5:14).

For Christians, these kinds of rites are not meant to be magical transactions in which objects or sacrifices given to God bring about a desired outcome. Instead, they are meant to focus attention on God and God's power over illness, misfortune, and sin.

Rites of passage

Rites of passage, or *life-cycle rituals*, transform a person or people from one life stage to another. As with rites of intensification and rites of affliction, rites of passage have a wide range of expression around the world. Rites of passage may involve moving a person from childhood to adulthood (often called *initiation rituals*), moving from one family into a new one (often through marriage), or even from life to death or an afterlife. Rites of passage take the person or people through phases in which social status is thought to change. Victor Turner (1920–83), following on the work of Arnold van Gennep, described a common structure to these rituals, consisting of three phases called separation, liminality, and reintegration.[11]

The first phase, *separation*, comes by symbolically or physically separating those going through the transition from their old identities. Audrey Richards's ethnography of the Bemba, a group in present-day Zambia, describes the

11. A description of this ritual can be found in Victor Turner, *The Ritual Process* (Chicago: Aldine, 1969), 94–113.

girls' initiation ritual as beginning with the girls entering a special initiation hut backward and crawling under blankets.[12] Initiates remained in the hut, out of sight of the community, for days or even months. They would have no contact with their previous life. Among some Native American groups, a young man would spend days or weeks alone, away from the village, on a vision quest to receive sacred knowledge from spirits with whom he would forever be linked. Among several pastoral groups of East Africa, such as the Maasai and Samburu, young men are initiated into a warrior phase by spending at least part of the time living in a separate village, making long-distance treks, and otherwise being separated from the community.

The second phase moves the person or people into an identity that is not yet the new one but also not the old. Turner called this the *liminal period*, in which the initiate was "betwixt and between," meaning the person was neither here nor there, this nor that. In many cultures people believe that while in this phase, a person is vulnerable, powerful, or both. Liminality sometimes allows or requires people to do things that under normal circumstances would be forbidden, harmful, or shameful. Among the Ndembu of Central Africa studied by Turner, the inauguration of a new chief involves a rite of passage from his old state as a member of the community, to his new place as chief. Turner observed that when an incoming chief returns to the village after a time of separation, a ritual specialist insults, harangues, and generally treats the chief-to-be with great disrespect. This behavior, which would be unthinkable under normal circumstances, is thought to be important in making the chief humble and able to relate to ordinary people once he ascends to the throne. During this phase, the future chief is not just a normal man in the community, nor is he a chief. He is betwixt and between roles and doesn't have a stable place in the community. He is treated as polluted, dangerous, and out of place. In this way, it makes sense for the people to humiliate him.

Reintegration marks the final stage when the initiate, chief, or other transformed person is welcomed back to the community in his or her new identity. In the case of the Ndembu chief-elect, when the period of insulting, criticizing, and harassing ends, a public installation, with all pomp and ceremony, publically establishes him as the leader of the people. Although they believe the humiliation is an important part of his becoming chief, once he *is* the chief to ever treat him in such a way means swift and severe punishment.

Anthropologists see these stages as characterizing other cultural phenomena as well, such as pilgrimage. When people travel to religiously significant places, it often involves leaving daily life, separating from friends and family, and undertaking a difficult and sacrificial journey. Once at the site, pilgrims

---

12. Audrey Richards, *Chisungu: A Girls' Initiation Ceremony among the Bemba of Northern Rhodesia* (London: Faber and Faber, 1956).

may give money, sacrifice physical comfort, and eliminate signs of social class or personal identity. The pilgrimage to Mecca, the Islamic holy city, is perhaps the most famous pilgrimage journey today. There, Muslims from around the world come together. Men wear a common white robe to erase social distinctions and mark their separation from the world. They spend many days in prayer and fasting, often walking miles to various holy sites and reciting specific verses along the way. While in this liminal phase, the pilgrims are supposed to abstain from many normal activities including shaving, nail-clipping, hunting or killing animals, and sexual relations. The qualities of the liminal phase are meant to heighten spiritual awareness and the efficacy of their sacred actions.[13]

One ritual familiar to most North Americans that contains all three elements is a traditional wedding. This ritual marks the passage of two individuals from different families into a new identity as a single couple/family. Traditionally, the ceremony is preceded with the bride and her attendants separated from their normal life, putting on distinctive clothing in some site where the groom is forbidden. (The belief that it is unlucky for the groom to see the bride before the ceremony heightens the separation phase). The ceremony begins with the groom and his men in the front of the church while the bride processes from the back. The groom and bride are symbolically separated from the guests by their clothing (tuxedo and white gown) and physical presence in the front. The family of the bride "gives" her to

13. For more on the pilgrimage to Mecca, see Mamdouh N. Mohamed, *Hajj & 'Umrah: From A to Z* (Beltsville, MD: Amana Publications, 1996).

the groom in a moment when the father of the bride takes her hand off his arm and places it on the arm of the groom, marking her transition from one patriline to the other.

The ceremony and subsequent reception continue to mark the bride and groom as different from other people as they remain in their unique wedding clothes, enter the room separately, and often sit at a separate table from the other guests. This stage has elements of the liminal phase, since it comes right after the ceremony but before the couple has consummated the marriage. The couple is legally married, but the fullness of married life has not yet begun. They are introduced as "Mr. and Mrs." and perform a few "married couple" acts, such as their first dance and feeding each other cake. One key element remains, however, before the couple assumes their place among other couples in society: the honeymoon.

The honeymoon represents liminality as the couple leaves for a secluded place, traditionally avoiding contact with family and friends. Unlike vacations from which people will send postcards or call home, the honeymoon has a kind of mysterious air as the marriage is consummated. Contemporary couples, for various reasons, may postpone their honeymoon or otherwise change the traditional understanding of the event, but it would be extremely rare (and likely considered weird) for friends or family to accompany the couple on their trip.

The reincorporation phase is perhaps the least symbolized in the ceremony, but it is not absent. In the classic movie version of the post-honeymoon ritual, it is only after this departure from "ordinary life" that the couple returns to enter their home as a couple. In a little-practiced but still-known tradition, the husband carries his wife across the threshold of their home, symbolizing their entrance into their new social status as a family.

The wedding ritual blends religious and secular elements. Other rituals, such as those involving worship and prayer, are explicitly religious, drawing meaning from a conception of the general order of existence. In baptism, for instance, Christians use water to symbolize spiritual transformation. Christians have debated for centuries just what that transformation means: whether it is strictly a symbol or an actual means of receiving grace, whether it is necessary for salvation, and whether it is meant for infants or adults. But despite diversity in how Christians understand and practice baptism, it is a widely accepted ritual. The physical elements of water, the presence of a priest, pastor, or fellow believer as facilitator, and the words spoken during the event are still just water, a person, and some words, but they become transformed by the context in which they are placed. This transformation of ordinary elements comes about because of prior commitments shared by participants. A person who has no beliefs about what is *really* going on during a particular ceremony would find the ritual meaningless.

Violating a Taboo

When I (Brian) was married in 1993, we chose to have a fairly traditional wedding. The ceremony was held in a church located near my wife's parents' house. The church was also a convenient half mile from the community center where the reception was held, which was attached to a hotel where we could spend our first night together before leaving on our honeymoon the next day.

The wedding went smoothly, the bride looked radiant (if I do say so myself), and everyone had a good time at the reception, which was complete with all the traditions expected in our community: throwing the bouquet, feeding each other cake, and a large-group version of the Electric Slide.

The next day, as we prepared to leave on our honeymoon trip, we realized that we had forgotten a few things at my wife's parents' house. Since it was close by, we had time to stop there on our way to the airport. As we entered the house in our traveling clothes, my wife's many siblings and other relatives were there eating breakfast. Immediately as we entered, the reaction was swift and forceful.

"What're you doing here?!"

"Hey you two, don't you have better things to do than come by and visit us?" (*wink wink*)

"I don't see you! You're not supposed to be here!"

There were other jokes and teasing, mostly of a slightly naughty nature, but it was clear that they did not expect to see us, nor did they think they should. We had violated the liminal state, coming back into normal society before we were supposed to. Of course, no one believed that spiritual forces would be disturbed or that ill fortune would be attached to our visit, but it struck me that we shared a sense that a taboo had been broken. We were all a little relieved when my wife and I grabbed our things, said quick good-byes, and dashed out to get back into the liminal space where we belonged.

In order for a ritual to have significance, the participants must be committed to the symbolism of the elements. These commitments are rooted in foundational myths.

Myth

A *myth* is any story with sacred significance. Using the word "myth" to describe Christian Scripture may strike believers as dismissive or offensive, because "myth" in popular English usage refers to fables or falsehoods. In anthropology, the word "myth" does not imply that something is not true, but rather that it is important. Myths are stories that tell people what is important, valued, and right.

Myths can be secular, just as rituals may be. The story of George Washington chopping down the cherry tree is a national myth of the United States, meant to convey the importance of truthfulness and the impeccable quality of our first president. The story of Abraham Lincoln walking several miles in the snow to return a few pennies overcharged to a customer in his store likewise has a mythic quality for the same reason. Historians believe the first story is not true, while the second probably is (although perhaps exaggerated). Either way, both stories convey important collective values to the nation.

Rituals rely on myths to give them significance. In some cases, rituals are a reenactment of a myth. On the Indonesian island of Bali, there are many well-known rituals in which people put on elaborate costumes representing demons, gods, and goddesses and act out the myths of creation or stories about the defeat of evil. Sometimes these ritual reenactments go on for days as the divine dramas are performed. Taking communion in a Christian context is also a reenactment, in which those taking the bread and cup often hear Scriptures specifically enjoining them to remember the historical act of Jesus breaking the bread and pouring the cup for his disciples. The Balinese do not necessarily believe the battle of demons and gods is "historical" in the same sense, but in both cases, the ritual assumes participants believe in the importance of the story.

Scholars of religion such as Mircea Eliade, psychologists such as Carl Jung, and many others have used myth as a way to understand society.[14] Anthropologists generally take one of two main approaches to the social understanding of myth. The first, associated with Bronislaw Malinowski's version of functionalism, sees myths as charters for social organization. Myths explain why things are the way they are and why people should perform certain rituals or hold to certain beliefs. The second view comes from Claude Levi-Strauss (see chap. 11). He agreed that myths help people organize the social world but claimed that, more fundamentally, myths organize human thought. He said myths organize the binary categories of thought—male and female, hot and cold, wrong and right—by which humans understand the world.[15]

In both views, myths are foundational to the religion and society with which they are associated. Many anthropologists in the past assumed people who rely on myths (people who are very "religious" or "traditional") are not aware of the ways that myths shape their lives. More recent work has demonstrated that people are often very aware of how myths sanction particular behaviors or shape the categories by which they think about the world. This awareness is reflected in the ways people change myths and rituals to serve new purposes.

Ritual Change

The fact that rituals are rooted in myths does not mean that rituals and myths are fixed and unchanging. The relative importance of particular

14. Mircea Eliade, *Myth and Reality* (Long Grove, IL: Waveland Press, 1998); also Carl Jung and Karl Kerényi, *Science of Mythology: Essays on the Myth of the Divine Child and the Mysteries of Eleusis* (1963; repr., New York: Routledge, 2002).
15. Claude Levi-Strauss, *Structural Anthropology* (1958; repr., New York: Basic Books, 1963).

myths changes, and as people's concerns or values change, so too do ritual forms. In contemporary North American wedding ceremonies, many have changed the traditional vows of a bride—to "love, honor, and obey"—into something more in line with their understandings of husband-wife relations (e.g., "love, honor, and cherish"). Increasing numbers of people in U.S. society, including Christians, question many elements of traditional marriage ceremonies. Innovation, creativity, and even idiosyncrasy flourish in contemporary weddings.

Some of the most dramatic examples of ritual change occur when people convert, for example, to Christianity from a non-Christian religion. Among the Ikalahan of the northern Philippines, most people converted from traditional ancestor religion to Christianity in the 1960s. Many people say they did not stop believing in the old spirits, but once they learned the story (myth) of Jesus and his power over these spirits, they felt free to change their ritual lives. Instead of sacrificing *carabao* (water buffalo), pigs, and chickens when people were ill, they prayed to God. Instead of calling the *mabaki* (ritual leader) to request the spirits' blessing for a new home or a newly planted field, they called the representative of Jesus, the pastor, to pray. They moved their ritual life into the church and away from the *cañao*, or traditional ritual circle.

It was not easy to decide how they might perform worship, prayer, weddings, funerals, and so forth, but they understood that rituals should point them toward God in terms that made sense in their own culture and history. For example, having a couple wear a tuxedo and white dress for a wedding, or putting a dead body in a funeral home for several days of "viewing" would have been alien and unhelpful for the Ikalahan seeking to clothe their (now Christian) conceptions of the general order of existence with an aura of factuality. Instead, such unintelligible symbols would have made their new beliefs seem *un*realistic.

In the decades since the first generation of Christians, Ikalahan believers continue to adapt, modify, and revise their ritual life to meet the needs of new generations of Christians. Ikalahan Christians have often collaborated with Delbert Rice, a North American missionary trained in cultural anthropology. Rice understood that though the people had become Christians and believed the Christian myths as central to their lives, their rituals should not necessarily be the same as lowland Filipino Christians, North Americans, or some other group. Today, some rituals of the Ikalahan church look similar to what is seen elsewhere in the Philippines or even in the United States (such as their Sunday morning service of singing, prayer, and sermon). Other practices—for example, the *tongtongan*, in which people accused of severe sins or civil crimes are disciplined by the elders and church leaders in a public process of punishment and reconciliation—reflect the unique Ikalahan culture and history. By intentionally considering cultural context as they worked out ritual life, often called "contextualization" (see chaps. 1 and 12), Rice encouraged Ikalahan Christians to consider how their ritual practices could reflect their own experience with God.

Christians and Religion

The first time many Christians meet a committed Muslim college professor or a devoutly Hindu social worker, they may find it strange that someone who is respected, intelligent, and admirable in their ethics could be so convinced about the truth of something radically different from our faith. It can be a challenge when a Christian asks, "Who am I to tell this person that what she believes is wrong? Why do I believe my religion is correct?"

Anthropology analyzes religion as a cultural system and offers holistic interpretations of how people incorporate religion into their lives. Anthropologists look at empirical data about how people live in the world and then theorize about what it means. This scientific approach doesn't answer the question of whether any religion or any particular religious belief is really true. Making a religious commitment and living a spiritual life requires faith, devotion, community, and theology.

Anthropological analysis reveals how the image of God, present in every human being, drives people everywhere to seek God. Even while we have radically divergent beliefs about the details of the "really real," common patterns of ritual, myth, and practice across cultures suggest that humans really are created to seek after truth and ultimate meaning (as described in Rom. 1). Humans everywhere live in communities bound together by moral orders, tell stories about how life began and what it means, and gather together in observance of what we believe.

Even those who feel called to cross-cultural boundaries in sharing their faith need to understand how symbols, myths, rituals, and other practices of religion work together to help people believe. Communicating meaningfully with others requires an understanding of one's own beliefs and practices. Being able to speak to the deep concerns in someone's life involves an understanding of how the symbols and practices of various faiths seek to answer those questions.

Studying religious diversity should unsettle us a bit, as it makes us recognize ways in which our own religious practices have come to reflect historical events, cultural norms, and personal preferences. God is never completely or perfectly represented in any manifestation of human devotion. Therefore, it should not surprise us that Christians have many different ways of expressing their religious commitments. Nor should we be afraid of the varieties of ways humans have worked out their longing to know the truth. We can explore and understand this human dimension in the many expressions of religious life around the world. Seeing differences and similarities in religions as cultural systems is a testament to the image of God in all of us.

Terms

animism: the idea that souls or spirits exist not only in humans but also in plants, animals, elements of nature, or even all of creation.

atheism: the belief that no god or supernatural being(s) exist.

cultural materialism: a theoretical approach that emphasizes ways in which humans adapt to the material conditions in which they live.

fetish: an item thought to carry spiritual power, such as a rabbit's foot.

initiation rituals: rites of passage that move a person from childhood to adulthood.

liminal period: the second phase of a rite of passage, placing the initiate in a space that is "betwixt and between" the old identity and the new identity.

magic: ritual practices that are believed to have effects on particular situations.

mana: a spiritual force that imbues all living things, a belief that is part of some animistic religions.

monotheism: the belief in one god.

myth: any story with sacred significance.

polytheism: the belief in many gods and/or goddesses.

reintegration: the third stage of a rite of passage in which the initiate is welcomed back to the community in his or her new identity.

religion: a system of symbols which acts to establish powerful, pervasive, and long-lasting moods and motivations in men [and women] by formulating conceptions of a general order of existence and clothing these conceptions with such an aura of factuality that the moods and motivations seem uniquely realistic (taken from Clifford Geertz).

rites of affliction: rituals directed at alleviating suffering or resolving a problem.

rites of intensification: rituals in which elements of society, belief, values, or behaviors are made more dramatic, intense, or real than in normal life.

rites of passage, or *life-cycle rituals*: rituals that transform a person or people from one life stage to another.

ritual (also called a *rite*): any patterned, repeated, predictable action.

separation: the first phase of a rite of passage, involving symbolically or physically separating those going through the transition from their old identities.

sorcery: evil done by a person who intended for it to happen.

symbol: an object, sound, action, or idea to which people assign arbitrary meaning; that is, there is no necessary relationship between the symbol and its meaning.

taboo: a behavior, artifact, or symbol that must be avoided in order to evade harm.

witchcraft: evil done by a person without her or his awareness.

Devotion 1

Lament as a Rite of Affliction

As a deer longs for flowing streams, so my soul longs for you, O God. My soul thirsts for God, for the living God. When shall I come and behold the face of God? My tears have been my food day and night, while people say to me continually, "Where is your God?" These things I remember, as I pour out my soul: how I went with the throng, and led them in procession to the house of God, with glad shouts and songs of thanksgiving, a multitude keeping festival. Why are you cast down, O my soul, and why are you disquieted within me? Hope in God; for I shall again praise him, my help and my God. (Ps. 42:1–6 NRSV)

The psalmist is despondent and complains to God about his inner state and the response of his community while he is in pain. Like other psalms of lament, Psalm 42 registers a profound complaint with God, makes a request for help, and praises God. When we read Psalm 42 alone or with a group, we are carried through the full cycle of affliction, from agony and distress to restoration and a renewed sense of God's presence. Christians throughout time have used the reading of Psalm 42 as a rite of affliction: a ritualized form of prayer and reflection that assists individuals and communities through times of suffering. Far from being empty or rote, this type of ritual renews faith by reconnecting despondent people with other believers who went before them and with God.

Devotion 2

Religious Symbols

For just as the body is one and has many members, and all the members of the body, though many, are one body, so it is with Christ. For in the one Spirit we were all baptized into one body—Jews or Greeks, slaves or free—and we were all made to drink of one Spirit. (1 Cor. 12:12–13 NRSV)

In 1 Corinthians 12, Paul extensively describes the metaphor of the body of Christ. Just as the body has many parts, each of which is essential, so is each person important in the church. The church is so important, in fact, that it may be likened to Christ's body. Paul uses the human body as a symbol, making it stand for something more than its literal reality.

Religious symbols help believers perceive what is "really real" about the world. The symbol of the body reminds believers that each person has an important role in the church, especially those who may be perceived as worthless or lowly. It provides a reminder that just as we need hands and feet to do our work in the world, Christ relies on his body (the church) to accomplish good works.

10

Globalization and Culture Change

After studying this chapter, you should be able to:

1. Define globalization and major theories of globalization.
2. Identify different colonial strategies and describe how they influenced culture change in the colonial and postcolonial eras.
3. Describe how globalization influences contemporary fieldwork.
4. Critically engage various Christian responses to globalization.

Introduction

In one sense, globalization is an ancient phenomenon. Archaeological evidence from the upper-Mississippi valley civilizations at Cahokia suggests that they traded with the people of northern Mexico almost 1,500 years ago. Around 350 BCE, Alexander the Great controlled an empire stretching from present-day Italy to the western border of China, facilitating trade, exchange, and the movement of knowledge throughout the vast area. Egyptians developed trade routes by sea and land, extending their reach thousands of miles throughout the ancient world almost two thousand years before the birth of Christ. Some scholars argue that the first truly global empire was the Arab and Muslim empire (around 700 CE), stretching from present-day Indonesia and China, across to Morocco and Spain in the westernmost parts of Africa

Globalization and Culture Change

Although all globalization is cultural change, not all cultural change comes from globalization. Even change inspired by nonlocal products or ideas may not be globalization if no connection is made to wider systems.

For example, in the (fictional) movie *The Gods Must Be Crazy*, members of a traditional Ju/'hoansi foraging society of southern Africa discover a Coke bottle dropped by a passing small airplane. Acquiring such an object with many uses (as a container, for crushing nuts, for starting fires by focusing the sun's rays) provides social and personal benefit, but since there is only one such object, it also introduces more competition and conflict. But the changes, both good and bad, are not a consequence of globalization. Until or unless their community develops an ongoing relationship with the manufacturers of Coca-Cola, or begins trading with others to acquire more Coke bottles, the object is just another object. Globalization requires some sort of articulation with a nonlocal/global system.

Notably, at the time the film was made, the Ju/'hoansi actors of the film were no longer living in the traditional style portrayed in the film. Their land rights were restricted, and many were living on reservations where hunting and gathering had become impossible. Many Ju/'hoansi mixed some foraging with agricultural and wage labor, others joined the military, and others received government rations. The movie concluded with a leader carrying off the Coke bottle—this symbol of the "outside" world—to be thrown away, allowing them to return to previous patterns of sharing and cooperation. In the real lives of the actors, however, globalization was profoundly changing their world and could not so easily be discarded.

and Europe.[1] We might consider the trade facilitated by these links to be the precursor of globalization.

Contemporary globalization is distinct, however, in its scope, rapid rate of development, and subsequent cultural consequences. Globalization today affects virtually everyone on the planet. Unlike ancient trade that served elites, today people in every stratum of society regularly use products, hear information, and consume food from places thousands of miles away. Nearly everyone is influenced by the decisions, preferences, or thoughts of people living on other continents. These connections can be as innocuous as eating Thai food at a county fair in Iowa, or as profound as the decision by an international group of bankers voting in Washington, D.C., to finance a dam-building project that will bring electricity to thousands of urban Haitians even as it displaces thousands more from the farmland and rural villages slated to be flooded.

Globalization today shapes how people around the world live, think, and act. In other words, globalization changes cultures. New technologies in communication and travel make the exchange of people, commodities, and information easier than ever before. Objects and ideas that used to have no meaning beyond their local context can now be viewed, sold, discussed, and altered around the world. *Commodification* is the transformation of concepts,

1. See Janet Abu-Lughod, *Before European Hegemony: The World System 1250 A.D.–1350 A.D.* (New York: Oxford University Press, 1989).

creations, and even cultures into goods that can be bought and sold, given and received. Commodification means that virtually everyone and everything can be part of a global system of economic and cultural exchange, whether they choose it or not.

Chapter 2 describes culture as a conversation, an ongoing process that always includes stability as well as change, negotiation, and adaptation. Anthropologists, then, analyze how people adapt their cultures to the problems and opportunities brought by globalization. In this chapter, we first define globalization and describe the history of the concept within anthropology and related fields. Then we present some of the concepts and methodologies anthropologists use to study globalization. Finally, we discuss mutual influences between Christianity and globalization, and how each presents the other with opportunities and challenges.

Globalization

Globalization is the integration of local, regional, and/or national production, exchange, and culture into a global system. In disciplines other than anthropology, scholars of globalization often focus on economics. They focus primarily on the international division of labor and distribution of production processes. Anthropologists certainly make economic life part of their analysis (some quite centrally), but they are also interested in the ways these processes intersect with cultural meanings and forms in specific places.

From international financial markets to the prevalence of foreign-produced goods in virtually all countries, few people today can survive without relying on the manufacturing, farming, mining, or service work of people across the globe. As an experiment designed to raise awareness of global interdependence, anthropology professor Emily McEwan-Fujita asked her Wheaton College students to go for a day without eating any refined sugar. Although some sugar is produced in the United States (sugar beets, honey, and a small amount of sugar cane from southern Florida), the vast majority comes from the Caribbean, Central America, and South America. Students, who largely relied on the college's food service, found it very difficult to find sugar-free foods. Breads, sauces, most soups, and even salad dressing contained processed sugar. Subsisting on steamed vegetables, dry salad, and meats that had not been marinated, smothered, or sauced

Professor Emily McEwan-Fujita had her Wheaton College students try to go for a day without eating anything containing refined sugar.
Monica Boorboor/Bigstock.com

Globalization is about culture change. James Watson found that the introduction of Western foods to Hong Kong shaped relationships between family members.
Goh Siok Hian/Bigstock.com

proved to be a strenuous and eye-opening experience for the students. They learned how dependent they are on others, and appreciated how other people's livelihood is dependent on their desire to consume the products they produce and distribute.[2]

As important as economics is, however, globalization is also a cultural phenomenon. In the early 1990s, anthropologist James Watson was not surprised to see Western-based restaurants such as McDonald's, the Hard Rock Café, and Chili's appearing in Hong Kong.[3] What surprised him were young children telling their parents what they wanted to order, or even explaining to their grandparents how to choose among the unfamiliar offerings. Formerly, within Hong Kong's social traditions, hierarchies of age and rank would have kept a child from speaking at the table at all, let alone deciding what to eat. In observing Hong Kong children taking authority for such decisions, Watson saw how economic change influenced culture far beyond a new fondness for hamburgers, pizza, and chicken fingers.

These sorts of changes are often lamented as *westernization*, a form of cultural homogenization in which Western cultural norms replace local culture, resulting in a loss of cultural diversity. Dubbed *McDonaldization* by sociologist George Ritzer, this effect is thought by some to be the hallmark of globalization.[4] Others see strong counterforces that exist alongside such homogenizing pressures. Political theorists Benjamin Barber and Samuel Huntington argue that people threatened with a loss of cultural identity often respond by rejecting these influences, even violently, reasserting their own cultural practices as incompatible with westernization. Both Barber and Huntington use the conflict between the Islamic world and Western democracies as the clearest example of this effect of globalization. (Barber's book about this phenomenon is entitled *Jihad vs. McWorld*.)[5]

As anthropologists study how people experience globalization in particular places, they find something far more complex than the movement of products, people, and ideas from the "West to the Rest." Individuals and communities exist in webs of mutual influence, where cultural influences flow from one

2. Emily McEwan-Fujita, personal communication with Brian Howell, October 2004.

3. James Watson, ed. *Golden Arches East: McDonald's in East Asia* (Palo Alto, CA: Stanford University Press, 1998).

4. George Ritzer, *The McDonaldization of Society* (1993; repr., Thousand Oaks, CA: Pine Forge Press, 2004).

5. Benjamin Barber, *Jihad vs. McWorld* (New York: Ballantine Books, 1996); Samuel Huntington, *The Clash of Civilizations and the Remaking of World Order* (New York: Simon & Schuster, 1996).

place to another through the movement of people (such as migrants, tourists, refugees, and missionaries), products, services, and images. If villagers in India drinking Coca-Cola instead of tea is called "westernization," what do we call suburbanites in Southern California doing Saturday morning yoga classes? Indianization? Just as people in the United States adopt, reject, transform, and redefine influences from around the world, people in Kenyan villages or Brazilian megacities put together influences from around the world to create and understand their local contexts.

Globalization is marked by multidirectional flows of goods and services, people, and information that make it a more complex process than either a grim capitalist plot to stamp out local cultures, on the one hand, or a universally welcomed world of free choices and cultural liberation, on the other. Globalization does have real and recognizable benefits for people. At the same time, it is not a benign process of people freely acting in their own self-interest. Central institutions such as governments and international governing bodies remain necessary to prevent excessive concentrations of power and wealth and to preserve people's freedom to exercise creativity and choice as new opportunities become available.

Theories of Globalization

Three important theories that try to explain globalization are modernization theory, dependency theory, and world-systems theory.

Modernization theory teaches that all societies move through stages of economic, political, and cultural development toward becoming industrialized, democratic, and "modern" societies. In this view, colonized societies were improving as they became more economically and politically complex and interdependent. The colonial rule by Western countries was necessary, it was argued, to move the "backward" economies of Asia, Africa, and Latin America through the stages of development Europe had experienced.

This was an optimistic (and ethnocentric) view similar to unilinear cultural evolutionary approaches to culture (see chap. 2). After World Wars I and II, it became clear that industrialization and economic growth did not mean societies became more "advanced" in any moral sense. Moreover, many former colonies remained deeply impoverished compared with their former colonial ruling states.

Modernization theory is not often employed as an overarching theory of development today, but many of its assumptions about progress, culture, and even race remain operative. *Neoliberalism* is a political and economic philosophy rooted in neoclassical economic theory (see chap. 6) that emphasizes free markets and democratic institutions as the path to human flourishing and economic development. In this view, some continue to view the history of the United States or other Western nations as the only route to economic development. This has been particularly true since 1989, when the collapse of the Soviet Union and its form of socialist communism seemed to leave Western democratic and market systems as the only viable model of economic and political life.

Dependency theory, advanced by scholars such as Andre Gunder Frank (1929–2005), argues that rather than nations necessarily moving from agricultural to industrial modes of production as global trade grows, some states become dependent on other states. The movement of global resources, the theory argues, creates permanent relationships of economic dependence between industrial and nonindustrial nations.

Dependency theory explicitly challenges some of the assumptions of modernization theory. For example, modernization theory suggests that colonial relationships invariably benefit the colonized. Dependency theory argues that rather than seeing colonized areas as inevitably progressing toward healthy economic development, the system of global capital creates poverty and sustained underdevelopment.

World-systems theory extends the premise of dependency theory, arguing that globalization may be conceptualized as a system of nations placed in the core, semi-periphery, and periphery of an interconnected global economy. Sociologist Immanuel Wallerstein (b. 1930) took concepts from dependency theory, Marxism (see chap. 11), and studies of nationalism to develop world-systems theory. In the world system, he suggested, core nations benefit tremendously while other nations are virtually destined to remain excluded from economic growth. World-systems theory argues that even after colonialism, global economic interrelationships are inherently exploitative of nations in the semi-periphery and periphery. Through a global division of labor, some nations become the suppliers of raw materials. Wealthier nations bring industries in farming, fishing, and mining to these peripheral countries in order to extract the needed materials. Local people derive wages but little else, as resources are sent to the consumer nations to be processed. People in core nations consume the goods, often processed in nations of the semi-periphery, while core-nation citizens engage in service industries such as finance, insurance, and health care. Some of the most skilled workers in the semi-periphery and periphery nations are drawn into the core, leaving the poorer nations even less able to contribute more than raw materials or manual labor to the global economy.

All of these theories were influential as scholars analyzed the nature and consequences of globalization. Economists continue to debate the effects of global exchange, free trade versus protected markets, and the limits or possibilities for continued economic growth. Anthropologists are likewise interested in the economic dimensions of globalization, but they have always sought to connect these economic changes to the cultural and social contexts in which they occur.

Colonialism and Culture Change

Today's globalization is rooted in colonialism. While forms of global trade have existed for millennia, it was not until the seventeenth century that the scale of global movements began to have widespread consequences. At that time, various European nations established comprehensive plans for controlling vast areas of Africa, Asia, and Latin America. Europeans wanted a supply of raw materials to support industrializing economies, and they wanted empires to establish national political power.

Colonialism was not, of course, a European invention. Throughout history large political states, from the Zulu nation in southern Africa to the Mongols of northern China, have used their strong numbers, economic organization, and political structures to invade and control other territories. But because of their technological capacity to extract resources from the lands they controlled, European colonialism led to greater economic and political entanglement than earlier instances of colonialism. In some cases, such as the Spanish strategy in much of Latin America and the British model for North America, colonial regimes encouraged thousands of people from their own countries to settle in these colonial territories. In other cases, such as the Portuguese approach in Brazil and Southeast Asia, the Spanish agenda in the Philippines, or the French in West Africa, the only Europeans who actually lived in the colonized territories were colonial administrators. These Europeans used local people to govern on behalf of the colonial regime.

Some scholars distinguish colonialism from imperialism to differentiate direct rule (colonialism) from indirect rule (imperialism). Others tend to reserve the term "colonialism" for what is sometimes specified as "settler colonialism," in which significant numbers of citizens from the ruling country live in the colonized land. In fact, within these various types, there are numerous variations in practice.

Underlying the various approaches were very different views of how colonial and local cultures should interact. The French colonial philosophy, for example, emphasized the "civilizing mission" (*mission civilicatrice*) of their colonization. Wherever the French extended their control, they sought to transform the people (specifically, the elites of the country) into "modern" and "rational" citizens in the French way. The British, on the other hand, tended to allow local cultural forms to remain in place, but resignified them toward the goals and purposes of British rule. That is, the British were likely to acknowledge (or appoint) a local "chief" who then was responsible for enforcing British law, taxation, and so forth. In other words, where the French tried to replace local culture with French forms, the British sought to infuse European culture *into* locally existing forms. Despite the different approaches of various colonial powers, what was common in each case was the creation of lasting economic and political links between the colonized countries and the European states whose economies came to rely on the extraction of their natural resources.

Insights about the cultural dynamics of colonialism help anthropologists understand culture change in postcolonial nations as well. Two key concepts are hegemony and resistance. Chapter 7 defines hegemony as the dominance of ideas or culture for the purpose of reinforcing inequality or control. When applied to colonialism, then, *colonial hegemony* refers more specifically to ways in which culture and ideology became means of colonial control, asserting widespread influence over dominated populations.

Anthropologists have studied how strategies and practices of imperialism and colonialism have played out in particular places, influencing economic, political, and cultural life, often in ways that could not be predicted or controlled by the colonizers themselves. For example, in addition to overt political domination, Belgian colonial rule in Rwanda involved shaping people's conceptions of their identities in ways that were favorable to the colonial power. John R. Bowen notes that prior to colonialism, "some [Rwandans] did consider themselves Hutu or Tutsi . . . [but] these labels were not the main sources of everyday identity. A woman living in central Africa drew her identity from where she was born, from her lineage and in-laws, and from her wealth. Tribal or ethnic identity was rarely important in everyday life and could change as people moved over vast areas in pursuit of trade or new lands."[6]

The colonial regime, however, created classifications it could use to categorize and govern the population. Similar to the way British colonial rule sought to bend local culture toward the objectives of colonial rule, Belgians found the minority Tutsis to be ready partners in their control of the majority Hutus. Moreover, according to Bowen, Belgians found the Tutsis more "appealing," as they tended to be taller; Belgians felt this trait made the Tutsis morally superior. Intensifying and exploiting ethnic divisions became a useful strategy for colonial rulers. This came to a tragic climax when those who felt oppressed by these increasingly rigid and imposed categories (the Hutus) rose up in armed conflict against the Tutsis, who were disproportionately represented in the ruling elite, leading to the 1994 genocide in which nearly one million people were killed.[7]

Hegemony involves assertions of power on every level of political and social organization, as well as cultural categories and values. It is resisted too on all these levels. *Resistance* includes not only rebellion or revolution of dominated populations, but the attitudes and behaviors of subordinated

6. John R. Bowen, "The Myth of Global Ethnic Conflict," *Journal of Democracy* 7, no. 4 (1996): 6.

7. Some Rwandans are seeking to resist these categories, including governmental leaders who have made the use of ethnic categories in public identification a crime in some cases. Changing cultural categories and public perceptions is difficult, however, and transformation is unlikely to occur any time soon.

people that thwart, or try to thwart, an oppressor's power. When dominated, people often resist through any means available. Besides direct armed rebellion, dominated populations engage in forms of resistance ranging from ethnic revival movements, asserting pride and positive identity in the face of racism or discrimination, to nonviolent resistance, such as that practiced by Mahatma Gandhi against British colonial rule in India or Martin Luther King Jr. against racism in the United States. Sometimes resistance is practiced on an individual level, such as work slowdowns, or personal dress or speech that expresses autonomy. Individual acts of resistance may not always affect the larger hegemony, but they preserve individual dignity and vision for times when political resistance becomes viable.

As people resignify or reinterpret the ideas of dominant groups, they produce a counterhegemony. Although the Hutus rose up against the Tutsis, they did not create a counterhegemony because they continued to act in accordance with the ethnic categories so effectively reinforced by the Belgians. But when Gandhi and King taught that political or racial identities were not as foundational as people thought, or could be reevaluated in terms of equality and pride, they were creating new categories, or at least transforming old ones. In this way, these were economic and political counterhegemonic movements, as people were drawn to practice new forms of "religious" behavior in an effort to gain economic and political equality.

Counterhegemonic movements may be led by visionary individuals in the face of national crises or widespread oppression, but they also may be organic responses to marginalization and culture change. For example, following World War II, new religious movements developed throughout the South Pacific. Known as *cargo cults*, these were small groups, often following local leaders with a prophetic message from ancestral or other spirits promising wealth ("cargo") to the followers of the new religion. In many cases, religious leaders taught that by performing rituals—sometimes based on the behavior of Westerners, other times in opposition to Western cultural norms—the people of their communities would receive the material blessing (the "cargo") seen among colonialists. In some cases, behaviors such as writing, reading the Bible, going to church, and wearing long pants were mimicked in hopes that those rituals would increase access to wealth. In other cases, the rituals bore little resemblance to Western behaviors, but the motivation seemed to be the same.

There is disagreement over what caused cargo cults to emerge at this time, but they were clearly a reaction to Western economic power and rapid social change. Some believe the sudden arrival and rapid withdrawal of Western goods and wealth as a result of World War II being fought among the formerly remote islands of the South Pacific caused local people to react, searching for financial and psychological stability. Others see it as an adaptation of previous exchange systems that incorporated new Western symbols to which South Pacific people were exposed during the war.

Both interpretations acknowledge that many of these movements inspired or directed followers to resist colonial rule. Some followers refused to pay the taxes imposed by distant colonial governments, while others obstructed economic "development" projects, such as logging and mining, that they saw as contrary to their own best interests. Though the explicit motives for these religious movements were directed toward spiritual beliefs, the cargo cults often served a simultaneous purpose as mechanisms of resistance to colonial hegemony. Subverting the intentions of colonial rulers, cargo cults created a way for people of the South Pacific to resist colonial power and actively respond to the dramatic and disorienting changes occurring around them.

Postcolonialism and Globalization

As direct colonial rule ended throughout the nineteenth and twentieth centuries, former colonies entered an era known as postcolonialism. *Postcolonialism* refers to the cultural and economic legacy of colonialism, including ongoing relationships between former colonies and colonizers. In cases where the economic or political influence of former imperial powers has remained particularly strong, some scholars apply the term "neocolonialism." *Neocolonialism*, meaning "new colonialism," describes a nation or group of people that is essentially a colony of another nation, despite the absence of direct or formal political control.

Before the Philippines outlawed foreign ownership of land in the late 1980s, some said the Philippines remained in a neocolonial relationship with the United States. United States–based companies such as Dole and Del Monte owned vast amounts of farmland throughout much of the country. Today, the economic influence of the United States in the Philippines is less direct, and the Philippine economy is more connected to many nations around the world. The land once owned by U.S. corporations, however, was sold to several wealthy families who had relationships with the former colonial rulers. The products were often processed and distributed by the companies who had originally owned the land, so the daily realities for many landless Filipino farm workers remained unchanged. At a structural level, however, the Philippines has shifted from a neocolonial to a postcolonial nation.

In terms of culture, postcolonialism often involves blending cultural influences from colonial powers with an independent national identity. In the Philippines, the influence of former colonial powers is expressed in cultural as well as economic and political terms. For example, English is one of the national languages, the political system is still based largely on the constitution written by U.S. colonial rulers prior to independence, and a massive

Filipino-American population (more than one million people of Philippine ancestry live in the United States) maintains relationships with families in the Philippines. As with colonialism itself, people in postcolonial states are not passive receivers of cultural influence from former colonial powers. At the same time, however, certain classes in these countries continue to draw from, remain attached to, and even celebrate cultural influences from the former colonial state. Gloria Macapagal-Arroyo, the Philippine vice president who became president after a popular revolt in 2002, was the daughter of Diosdado Macapagal, a former Philippine president who had once worked for a U.S. law firm and served in Washington, D.C., as the Philippine ambassador. Macapagal-Arroyo herself was a graduate of Georgetown University in Washington, D.C., where she was a classmate of former U.S. President Bill Clinton. Such close relationships between national elites and former colonial powers are not unusual. Whether Indian elites with Oxford degrees, Senegalese leaders who studied at the Sorbonne, or Latin American generals receiving anti-insurgency training in Columbus, Georgia, elite members of postcolonial nations often receive education and socialization from former colonial powers.

Another major cultural dynamic of postcolonialism is cultural hybridity. The term "hybridity" is borrowed from botany, describing two plants that are combined to create a new plant. (Many roses are hybrids, as are fruits such as the "tangelo"—a tangerine crossed with a grapefruit or pomelo.) *Cultural hybridity* refers to the cultural practice of combining and assigning new meanings to previously separate beliefs, practices, or ideas. Whether in plants or people, hybridity is the emergence of a novel thing out of two or more existing ones.

Cultural hybridity is a hallmark of the postcolonial condition in which, following decades or centuries of colonial rule, people have so deeply internalized cultural norms and practices from the colonial power that they feel natural and normal. At the same time, people resent the imposition of foreign cultural practices and want to reclaim local distinctives. The negotiation of what to keep, how to change, what is "us" and what is "them" is a never-ending process in the postcolonial, globalizing world.

India provides a powerful example of cultural hybridity. Modern India is literally a colonial creation. Prior to the arrival of European colonialists, the area now known as India was not organized around a central government or monarchy. Villages maintained a degree of political autonomy, even within kingdoms or sultanates. People living on the subcontinent associated themselves with local cultures and languages and didn't think of themselves as belonging to one nation stretching from Punjab in the northwest, to Bengal in the northeast, to the tip of Tamil-Nadu in the south. The British created the idea of India as a single place. Just before the end of British rule (almost simultaneous with it), the area known as British India was

Fig. 10.1 The Nation of India, Pre- and Post-British Colonialism

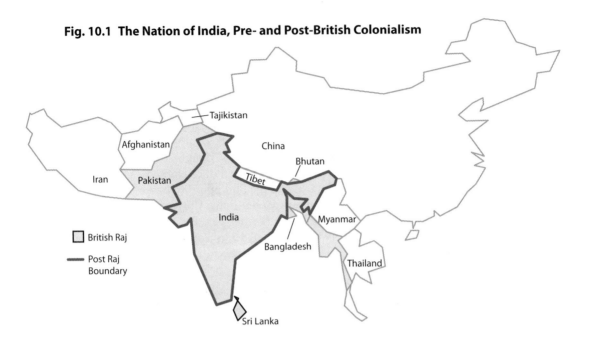

partitioned into what are now the modern-day countries of Pakistan, India, and Bangladesh.[8]

Although Britain has left an indelible impact on Indian life, India has not become an enormous replica of Britain, but with warmer weather. The game of cricket, for instance, is an identifiably British practice flourishing in India, but Indians have infused it with their own meanings. They are engaging in what some scholars have called *decolonization*, the process of separating the colonial meanings, associations, or imprint from a colonial cultural practice or artifact and reimagining the practice or artifact as a local, indigenous phenomenon. Postcolonial scholars note how the ability to play (and win) at the sport of the former colonizer gives many Indians a sense of national pride and superiority over the former ruler. Scholars studying people of Indian descent living outside India note that these populations are particularly devoted to the national success of Indian cricket teams. Among Indians everywhere, notes anthropologist Arjun Appadurai, cricket has gone from being a leisure activity of the British colonial elite to a passion of the masses.[9] Matches between Pakistani and Indian teams carry particular weight as the pride of each competing postcolonial nation becomes wrapped in a sport developed by the former colonizer.

8. After the partition of British India in 1947, present-day Bangladesh was called East Pakistan. It was renamed Bangladesh in 1971.

9. Arjun Appadurai, *Modernity at Large: Cultural Dimensions of Globalization* (Minneapolis: University of Minnesota Press, 1996), 89–113.

The Anthropology of Globalization Today

Because people everywhere are touched by globalization, anthropologists research the cultural dimensions of globalization, including new forms of media, travel, and economic relationship. Anthropologists study culture change, rather than simply cultural difference, as globalization has become an overarching context for most anthropological research. Anthropologists have to adapt research methods originally conceived for villages or small populations to encompass new global interactions.

Multisited research involves ethnographic fieldwork in two or more places, or studying a group that, by definition, does not have a specific place. Research on tourism, short-term missions, international adoption, migration, pilgrimage, consumption, and production relies on multisited ethnography to understand how the movement of people affects the individuals who move, the places they come from, the places they go, or even the process of travel. The image of a lone anthropologist setting out to contact an isolated band or tribe is an evocative one, true to the discipline's origins, but in today's globalized world, an anthropologist is more likely to travel between urban and rural sites, or between a village in Bangladesh and extended family members in Detroit. In multisited ethnography, anthropologists may follow a group of people (e.g., displaced Sudanese children or corporate elites), a thing (e.g., sugar, oil, or donated organs), or an idea or metaphor (e.g., freedom, romance, or racism). They may even do fieldwork without a physical site, studying internet or cell phone communications.

Multisited ethnography has been particularly helpful in the study of *diasporas*, populations living outside their traditional homelands. Some diasporas, such as Indians and other South Asians, maintain strong links to a homeland. To the extent that members of a diaspora move between two or more places, they become *transnational*, a term that describes people who move and live between two or more nations, or people who maintain cultural beliefs, practices, products, and networks connected to their homeland. Even if they do not physically travel across national boundaries, by maintaining cultural practices while living in diaspora and using items connected to their homeland, transnational populations blur the boundaries between one nation and another.

Anthropologists of globalization also study processes and effects of deterritorialization. *Deterritorialization* is the transnational movement of people, ideas, goods, and images that results in a disassociation between the people or things and the place from which they originate. Multinational corporations, though they are based in specific countries, often work very hard to deterritorialize their brands. Playing with Legos™, for instance, is not considered a Danish practice. Most people who use Nokia mobile phones could not name the country where the Nokia Corporation is based (Finland).

These companies want their toy blocks and cell phones to become such familiar aspects of life that they no longer convey a sense of being from some specific country.

Another way deterritorialization occurs is through the commodification of ideas, behaviors, and even cultures that are packaged for consumption by people anywhere. Hip-hop dance and music began as an artistic form in the South Bronx, a borough of New York City. Born out of economic and social marginalization and characterized by particular clothing, mannerisms, dances, music, and even attitudes, this youth movement became widely popular as a rebellion against an older generation and against the racism and class stratification of the United States. Elements of hip-hop became popular outside the groups that originated it, inspiring clothing and music available throughout the world. Anyone could be hip-hop by buying the right clothes, music, and learning the dances and physical mannerisms. In this way, hip-hop was commodified and its messages of social resistance were expanded (some might say lost) far beyond their original context.

Deterritorialization happens to people as well as to things. In addition to the people who belong to a diaspora, individuals who cross cultural boundaries often experience a deterritorialized existence. Aihwa Ong, an anthropologist born and raised in Malaysia but educated and working in the United States, has written about "flexible citizenship" to understand elite businesspeople who live and work in a variety of cultural and national contexts.[10] Others have argued that these world travelers comprise a class of "cosmopolitans" who are not fully a part of a single cultural context but weave together elements from many and become skilled at choosing what to emphasize in a particular setting. The children of these families, including missionaries who work outside their home countries, often are deeply familiar with several places. Among Christians, missionary children are sometimes called "third culture kids" as a way of naming their transnational identity. Anthropologists also study *interstitial zones*, places where two or more cultural contexts overlap and intersect, creating a new, generally ambiguous cultural context. Mexican citizens who daily cross the border into the United States to work, returning to Mexico each night, live in an interstitial zone. It shapes a unique sense of identity that some have dubbed "Amexican."[11]

As people adopt global products and practices for themselves, they turn globalization into a process of localization. *Localization* is the cultural practice of translating ideas, artifacts, or behaviors from elsewhere into localities.

10. Aihwa Ong, *Flexible Citizenship: The Cultural Logics of Transnationality* (Durham, NC: Duke University Press, 1999).

11. A *Time* cover story quotes the mayor of Laredo, Texas, as saying, "The border is not where the U.S. stops and Mexico begins. . . . It's where the U.S. blends into Mexico." Nancy Gibbs et al., "La Nueva Frontera: A Whole New World," *Time*, April 4, 2006, www.time.com/time/magazine/article/0,9171,1000093-3,00.html (accessed August 18, 2009).

Over time, things that were deterritorialized are *re*territorialized in their new home. This may occur as the original practice or product is modified to include elements from the new context. For example, the Oak Brook, Illinois-based McDonald's corporation adapts its menu in new markets to reflect local tastes: the salmon burger in Norway or the teriyaki burger of Japan. More significantly, however, in places where kinship ties are emphasized, such as mainland China, McDonald's often employs a hostess known as "Auntie McDonald" to welcome guests (especially children) and make sure everyone is having a good time. Likewise, McDonald's customers have developed their own understandings of the place, using it as an after-school hangout for teens or a preferred location for children's birthday parties, rather than a quick and easy meal as is customary in the United States. In his book from which these ethnographic examples are taken, Watson tells the oft-repeated story of some Japanese children visiting the United States for the first time. The children were surprised but pleased to find that, even in the United States, they were still able to eat at their favorite Japanese restaurant: McDonald's.[12]

Christians Respond to Globalization

At the end of the twentieth century, protests took place across the world as an eclectic coalition of labor rights activists, environmentalists, anti-immigration nationalists, human rights advocates, and antiwar demonstrators began regularly gathering in major cities where leaders of powerful nations or the heads of international organizations met. The disparate groups came together around the conviction that globalization was harmful to people and the planet. Some were concerned that corporate interests were gaining too much influence at the expense of elected governmental bodies. Others were opposed to the consolidation of power into the hands of nonelected, quasi-governmental organizations such as the World Bank and the International Monetary Fund. A violent 1999 protest against the World Trade Organization in the U.S. Pacific Northwest—dubbed the "Battle of Seattle"—initiated years of increasingly organized protest against globalization. These antiglobalization movements gained such strength that in 2006, Douglas Kellner, a prominent scholar of globalization, concluded, "The current forms and scope of worldwide resistance to globalization policies and processes is one of the most important political developments of the last decade."[13]

12. James L. Watson, ed., *Golden Arches East: McDonald's in East Asia*, 2nd ed. (Stanford, CA: Stanford University Press, 2006).

13. Douglas Kellner and Richard Kahn, "Resisting Globalization," unpublished manuscript, 2006, www.gseis.ucla.edu/faculty/kellner/essays/resistingglobalization.pdf (accessed June 1, 2009).

Studying Globalization at Home

Studying globalization doesn't have to involve traveling to foreign countries. U.S. anthropologists who study the United States (also called domestic anthropology, referring to anthropology done in the nation of which the anthropologist is a citizen) consider how global trends influence people close to home. In my (Jenell's) research on ghetto formation in Washington, D.C., I studied several global trends that affected the residents of Northwest One, a neighborhood ten blocks north of the U.S. Capitol.

Though U.S. slavery ended over one hundred years before the research began, the global slave trade of the modern era continues to shape daily life in the United States. The slave trade that brought Africans to the United States lasted for hundreds of years, and when it finally ended, it gave way to new systems of inequality that perpetuated the degradation, segregation, and poverty of African Americans. Research informants—living in Washington, D.C., in the mid-1990s—were part of a larger ethnic group (African Americans) who had enjoyed full citizenship for only thirty years. Prior to the Civil Rights Act, this group had lived under slavery and then legal discrimination, processes that networked Europeans, Africans, and South, Central, and North Americans together in a pursuit of economic growth that relied upon human exploitation.

My research sought to understand how resident activists had strategized to improve local conditions of life in the post–civil rights era. One of the most important activists was Miss Munlyn, and I spent hours listening to her life story and her neighborhood work.

She and other activists drew upon the nonviolent strategies of Indian revolutionary Mahatma Gandhi and U.S. civil rights leader Martin Luther King Jr.—for example, they staged a "We Refuse to Leave" campaign that involved sitting across a major roadway to block traffic and draw attention to their cause, opposition to proposed urban renewal programs that would displace neighborhood residents.

I also noticed changes in names over time, both in interviews and in archival data. At various times, African Americans referred to themselves, or were referred to by others, as Negroes, Colored, Black, Afro American (hyphenated or not), and African American (hyphenated or not). As a white person doing fieldwork in an African American neighborhood, I had to choose my words carefully (I tried to listen first, and then use whichever term others were using in a given situation) and respond courteously when corrected. Changing names of U.S. racial and ethnic minorities reflect global trends. "Negro," for instance, emphasizes the international slave era in which the line between slave and free was drawn according to skin color. Names that end with "American" reflect the era of freedom, when Americans of African descent were recognized as full citizens. The prefix, African or Afro, and the hyphen, reflect concerns about retaining historical identity and establishing a connection (tight or loose) between the African and the American parts of identity.

In my fieldwork I found that, from naming practices to activist strategies to the very presence of urban ghettos, globalization is evident even in a local neighborhood.

Like globalization itself, however, these antiglobalization efforts are complex movements. The part of the movement focused on resisting the power of transnational corporations has been termed the "anticorporate globalization movement." Others have focused on human rights and called their work a "social justice movement." While some argue for a return to a more locally based, less technologically dependent way of life, most of the antiglobalization movements rely on global media such as the internet, cell phone technology, and the circulations of images and ideas in order to draw together far-flung networks of like-minded people.[14]

The irony of so-called antiglobalization resistance being rooted in technologies facilitating or synonymous with globalization is not lost on these activists. For this reason, many prefer to speak of "globalization from below" or "grassroots globalization," rather than simply employing an antiglobalization rhetoric.

These movements stress local responses to globalization rather than resistance to globalization per se. Sociologist Jackie Smith described this as the "Comprehensive Globalization Movement" (CGM), a term that emphasizes not simply the globalization of corporate influence, commodities, and economics, but also social and political globalization. She argues that where the antiglobalization label can be an easy target for those who see such movements as negative responses and unrealistic nostalgia in the face of economic progress, the CGM is about including more voices in the processes affecting their lives. "If one had to identify a common thread among the demands of activists in this movement, it would be a demand for democracy."[15] Anthropologists argue that democracy, literally meaning "rule of the people," can take many forms, from informed politics in small-scale band societies to large representative voting systems. Nevertheless, the notion of including more people in the process of governance and preventing power from becoming concentrated into the hands of a few is one positive response to forms of globalization that leave many people outside decision-making processes.

As Christians respond to globalization, they share some common concerns for human rights, social justice, and care for the environment. Some believers, such as Ron Sider, Joan Chittister, Shane Claiborne, and most notably Mother Theresa have insisted that Christians have a responsibility to reject unsustainably consumptive lifestyles and a growth-oriented economic model in favor of simple and sustainable living. Writer and Christian Wendell Berry, for instance, left his life as a professor of literature in favor of farming in Kentucky on land owned by his family for generations.[16] Through his writing, he encourages people to challenge corporate models of consumerism, mobility, and industrial agricultural social organization. His life demonstrates the importance of local living that is responsive to human and natural environments.

In contrast, others have pointed to the ways globalizing technology and economic growth has benefited human flourishing. They also note how global media have been useful in sharing the gospel message around the world. These

14. See Wendell Berry, *Another Turn of the Crank* (Washington, DC: Counterpoint Press, 1995).
15. Jackie Smith, "Behind the Anti-Globalization Label," *Dissent*, Fall 2001, http://dissentmagazine.org/article/?article=896 (accessed June 1, 2009).
16. Berry, *Another Turn*.

Christians argue that the church should be at the forefront of mastering the use of global media and modes of exchange rather than trying to diminish their place.[17]

As Christians, we are part of a global religious movement. As discussed in more detail in chapter 2, crossing cultural, linguistic, economic, and political boundaries has been part of the Christian church from its beginning among the believers in Jerusalem. Christian anthropologists, missiologists, and theologians have celebrated the potential for global voices to be increasingly included in the life of Christians everywhere.[18]

Within that potential, however, is always the danger that some Christians today may too easily accept global inequalities. Like the Colossians who risked being taken captive by "hollow and deceptive philosophy" (Col. 2:8), Western Christians may enjoy the benefits that global trade and travel have brought to them without considering how inequality and poverty may be supported by these very things. In fact, some secular anthropologists are convinced that the economic effects of nineteenth-century mission activity were far more important than religious effects. Just as the histories of modern capitalist society and Protestant Christianity are intimately intertwined, the history of global evangelism and colonial exploitation cannot be separated. Even today, many living in postcolonial African nations see European and U.S. mission work as directly linked to economic exploitation that continues today. In the words of one black South African, "When the white man came to our country, he had the Bible and we had the land. The white man said to us 'let us pray.' After the prayer, the white man had the land and we had the Bible."[19] When Christians fail to atone for this history or even acknowledge it, we make it difficult to argue that Christianity is not a tool of colonialism or global hegemony.

Globalization is a diffuse and complex process in which Christians are, and must remain, intimately involved. There are no simple answers as to how economic, political, and social life can better reflect God's justice, but certainly Christians must ask difficult questions and be willing to make changes where appropriate. Anthropology contributes insight into how globalization affects people and their ways of life—knowledge that can help Christians be increasingly aware of globalization and their responses to it.

17. See, for example, Brian Griffiths, *Globalization, Poverty and International Development* (London: Acton Institute, 2006).

18. An excellent collection of essays around many issues related to globalization and the church can be found in Craig Ott and Harold Netland, eds., *Globalizing Theology: Belief and Practice in an Era of World Christianity* (Grand Rapids: Baker Books, 2006).

19. Takatso Mofokeng, "Black Christians, the Bible and Liberation," *The Journal of Black Theology in South Africa* 2, no. 34 (1988): 34–42.

Christian Anthropologists and Globalization

Christian anthropologists respond to globalization in many different ways and are influenced by it as well.

Some Christian anthropologists embody globalization in their personal identities and make globalization a focus for their research. Having studied in both Kenya and the United States, Mwenda Ntarangwi is an anthropologist whose education spans the globe. In his book, *East African Hip Hop: Youth Culture and Globalization*, Ntarangwi analyzes how young musicians in Kenya, Uganda, and Tanzania maximize globalization's potential for making and sharing music. He found that music empowers youth to address issues such as economic inequality, African identity, and AIDS. His three years of fieldwork included interviews, analysis of live performances and songs, and participant observation among musicians.[1]

Anthropologist Katrina Greene also looks for ways to apply anthropological insight to real-world problems and opportunities caused by globalization.[2] Her fieldwork in South Africa focused on how women engage in collective savings and credit practices to finance and develop small businesses, invest in the Johannesburg Stock Exchange, and supplement the government housing subsidy in order to construct houses. South Africa is a postcolonial state that, at the time of Greene's initial fieldwork, had made a massive political transition to a post-apartheid democracy. Greene considered this political context as well as ways in which local women blended "traditional" cultural practices with emergent post-apartheid economic opportunities. Through ongoing field research, Greene has continued to examine how neoliberal economic practices as well as the ideology of individual economic aggrandizement have affected the status and viability of various collective savings and investment activities in South Africa.

Katrina Greene (standing second from the left) is pictured in Vrygrond—an informal settlement located outside of Steenberg in Cape Town, South Africa—with friends and attendees at an Amabhaso, a traditional gift-giving ceremony. In such informal settlements, people live in self-constructed houses made out of corrugated iron, tin, plastic, and other scrap materials. The Amabhaso is a tradition of the Xhosa tribe that is a combination of a bridal shower and an engagement party. Invited guests bring gifts for the bride (standing second from the right) and the groom as well as eat together to celebrate the couple's engagement. Women and men attend the Amabhaso.
Photo: Katrina Greene

Christian anthropologists are also influenced by globalization. As a graduate student at Boston University, Sarah Tobin did fieldwork among Muslims in Jordan. To the extent that fieldwork involves culture shock and long periods of time away from home, her twenty-first-century fieldwork was the same as it was for early anthropologists. But Tobin blogged her fieldwork, which drew her friends, family, and even research informants into the process of reflection and analysis. In this way, through globalized forms of communication, the Muslims among whom she worked did not become "exotic others," even to Tobin's family and friends in the United States. They became real participants in the ethnographic process. Globalization has the potential to shape both anthropologist and research informants in ways that produce a pool of shared knowledge.

1. Mwenda Ntarangwi, *East African Hip Hop: Youth Culture and Globalization* (Urbana: University of Illinois Press, 2009).

2. Katrina Greene, "Is It Possible to Overcome the 'Tragedy of *Ubuntu*'?: The Journey of a Black Women's Economic Empowerment Group in South Africa," presented at the Society for Economic Anthropology 2008 Annual Conference, Cincinnati, Ohio, April 3–5, 2008.

Terms

cargo cults: religion that involves local leaders with a prophetic message from ancestral or other spirits promising wealth ("cargo") to the followers of the new religion.

colonial hegemony: ways in which culture and ideology became the means of colonial control, asserting widespread influence over dominated populations.

commodification: the transformation of concepts, creations, and even cultures into goods that can be bought and sold, given and received.

cultural hybridity: the cultural practice of combining and assigning new meaning to previous beliefs, practices, or ideas. The emergence of a new cultural form out of two or more existing ones, leaving both forms changed without erasing the old.

decolonialization: the process of separating the colonial meanings, associations, or imprint from a colonial cultural practice or artifact and reimagining the practice or artifact as a local, indigenous phenomenon.

dependency theory: the view that globalization results in some states becoming dependent on others.

deterritorialization: the transnational movement of people, ideas, goods, and images that results in a disassociation between the people or things and the place from which they originate.

diaspora: a population living outside its traditional homeland.

domestic anthropology: anthropology done in the nation of which the anthropologist is a citizen.

globalization: the integration of local, regional, and/or national production, exchange, and culture into a global system.

interstitial zone: a place where two or more cultural contexts overlap and intersect, creating a new, generally ambiguous cultural context.

localization: the cultural practice of translating ideas, artifacts, or behaviors from elsewhere into localities.

modernization theory: the view that all societies move through stages of economic, political, and cultural development toward becoming industrialized, democratic, and "modern."

multisited research: research that involves ethnographic fieldwork in two or more places, or studying a group that, by definition, does not have a specific place.

neocolonialism: "new colonialism," meaning that a nation or people is essentially a colony of another nation, despite the absence of direct or formal political control.

neoliberalism: a political and economic philosophy rooted in neoclassical economic theory emphasizing free market and democratic institutions as the path to human flourishing and economic development.

postcolonialism: the cultural and economic legacy of colonialism, including ongoing relationships between former colonies and colonizers.

resistance: the attitudes and behaviors of dominated people, as well as instances of rebellion or revolution, that thwart, or try to thwart, an oppressor's power.

transnational: describes people who move and live between two or more nations, or people who maintain cultural beliefs, practices, products, and networks connected to their homeland.

westernization (also called *McDonaldization*): a form of cultural homogenization in which Western cultural norms replace local culture, resulting in the loss of cultural diversity.

world-systems theory: the view that the world may be conceptualized as a system of nations placed in the core, semi-periphery, and periphery of an interconnected global economy.

Devotion 1

Israelites in Diaspora

By the rivers of Babylon we sat and wept when we remembered Zion. There on the poplars we hung our harps, for there our captors asked us for songs, our tormentors demanded songs of joy; they said, "Sing us one of the songs of Zion!" How can we sing the songs of the Lord while in a foreign land? (Ps. 137:1–4)

Psalm 137 is a psalm of lament, in which the psalmist remembers when the Israelites lived in diaspora under Babylonian domination. He recalls a particularly desperate time when the Babylonians mocked and tried to force the Israelites to sing one of their holy songs of joy. The Israelites were despondent: "How can we sing the songs of the Lord while in a foreign land?" This is a lament of a colonized people that poignantly expresses how difficult it is for a group of people to be dispersed and conquered by another culture. Though they had hung up their harps, they did remember their songs and asked God for justice on their behalf.

In anthropological terms, the question in verse four is a question of localization. Translating treasured cultural beliefs and practices into a new situation—especially one in which your group is oppressed—is extremely difficult. Throughout the world today, millions—including many Christian brothers and sisters—live in diaspora, displaced from their homelands by wars, economic and natural disasters, and persecution. They struggle, even now, to answer the question, "How can we sing?"

This psalm of lament doesn't resolve the issue but voices its importance, then and now.

Devotion 2

Israelites Practice Resistance

The king of Egypt said to the Hebrew midwives, whose names were Shiphrah and Puah, "When you help the Hebrew women in childbirth and observe them on the delivery stool, if it is a boy, kill him; but if it is a girl, let her live." The midwives, however, feared God and did not do what the king of Egypt had told them to do; they let the boys live. Then the king of Egypt summoned the midwives and asked them, "Why have you done this? Why have you let the boys live?" The midwives answered Pharaoh, "Hebrew women are not like Egyptian women; they are vigorous and give birth before the midwives arrive." So God was kind to the midwives and the people increased and became even more numerous. And because the midwives feared God, he gave them families of their own. (Exod. 1:15–21)

The Hebrews were living as an ethnic minority population within the Egyptian kingdom, laboring as slaves under cruel overlords. Things could hardly have gotten worse, but they did. The Egyptian Pharaoh commanded Shiphrah and Puah, the Hebrew midwives, to kill all newborn Hebrew boys.

Shiphrah and Puah practiced resistance. They disobeyed this unjust order and when questioned about it, they lied. Their acts of resistance protected the Hebrew people as a whole, and God blessed the entire group, Shiphrah and Puah included. They also preserved Moses's life, because he was a boy born at this time. The midwives' resistance escalated into the Hebrews' massive resistance movement that ultimately resulted in their freedom, the story of which is recorded in Exodus.

Politically, this situation differs from that of modern-day colonialism, but on a human level it was very similar. The anthropology of globalization, colonialism, along with concepts of hegemony and resistance, help us see the injustices that result when one culture dominates another. At the same time, they highlight the possibility of righteousness in the face of evil.

Theory in Cultural Anthropology

After studying this chapter, you should be able to:

1. Explain the role of theory in anthropological research.
2. Identify key theoretical perspectives in anthropology.
3. Discuss how Christians can engage anthropological theory in thinking about faith and society.

Introduction

Everyone has a theory of culture, although most do not know it. Every time someone uses the word "culture," she or he does so with an implicit view of what culture is and how it works. If we say we respect culture, want to protect culture, change culture, or avoid culture, we are invoking a theory of culture. Most of the time these theories are unacknowledged, based on our assumptions about what people are like, why they do what they do, and how culture influences them. Anthropologists examine these assumptions and systematize their understandings into scholarly theories of culture.

This chapter presents theory in cultural anthropology. First, we define theory. Then, we describe the social philosophies that provide foundations for anthropological theory. Next, we turn to early anthropological theories that are important in the history of the discipline, before going on to describe several important streams of contemporary theory, including positivist anthropology, symbolic anthropology, and postmodern anthropological theory. Finally, we describe some of the problems and possibilities for Christians as they work with anthropological theory.

Theory in Anthropology

Anthropologists were among the first scientists to conceptualize culture and describe its dynamics. For anthropologists to really make sense of what they see, they need an explicit theory of why things happen and what they mean. For example, an anthropologist might observe people shopping and note the items purchased. Her question then becomes, "Why do people buy what they buy?" The people themselves may answer, "Because we like this," or "That's what people here do." The anthropologist considers the people's own views of their behavior and also considers scholarly theory. Are consumption patterns created by rational actors who know what they want? Is it a result of socialization in which they've been taught to buy that thing? Are people in the society encouraging others to buy it? Do people seek to impress their friends and neighbors to achieve social prestige? Theory helps the anthropologist move beyond impressions or opinions to a more systematic explanation of social phenomena.

In popular language, calling something a "theory" means it is a guess or just one person's opinion (as in, "My theory is that professors don't have enough to read; that's why they assign these papers"). In science, however, theory represents the highest level of scientific explanation. A *theory* is a formal description of some phenomenon in the world that explains how that thing works. Strong theories are able to explain data in a comprehensive and persuasive way. As new data are discovered, a strong theory explains the old data as well as the new.

Consider, for instance, theories about why objects fall to the ground when dropped. The Greek philosopher Aristotle (384–322 BCE) believed all objects want to return to their natural place. This means that if a solid object, such as a pen, rolls off a desk, it drops to the ground because it is seeking the center of matter at the center of the earth; it just wants to go home. According to this theory, gases, steam, smoke, and the like seek their natural place in the heavens; therefore, they go up.

This theory made good sense of the data known by the ancient Greeks, but as new knowledge of astronomy emerged, the old theory didn't explain the new data. For example, instead of the stars moving as if the earth were the center of the universe, it appeared that the earth actually moves around the sun. Later Greek and Arab astronomers began to suggest the existence of a force of attraction between planets and stars. In the seventeenth century, Isaac Newton (1643–1727) took all the data he knew—from Aristotle, through Avicenna,

Copernicus, and Galileo—and developed his universal theory of gravitation. Later, in the twentieth century, Albert Einstein (1879–1955) radically revised Newton's theory with the theory of general relativity. What made each iteration of this theory work (and rise to the level of theory) was its ability to explain what people observed and help predict what would be seen.

A theory can never be proved once and for all. Theories are always being contested and refined, replaced by new theories that explain everything the old theory did, plus anything the old theory could not. Some scientists, such as Karl Popper, posit *falsification* as the principle of science: that is, scientific theories cannot be proven, only falsified.[1] Thomas Kuhn, however, argued that theories are not falsified but replaced.[2] Theories may be well established, such as germ theory or atomic theory, or they may be more contested, such as string theory and other innovative ideas in theoretical physics. What makes a theory accepted is its ability to bring empirical data together into an explanatory whole, as well as its persuasiveness within a particular paradigm or worldview of both science and society.

Within cultural anthropology, numerous theories are employed at any given time. Anthropologists choose theories based on factors such as their research interest, fieldwork context, and personal values. One important factor that shapes an anthropologist's choice of theory is whether he or she is seeking a nomothetic explanation or an idiographic explanation of the phenomenon in question. A *nomothetic explanation* is a generalization, a natural law that predicts and explains culture change and human behavior. Just as chemists use the scientific method of hypothesis testing, this sort of anthropological theory presents testable theories of culture change or social organization. This was the primary approach of early anthropologists, and many anthropologists continue to view the discipline primarily in these terms. Their work often involves the study of material and measurable aspects of social life.

An *idiographic explanation* provides a rich description of a particular case. The understanding gained from such work is not meant to be directly compared across contexts nor generalized to all contexts. Instead, it provides a detailed understanding that becomes background for future research on related issues in other settings.

Research that is directed toward idiographic explanation relies on theory differently than research designed for nomothetic explanation. Clifford Geertz (1926–2006) uses a medical analogy, comparing a medical researcher investigating disease causation with a clinician engaged in diagnosis. The medical researcher wants to definitively state what causes a disease: a person infected by virus A will have disease B. Theories are tested in the laboratory and, if

1. Karl Popper, *The Logic of Scientific Discovery* (New York: Basic Books, 1959).
2. Thomas Kuhn, *The Structure of Scientific Revolutions* (Chicago: University of Chicago Press, 1970).

not borne out by the data, are revised or discarded in favor of a new theory. The clinician, on the other hand, is faced with a person who presents a variety of symptoms—sore throat, fever, achy joints, red blotches. The clinician asks questions and compares what she sees to other patients she has seen, or case studies written by other diagnostic clinicians who have seen similar patients. Her goal is to understand this particular patient, including the patient's history, context, and idiosyncrasies, and she incorporates the lab researcher's findings as appropriate. Her comprehensive study will become part of the medical knowledge that will help other clinicians see how this disease is similar and distinct in the experience of individual patients.

The medical researcher is more like an anthropologist seeking a predictive generalization (nomothetic explanation), and the clinician is more like an anthropologist developing a rich ethnographic description of a culture (idiographic explanation). Geertz argues that, "in ethnography, the office of theory is to provide a vocabulary in which what symbolic action has to say about itself—that is, about the role of culture in human life—can be expressed."[3] Over the years, social and cultural theory has served both purposes—prediction and description—and anthropologists continue to incorporate both into research today.

Anthropologists cannot conduct "theory-free" research. All researchers—in disciplines ranging from biology and physics, to psychology and anthropology—conduct research in terms of theory.[4] In nomothetic research, data are brought to the theory in an effort to test the continued validity of the theory. In idiographic research, ethnographic data are interpreted through a theoretical perspective in order to create a convincing explanation of particular phenomena such as social or cultural change, views of health, politics, religion, or any other realm of human life. Subsequent anthropologists investigating the same or similar phenomena may apply the same theory or a new one as a way of adding to the "consultable record of what [humanity] has said."[5]

Foundations of Anthropological Theory: Marx, Durkheim, and Weber

Like other social sciences, anthropology has roots in the eighteenth century, when European philosophers wrestled with the rapid changes occurring in

3. Clifford Geertz, *The Interpretation of Cultures* (New York: Basic Books, 1973), 27.
4. Grounded Theory (GT) is considered by some to be an exception. GT encourages anthropologists and other qualitative researchers to gather data first, and develop theory as it emerges from the data. Whether or not this is "theory-free" research is arguable. For a description of GT see K. Charmaz, *Constructing Grounded Theory: A Practical Guide through Qualitative Analysis* (Thousand Oaks, CA: Sage Publications, 2006). For a critique, see Gary Thomas and David James, "Re-inventing Grounded Theory: Some questions for theory, ground and discovery," *British Educational Research Journal* 32, no. 6 (2006): 767–95.
5. Geertz, *Interpretation of Cultures*, 30.

their nations as a result of the Industrial Revolution. Agrarian life was changing rapidly as millions moved into cities for factory work. Globalization was exploding through the colonial expansion of European nations, which exposed Europeans to new information about the world and embedded them in new economic relationships that included the exploitation of natural and human resources. From that time until the present, scholars have theorized about how best to understand cultural and social diversity. Karl Marx, Emile Durkheim, and Max Weber are three philosophers whose work provided foundational philosophy for cultural anthropology.

German philosopher and historian Karl Marx (1818–83) constructed a complex theory to explain and predict the development of all human societies. According to him, societies moved through stages of development driven by economic relations between classes. Capitalism, in rapid development during his time, represented one stage of development that he said would eventually give way to communitarian social forms. These communitarian social arrangements would provide human beings with economic equality and social harmony.

Marx wrote a great deal, subtly changing and refining his ideas. Many scholars refer to the "early Marx" and "late Marx" as distinct bodies of writing and thinking. In one of his earlier works, *The German Ideology*, Marx explained his belief that human beings gain consciousness through working together.[6] He argued that stratification of work and wages results in social class stratification, in which classes struggle against each other for control of economic resources. Class conflict fuels social change. He argued that every society and every form of social and cultural life in history could be understood in terms of the economic systems and conflict they produce. His most significant work, *Capital: A Critique of Political Economy*, is a detailed explanation of capitalism as a system of exploitation in which those who own the "means of production" (such as land and factories) are able to extract surplus value from workers by compensating workers with wages far below the value of goods and services produced with their labor.[7]

A significant element of his theory for later anthropologists was his view of human nature. Unlike Christian views of human beings as originally good but now sinful, or other philosophies that assert that the intrinsically good human race has been somehow corrupted, Marx began with the idea that human beings are, at root, socially created, neither inherently good nor bad. Human nature, he argued, is a flexible capacity that changes over time. Anthropologists have also drawn from his idea that social conflict caused by

6. Karl Marx, *The German Ideology* (New York: International Publishers, 1972).
7. Karl Marx, *Capital: A Critique of Political Economy* (1867; repr., New York: International Publishers, 1967).

inequality is a key organizing principle for culture. Anthropologists have argued that class-based inequalities underlie social conflict, including those between genders, ethnicities, races, and other social statuses.

Fifty years later, French scholar Emile Durkheim (1858–1917) also faced the question of how to understand European industrial societies.[8] Like Marx, he believed that researchers could discover laws of social life and could use those laws to make predictions about social change. He argued that scientists could apply the same rigorous methodologies to the study of society as they used in astronomy, biology, or chemistry. Like other thinkers of his day, he believed that societies evolve from simple to complex. He posited that European societies had advanced from the simple (what he called "elementary" or "primitive" forms) to the complex forms emerging at the end of the nineteenth century. Unlike Marx, who predicted utopia after an exploitative and oppressive capitalist phase, Durkheim did not place any value judgment on capitalist industrialism.

For both Marx and Durkheim, phenomena such as religion and the arts are products of underlying social or material causes, not reflections of spiritual or metaphysical causes. A major departure for Durkheim was to argue that social organizational forms do not originate from some proximate cause, such as economic relations. He called society "a thing in itself," or *sui generis*. This meant society is not the outcome of individual choices all added together. Rather, society is the thing that creates those individual choices in the first place (or at least the opportunity to make individual choices.) Studying individual thought (psychology) or individual economic choices (as most economists did in his time) would not explain why society and culture looked as they did. What can be studied, he believed, are the unique forms of social life, or what he called "social facts," that differentiate one society from another. Durkheim said society is like an organism with various parts that all work together for the health of the whole. Durkheim's theory provided an important perspective for anthropologists as they sought to explain seemingly irrational or inexplicable behaviors in communities around the world.

Max Weber (1864–1920), a German social philosopher and contemporary of Durkheim's, also wanted to explain the rapid changes in European societies. In contrast to Durkheim and Marx, Weber gave more credence to the power of ideas in shaping social organization. That is, unlike Durkheim and Marx, who sought to reduce social analysis to single variables, Weber believed a multivariate approach was best.

Weber is particularly known for his analysis of modern industrial capitalism, in which he connected the ethos of investment, frugality, and discipline

8. Emile Durkheim, *Suicide: A Study in Sociology* (1897; repr., Glencoe, IL: Free Press, 1951).

Choosing Theory

When I (Brian) started graduate school, I knew what I wanted to study—the relationship of Christianity and social change—but I did not know *how* I wanted to study it. At Washington University in St. Louis, where I did my graduate work, there were two excellent faculty members with very different theoretical perspectives. I arrived planning to work with one who employed rational choice theory in her work. This perspective tended toward positivism and nomothetic explanations. She encouraged me to explore the relationship between prohibitions on alcohol use inspired by Christian conversion and community change, particularly economic change. She was a brilliant scholar and, at first, this seemed good. As I went on, however, I felt that this perspective did not allow me to consider aspects of Christianity that I found most interesting, such as how people experience their relationship with God, and the ways people negotiate the meanings of their faith together.

The other faculty member with whom I worked studied Islam in Southeast Asia using an approach that blended Weberian theory with postmodern theory. This view emphasized how ideas, language, and culturally specific views of the world shaped human life and action. My professor did not ignore economic influences, but these were not the factors he found most helpful in explaining how the people he studied made choices about how to be Muslim in their context.

Eventually I found the Weberian and postmodern approaches to be more powerful theoretical perspectives in helping to explain how the Southern Baptist Christians of the northern Philippines (where I eventually did my research) interpreted their Christianity. My choice of a theoretical framework guided my entire research project, leading me to ask questions I would not have asked had I employed another theory. Although I sometimes wonder what direction my life would have taken had I become a rational choice theorist, all anthropologists eventually choose the theory that seems best given their interests, dispositions, and research questions.

necessary for the growth of capitalism to the doctrine of predestination as articulated by John Calvin.[9] Weber emphasized the "Protestant Ethic"—the belief that members of God's elect should live disciplined lives focused on the afterlife rather than on enjoyment in the present—as an indispensable component in the development of capitalism, industrialization, and the radical reordering of European society in the eighteenth and nineteenth centuries. Weber's analysis was geared more toward explaining modern Western cultural and social life, but his use of religious, philosophical, and political ideas as foundations for cultural change became an important philosophical touchstone for later anthropological theory.

A key concern for all social theorists is the relationship between society (the large-scale organization of social life) and culture (the ideas, symbols, and interpretations people have about the world). Some theorists, such as Marx, gave absolutely no role for culture in shaping how people live. Marx's theory is sometimes called mechanistic insofar as it argues that all human ideas, symbols, art, religion, and even family systems are products of ma-

9. Max Weber, *The Protestant Ethic and the Spirit of Capitalism*, trans. Talcott Parsons (1905; repr., New York: Scribner, 1958).

terial relations.[10] There is an almost mechanical cause-and-effect relationship between the material world and the ideas humans have.

Other theorists said culture and ideas are far more important as influences on human life. A contemporary of Marx's, Wilhelm Dilthey (1833–1911) argued that humans only ever understand the world through the symbols and ideas in their minds. Therefore, the symbolic world (culture) is actually "more real" than the material world in which we live.[11]

Today, many view these theories as overly reductionistic, interpreting complex processes through just a few variables. Even most anthropologists who use Marxian theory see culture as an independent influence on human life, one that is not *wholly* a product of material relations. Yet the underlying emphases have remained important in the development of subsequent schools of thought and anthropological theory.

Early Anthropological Theories

Influenced by Marx, Durkheim, Weber, and other philosophers, early anthropologists developed theories of culture. They were trying to understand and explain cultural diversity, the scope of which was becoming evident to Europeans and Americans because of colonialism and globalization. They were also interested in culture change, particularly general rules for cultural development. This section surveys five important early anthropological theories: unilinear cultural evolution, diffusion, historical particularism, functionalism, and structural-functionalism.

In the tradition of Marx and Durkheim, early scholars of cultural diversity explained the development of culture in general, universal terms. *Unilinear cultural evolution* (introduced in chap. 2) posited that all cultures evolve from simple to complex along a single trajectory of progress. This approach sought to make "objective" comparisons of societies with scales of development. The British anthropologist Edward B. Tylor (1832–1917) constructed his scale largely according to religion. He believed levels of religious development could be used to classify particular stages of cultural progress (see chap. 9).[12] American anthropologist Henry Lewis Morgan (1818–81), reflecting a more Marxian emphasis on economics and material life, placed cultural development on a scale from "savagery" to "barbarism"

10. See Jeffrey Alexander and Steven Seidman, *Culture and Society: Contemporary Debates* (Cambridge: Cambridge University Press, 1990): 1–30.
11. Wilhelm Dilthey, *The Philosophy of History in Our Time*, ed. Hans Meyerhoff (Garden City, NY: Doubleday, 1959).
12. Edward B. Tylor, *Anthropology: An Introduction to the Study of Man and Civilization* (New York: D. Appleton, 1916).

to "civilization," including such subdivisions as "upper savagery" and "lower barbarism."[13]

A competing explanation at the time, *diffusionism*, stated that cultural artifacts or activities (known as *cultural traits*) spread from more advanced to less advanced societies. In this view, people do not innovate cultural traits, rather, they borrow cultural traits from other societies. Strict diffusionists afforded virtually no role for creativity, innovation, or adaptation in culture.

Each of these theories offered a mechanism and explanation for the ethnographic data of cultural diversity and the observation that cultures had changed over time. Today, however, both cultural unilinear evolution and diffusion have been critiqued for their ethnocentrism and racism, as well as their failure to account for new historical and cultural data. The anthropologists espousing these theories were ethnocentric because they were using their own culture as the norm from which other cultures were interpreted. Some theorists explicitly argued that Europeans and European Americans represented the highest form of cultural development. If other, lower forms of cultural life were to advance, they would need to be taught by people from the more advanced cultures.

Most forms of diffusionism and unilinear cultural evolution were eventually discredited as cultural anthropologists and archaeologists accumulated more data from diverse cultural contexts. It became clear that not all societies moved through the same stages of development. The old theories were not sufficient to explain the new data, so new theories emerged. Franz Boas (1858–1942) was a German émigré to the United States who originally trained as a physicist before turning to anthropology. Sometimes called the founder of American anthropology, Boas founded the anthropology program at Columbia University, the first PhD-granting anthropology program in the country. He challenged both the unilinear and diffusionist theories, arguing that they relied on speculation and circular reasoning rather than careful data collection.[14]

His theory of independent cultural adaptation, which came to be called *historical particularism*, argued that each culture is a unique representation of its history and context. Boas and his students, such as Alfred Kroeber (1876–1960), Ruth Benedict (1887–1948), and Margaret Mead (1901–78), stressed the historical, context-specific, and environmentally responsive aspects of cultural development, amassing large amounts of ethnographic data through long-term fieldwork to support their conclusions. Their work is sometimes referred to as "salvage anthropology," because these anthropolo-

13. This is not to say that Morgan drew on Marx's writings. In fact, Marx's colleague and collaborator, Friedrich Engels, used Morgan's writings in an explanation of the development of family. The work of Morgan and other unilinear evolutionists expressed similar theoretical presuppositions and arguments about human life. See Lewis Henry Morgan, *Ancient Society* (1877; repr., Cambridge, MA: Belknap Press of Harvard University Press, 1964).

14. Franz Boas, *Race, Language, and Culture* (New York: Macmillan, 1940).

gists were preserving as much cultural knowledge as possible at a time when indigenous cultures, especially in North America, were either dying out or becoming assimilated. Some have argued that Boasian anthropology is actually "atheoretical" (that is, without theory), since it emphasizes specificity over generality, but following Durkheim, Boas believed cultures could be studied scientifically. Though he and his students were suspicious of generalized theories of human cultural development, Boas believed that by collecting enough ethnographic data, patterns would emerge, leading to law-like (nomothetic) explanations of social life.

British anthropologists in the early twentieth century likewise began rejecting unilinear and diffusionist approaches as ethnographic data began to contradict the hierarchical underpinnings of these views. Bronislaw Malinowski (1884–1942), a Polish ethnologist who later taught at the London School of Economics, became a prominent figure in the development of anthropology when he argued that rather than viewing the cultural traits of non-Western people as undeveloped, they should be seen as adapted to the needs of the environment. Malinowski became stranded in the British-controlled South Pacific when, during a trip there, the outbreak of World War I made him an "enemy combatant." Unable to leave, he spent several years in the islands, learning the language and becoming intimately acquainted with the lives of the people there. His first book, *Argonauts of the Western Pacific*, became a classic due to its extraordinary level of detail and almost storybook quality.[15]

Functionalism, the theory that emerged from this research, argues that culture develops in response to human needs. Malinowski came to believe that all the diverse customs and behaviors of cultures around the world served a function, meeting people's need for food, comforts, reproduction, safety, relaxation, movement, and growth. Rather than viewing band and tribe societies as irrational, underdeveloped, or primitive, and industrialized societies as advanced or civilized, all cultures could be understood in terms of how they meet human needs.

Alfred Radcliffe-Brown (1881–1955), a colleague of Malinowski, advanced a similar theory. Radcliffe-Brown, however, drew more heavily on the work of Durkheimian theory, emphasizing the life of the society over the individual.[16] Radcliffe-Brown's early work among the Andaman islanders far off the coast of Thailand employed ethnographic data to demonstrate how the cultural traits deemed primitive by evolutionists and diffusionists preserved the cohesion of social order. His theory, *structural-functionalism*, stipulated that

15. Bronislaw Malinowski, *Argonauts of the Western Pacific: An Account of Native Enterprise and Adventure in the Archipelagoes of Melanesian New Guinea* (New York: Routledge & Sons, 1922).

16. Alfred Radcliffe-Brown, *The Andaman Islanders* (1922; repr., New York: Free Press, 1964).

the functions of particular beliefs or behaviors should not be understood as meeting individual needs but as supporting a social need for order and cohesion.

Both the Boasians in the United States and the functionalists and structural-functionalists of Britain pushed anthropologists to emphasize ethnographic fieldwork and the collection of empirical data to support conclusions and theory. Original fieldwork became the standard for becoming an anthropologist; no longer could an anthropologist base his or her research on travelogues, missionary letters, or secondhand information. The emphasis on society in British anthropology, and culture in U.S. anthropology, however, became a strong division between the two. British scholars believed the U.S. emphasis on culture undermined the status of the discipline as a science by emphasizing an immaterial quality (culture) over the concrete (society). U.S. researchers, however, saw their work as scientific because it relied on ethnographic data to document and interpret culture.

In the second half of the twentieth century, division continued between anthropology as a science in search of nomothetic explanations versus a process of interpretation and cultural understanding. In early anthropology, this was a division between U.S. and British approaches. Later in the twentieth century, it became a division between materialist and biological theories on the one hand, and multivariate, interpretive theories on the other.

Positivist Anthropology: Materialism and Structuralism

In the United States, Boas and his students worked to discredit evolutionary and racist views of cultural hierarchy and change. The questions behind those theories remained important, however, such as why certain cultural traits exist, how cultures change over time, and whether processes of change are unique to each culture or common to all. Some anthropologists pursued these questions with a *positivist* approach, seeking universal, nomothetic explanations based on empirical evidence. One branch of positivist anthropology includes materialist theories such as cultural ecology, cultural materialism, and sociobiology. Another branch of positivist anthropology includes structuralism.

Cultural ecology teaches that culture can be understood in terms of how people adapt to and interact with the natural environment. Leslie White (1900–1975) drew on the work of Karl Marx to argue that cultures change as people develop technologies to capture energy from the environment more efficiently.[17] His contemporary, Julian Steward (1902–72), disagreed that these developments are universal stages but concurred with the theory that ma-

17. Leslie White, *The Evolution of Culture: The Development of Civilization to the Fall of Rome* (New York: McGraw-Hill, 1959).

Thomas Headland has used biometric data, environmental and ecological studies, and culture in understanding the relationship of Agta culture to environment in over forty years of research in the Philippines. Here he is measuring the height of an Agta woman in 1994.
Photo: Thomas Headland

terial life is the basis for cultural change.[18] Their work contributed to the development of cultural ecological theory, an approach that emphasizes how human interaction with the material environment (i.e., human ecology) drives cultural change.

Later anthropologists developed the overall perspective of cultural ecology into more specific theories including cultural materialism and sociobiology. *Cultural materialism* theorizes that culture is driven by the material, ecological, and economic adaptations humans make. Marvin Harris (1927–2001) argued that humans use an unconscious cost-benefit analysis to adapt cultural beliefs toward economically rational ends.[19] These adaptations could survive beyond their usefulness, in some cases, but understanding cultural traits and culture change should be derived from an understanding of how behaviors, beliefs, and institutions benefit (or benefited) people in basic material ways (see the example of the "sacred cow" in chap. 9).

Sociobiology is a theory that takes materialist explanations of culture to an extreme. *Sociobiology* teaches that culture is rooted in the human drive for evolutionary advantage and genetic survival. For example, sociobiologists have argued that women are more selective about sexual partners and enforce monogamy because they have a limited number of ova (eggs) for use in repro-

18. Julian Steward, *Theory of Culture Change: The Methodology of Multilinear Evolution* (Urbana, IL: University of Illinois Press, 1955).

19. Marvin Harris, *Cows, Pigs, Wars, and Witches: The Riddles of Culture* (New York: Random House, 1974).

ducing. Since men can ordinarily produce sperm throughout their lives, they gain reproductive advantage by having as many sexual partners as possible, making them prone to infidelity and proponents of polygyny. Ethnographic data have been used to support this idea, although strong sociobiological accounts of human sexual decision making can be contradicted by other ethnographic examples. Moreover, while this theory works to explain some sexual behavior or gender stereotypes, it is often less helpful for addressing questions of religious practices, political conflict, or cultural change.[20]

Structuralism is a positivist theory that links the material to the cultural in a different way. *Structuralism teaches that human biology, specifically brain structure, drives culture.* Working from the linguistic approach of Ferdinand de Saussure (chap. 3), anthropologist Claude Levi-Strauss (1908–2009) believed that the human brain is structured by rules of opposition.[21] Language, with its orderly rules, is one manifestation of this biologically based human tendency to structure life in oppositions such as cold and hot, raw and cooked, or nature and culture. Culture, he argued, reflects this structuring in all cultural forms from kinship terminology and political systems to mythology and religion.

Good

Structuralism was enormously influential in the 1960s and found an eager audience in other disciplines. Historians, literary scholars, and sociologists appreciated the power of structuralist explanations to make subjective analysis more objective and scientific. Structuralists in every field argued that myths, works of art, literature, and more could now be studied with scientific rigor by uncovering and mapping the structure that could be found within.

There are significant differences between cultural ecology, cultural materialism, sociobiology, and structuralism, but all of these positivist approaches to anthropology work from the idea of naturalism. *Naturalism is the belief that all that exists are the natural phenomena that can be touched, seen, or otherwise physically experienced.* Although naturalism does not view religion or the supernatural world as real in and of itself (religion is often interpreted as just an expression or after-effect of natural phenomena), Christian scientists often work fruitfully within naturalistic scientific paradigms. Christian sociologist Peter Berger says that social scientists—even Christian ones—should employ "methodological atheism."[22] That is, even though the researcher is

---

20. For an example of sociobiology, see Edward O. Wilson, *Sociobiology: The New Synthesis* (Cambridge, MA: Belknap Press of Harvard University Press, 1975). Within cultural anthropology, the field of evolutionary psychology has adapted many of the insights of sociobiology to questions of culture. This approach has drawn many adherents and critics in cultural anthropology. See Jerome Barkow, Leda Cosmides, and John Tooby, eds., *The Adapted Mind: Evolutionary Psychology and the Generation of Culture* (New York: Oxford University Press, 1992).

21. For an example of ethnographic data interpreted with structuralist theory, see Claude Levi-Strauss, *Tristes Tropiques* (New York: Atheneum, 1974).

22. Peter Berger, *The Sacred Canopy: Elements of a Sociological Theory of Religion* (Garden City, NY: Doubleday, 1967), 100.

committed to a belief in God, the research should be done in such a way as to assume natural laws and material phenomena are all that exist in a given context. This approach asserts that, given a consistent method, any researcher should come to the same conclusion as any other.

Many anthropologists conduct research with positivist approaches. However, beginning in the mid-1960s, other anthropologists encouraged a shift away from positivism, naturalism, and nomothetic explanations in favor of interpretive, symbolic, and idiographic explanations.

Symbolic Anthropology

Symbolic anthropology (also called *interpretive anthropology*) views culture as a system of symbols that people create, alter, and share with each other. In contrast to the Durkheimian and Marxist approaches to anthropological theory that stressed the scientific method and universality of analysis, anthropologists taking up Weber's emphasis on ideas and multicausality opened the door for new approaches. Interpretive anthropology focuses on understanding the symbolic worlds of others and describing them in depth minimizing the importance of constructing generalized theories of culture and culture change.

Clifford Geertz (1926–2006) was arguably the most influential scholar in promoting interpretive or symbolic analysis as the overall agenda for anthropology as a discipline. Specifically invoking the multicausal and idea-oriented (as opposed to economics or material-oriented) social theory of Max Weber, Geertz urged anthropologists to move away from efforts to explain and predict, turning toward description and interpretation. Geertz's work has been called "dramaturgical" because he saw human social life as akin to a drama in which people take roles and play parts on the cultural "stage." His work has also been classified as semiotic analysis, focusing on the signs—or meanings—people give to elements of the world around them.[23]

Mary Douglas (1921–2007) was another important symbolic anthropologist.[24] A devout Catholic, Douglas famously analyzed Old Testament purity laws in terms of how classifying particular things "clean" and "unclean" served to organize society rather than to reflect anything inherent in the object itself. She built on Durkheim's view of society as an integrated whole, but unlike those who emphasized social institutions and practices as key to social order, Douglas focused on the ways symbolic meanings of objects and actions served this role. In the United States, another Catholic anthropologist, Victor Turner

23. Clifford Geertz, *Local Knowledge: Further Essays in Interpretive Anthropology* (New York: Basic Books, 1983).

24. Mary Douglas, *Implicit Meanings: Essays in Anthropology* (London; Boston: Routledge & Paul, 1975).

(1920–83), engaged in similar analysis, analyzing social dramas in which actions and objects were given particular meanings for the sake of social order.[25]

Sherry Ortner (b. 1941), an anthropologist who has written on the development of theory in the latter half of the twentieth century, points to three significant movements in cultural theory during the emergence of symbolic anthropology.[26] First, "the power shift." As anthropologists began highlighting gender, ethnicity, race, and class as social constructions of inequality, they became aware of the need to account for the ways dynamics of social control—power—were integrated into cultural contexts, cultural change, and even ethnographic representation itself. Second, "the historic turn" was a new emphasis on the importance of history in revealing how people's understandings and symbols change over time. Third, the "reinterpretation(s) of culture" refers to a foundational rethinking of the culture concept as anthropologists and others wrestled with the rapidly changing, globalizing, and extraordinarily heterogeneous cultural worlds in which most people live today. These three shifts brought in new theoretical approaches that no longer rested on the modernist belief that human reason and scientific method alone could lead to adequate understandings of the world.

Postmodern Anthropological Theory

Postmodern theory is an umbrella term for theories built on the premise that positivist or so-called objective views of human phenomena are inherently limited, and that they are therefore not unbiased in the ways proponents believe them to be. Anthropologists generally were early adopters of postmodern approaches to cultural analysis, due in part to a long-standing awareness of the pervasive influence of culture on human knowledge. By bringing questions of power, history, and the culture concept itself into the center of anthropological analysis, many anthropologists moved away from nomothetic explanations. Postmodernism is an expansive concept that takes on different meanings in different disciplines, but postmodern approaches in anthropology are arguably rooted in Geertz's call for anthropologists to redirect their attention from cultural explanation to cultural explication. Three important strands of postmodern theory in cultural anthropology include cultural Marxism, feminism, and perspectivalism.

Cultural Marxism (also called *Marxian theory*) draws on Karl Marx's concepts of power, inequality, and class struggle to understand cultural change. Cultural marxists analyze all forms of social inequality, including economic disparity, and also inequality in social status, the oppression of women, the

25. Victor Turner, *The Anthropology of Experience* (Urbana, IL: University of Illinois Press, 1986).

26. Sherry Ortner, *Anthropology and Social Theory: Culture, Power, and the Acting Subject* (Durham, NC: Duke University Press, 2006), 3–5.

domination of particular ethnic groups, and so forth. Here the lowercase "m" indicates these anthropologists are not necessarily Marxist in their politics or overall view of history. Instead, they rely on Marx's foundational insights about social structure and culture change to interpret social inequality in the contemporary world. While this distinction is sometimes made, it should be noted that lower and uppercase derivatives of the name Marx are generally interchangeable in an anthropological context.

Feminist theory highlights the importance of gender as an analytic concept and the importance of including women's presence in cultural analysis (see chap. 5). Most anthropologists who use feminist theory are also feminist in their personal values, but feminism as a political stance or a social identity is different from feminist theory as a scientific paradigm. Feminist theory says that gender categories are important to describe and analyze in ethnographic research and/or that women's points of view and experiences should be equally represented in ethnographic accounts. A great deal of ethnographic research assumed that men's experiences represented the whole.[27] Moreover, it was assumed that a man doing ethnographic fieldwork would have the same access, interpretation, and understanding as a woman fieldworker.

Feminist anthropologists were some of the first to emphasize the importance of recognizing power and privilege, not only within the society being studied, but also between the anthropologist, his or her subject, and the reader of an ethnography. Researchers began focusing more intentionally on the experiences of women in the societies they studied. They understood that inequality and differences in social power often mean that men and women do not have the same perspective or experience, even within the same society. They also contributed to the "historic turn" by highlighting the place of gender relationships in history and pointing out how the telling of history often places men's experiences and men's language as central to cultural narratives.

In this way, feminists were among the first to argue that anthropological research itself is always positioned, meaning that the identity, background, and experiences of the researcher are relevant to conclusions and analysis being made.

Perspectivalism is an anthropological theory that highlights the positionality of knowledge. Also known as *standpoint theory*, this view states that knowledge is generated by a knower who is positioned in a particular place and time, and therefore reflects a specific and limited perspective. Objective knowledge—conceived as knowledge that is complete and unrelated to the identity of the knower—is not possible. Perspectivalism is a theory in other disciplines as well, such as philosophy, literature, and sociology. Within anthropology, it has led some to experiment with the form and purpose of

27. See, for example, Annette Weiner, *Women of Value, Men of Renown: New Perspectives in Trobriand Exchange* (Austin: University of Texas Press, 1983).

Engaging Anthropological Theory as a Christian

My (Jenell's) fieldwork among low-income African Americans in Washington, D.C., was motivated by my Christian faith. Asking the question, "Who is my neighbor?" led me to study how neighborhoods form over time, and how people (who, during fieldwork, became my neighbors) organize to improve the place they call home. My faith also enlivened my fieldwork and girded my ethical practice, helping me to become a compassionate listener in interviews and even a practical helper, cleaning up after community meetings, babysitting for informants, and sharing meals and celebrations with neighbors.

When it came to theory, however, I faced some problems. How could a Christian anthropologist rely on theories grounded in Marxism, feminism, or postmodernism? I first compared Christian doctrine and Scripture with secular anthropology theories. I evaluated anthropological theories in terms of how "Christian" they were—that is, in what ways they harmonized with or diverged from Christian understandings. This approach was mistaken. First, I was comparing apples and oranges. Christianity is a living way of life, not a static philosophy or theory that can be neatly compared with modern scientific theories. Second, I had too keen an eye for difference, highlighting ways in which anthropological theories failed to be Christian. This maximized antagonism, when what I really needed was a way for my faith and my anthropology to collaborate harmoniously.

In the end, I relied on Marxian theory to analyze my data. Marxian theory emphasizes social conflict—ways in which modern capitalism sorts people into social classes and how social class influences all parts of life. Marxian theory certainly doesn't affirm Scripture or promote Christianity, but its detailed approach to understanding injustice helps me—as a white, middle-class, North American woman—live as a good neighbor in a world divided by class, race, ethnicity, and other social statuses. At times, Marxian theory offends my faith, such as its tendency to denigrate the privileged social classes or its view of religion as merely a byproduct of economics. At those times, whether in a classroom or in writing, I can assert my point of view in ways that can potentially shape the development of theory. Discussing and adapting theory is an essential part of developing the discipline.

I once thought that comparing Christianity with secular theories in a way that ultimately crowned Christianity the victor was a way of promoting the faith. Now I see it as a competitive, even arrogant approach that really diminishes the faith by reducing it to a philosophy and using it in ways that are not humble, kind, or other-centered. Relying on Marxian theory to interpret data allowed me to build an anthropological argument that was acceptable in the discipline, instructed me in detailed analysis of social systems, and harmonized with my Christian values of neighborliness and care for others.

ethnography. In the mid-1980s, James Clifford and George Marcus published a collection of essays questioning what it means to "write culture."[28] Advocating experimental forms of ethnographic representation, they suggested that traditional anthropological research obscured the voices of those being represented, necessarily misrepresenting or adding layers of interpretation between the reader and subject. All ethnographic knowledge, Clifford and Marcus argued, is partial knowledge and must be represented as such.

Perspectivalism has influenced cultural anthropology by increasing reflexivity in ethnographic writing. *Reflexivity* is the inclusion of the anthropologist's

28. James Clifford and George Marcus, *Writing Culture: The Poetics and Politics of Ethnography* (Urbana, IL: University of Illinois Press, 1986).

perspective and experience in ethnographic writing. By including first-person narrative of the experiences, feelings, and responses of the ethnographer, along with the ethnographic data, the reader is better able to assess the role of the ethnographer in the generation and presentation of data. Postmodern anthropologists do not attempt to tell the whole truth or the objective truth about their subject; they would say this is not possible. Instead, they strive for comprehensive, ethical research presented in a way that allows the reader to understand the perspective of the researcher as well as the data.

Some fear that the abandonment of objectivity removes any capacity to assess the validity of research. While some philosophers have certainly made this case, postmodern anthropologists argue that, first, by attending to standards of reflexivity, ethnographic detail, and methodology, readers may evaluate anthropological analysis. Secondly, the attention to comprehensive analysis, as opposed to objectivity, makes the role of theory even more important. Strong cultural anthropology is that which speaks to key anthropological questions in particular areas—How do concepts of time change for people who move from farm labor to factory work? What sorts of alliances and communities form among residents of squatter settlements in the slums of megacities? How do Muslim men in the United States address the issues of marriage, gender, and family as a consequence of living as religious minorities in a non-Islamic country?—in terms of explicit theories of culture, culture change, identity, personhood, and agency.

Postmodernism often has a negative ring to Christian ears, since some versions of postmodernism deny the existence or accessibility of truth. At the same time, many aspects of postmodern thinking have proven helpful for Christians, and particularly for Christian anthropologists, who see the importance of acknowledging perspective and highlighting social inequality in analysis.

Symbolic anthropology and postmodern theory provide a new way to understand culture change and power dynamics, but seem to some to be limited and impervious to generalities. Functionalist, structural-functionalist, and structuralist explanations of culture are comprehensive and scientific, but often seem less able to make sense of innovation, cultural change, and human agency. Ecological, materialist, and other positivist approaches frequently produce predictive measures and falsifiable studies, while at the same time are also critiqued for ignoring agency, inequality, and power. Dialogue continues today about positivist and symbolic approaches to anthropology, both of which are vibrant.

Christians Engaging Anthropological Theory

Some Christians, such as those studying the nutritional provisions of rain forest–dwellers in the Philippines or the changes in economic life spurred by new techniques of pottery production in southern Mexico, have found little intersection between their Christian commitments and the theories guiding their scientific anthropological research. Others, such as my (Brian's) research on Protestants in the Philippines and short-term mission trips, or my (Jenell's) research on identities of race, gender, and sexuality, find anthropological theory to be a major arena for considering the intersection of Christian faith and categories of cultural theory. All professional anthropologists, regardless of research or scholarly focus find themselves part of a larger anthropological community in which colleagues are asking vital questions about the meaning of human life, acceptable research ethics, human nature, and the assumptions anthropologists may hold about the nature of reality. Every Christian in anthropology must consider the relationship of faith and theoretical perspectives in the discipline.

Anthropologist Eloise Hiebert Meneses studies low-caste market women in India and also writes about anthropological theory. She argues that Christianity and anthropology are two distinct viewpoints, each of which calls for ultimate commitment.[29] She describes anthropology as foundationally committed to atheism, naturalism, and evolution, all three of which are incompatible with Christian truth. She argues against attempts to harmonize, integrate, or amalgamate Christianity and anthropology as if they are equals. One must be subordinate to the other, and in her view, Christianity deserves ultimate commitment. Anthropology should be taken as a secondary commitment that may be appropriated for Christian purposes. In line with her perspective, Hiebert Meneses has developed explicitly Christian theories of culture that guide her ethnographic analysis.[30]

In contrast, anthropologist and missiologist Robert Priest argues for the inclusion of Christian perspectives in anthropological theory and approaches to knowledge.[31] He uses symbolic anthropology to describe the place of Christian perspectives in cultural anthropology, asserting that despite the openness of the postmodern climate to all perspectives, Christianity is too often marginalized and maligned. He presses postmodern anthropologists toward consistency, arguing that Christian perspectives should be given the same respectful attention that views from other religious, ethnic, political, and ideological perspectives receive.[32]

29. Eloise Hiebert Meneses, "No Other Foundation: Establishing a Christian Anthropology," *Christian Scholar's Review* 29, no. 3 (2000): 531–49.

30. Eloise Hiebert Meneses, "Faithful Witness: A Postcritical Epistemology for Christians," *Direction Journal* 36, no. 2 (2007): 129–43.

31. Robert J. Priest, "Missionary Positions: Christian, Modernist, Postmodernist," *Current Anthropology* 42, no. 1 (2001): 29–68.

32. For a related argument, see also Brian M. Howell, "The Repugnant Cultural Other Speaks Back: Christian Identity as Ethnographic 'Standpoint,'" *Anthropological Theory* 7, no. 4 (2007): 371–91.

Christians employ every sort of theory in anthropology, from materialist and ecological approaches, to feminist, cultural marxist, and other postmodern theories. Theory in anthropology, like theory in science generally, provides a way to understand data, whether symbolic, material, or historical. For Christians, the various theoretical approaches can aid in understanding the data without contradicting or erasing faith commitments.

Terms

cultural ecology: an anthropological theory that teaches that culture can be understood in terms of how people adapt to and interact with the natural environment.

cultural Marxism (also called *Marxian theory*): a postmodern theory that draws on Karl Marx's concepts of power, inequality, and class struggle to understand cultural change.

cultural materialism: a theory that understands culture as driven by the material, ecological, and economic adaptations humans make.

cultural traits: cultural artifacts or activities.

diffusionism: an early anthropological theory stating that cultural traits spread from more advanced to less advanced societies.

falsification: the view that scientific theories cannot be proven, only falsified.

feminist theory: a contemporary theory that highlights the importance of gender as an analytic concept and the importance of including women's presence in cultural analysis.

functionalism: an early anthropological theory that says culture develops in response to human needs.

historical particularism: an early anthropological theory that argues that each culture is a unique representation of its history and context.

idiographic explanation: a rich description of a particular case.

naturalism: a belief that all that exists are the natural phenomena that can be touched, seen, or otherwise physically experienced.

nomothetic explanation: a generalization, a natural law that predicts and explains culture change and human behavior.

perspectivalism (or *standpoint theory*): an anthropological theory that highlights the positionality of knowledge; that is, knowledge is generated by a knower who is positioned in a particular place and time and who reflects a specific and limited perspective.

positivism: an approach to anthropology that involves seeking universal, nomothetic explanations based on empirical evidence.

postmodern theory: an umbrella term for theories built on the premise that positivist or so-called objective views of human phenomena are inherently limited, and that they are therefore not unbiased in the ways proponents believe them to be.

reflexivity: the inclusion of the anthropologist's perspective and experience in ethnographic writing.

sociobiology: an anthropological theory that teaches that culture is rooted in the human drive for evolutionary advantage and genetic survival.

structural-functionalism: an early anthropological theory that says the functions of particular beliefs or behaviors may be understood in terms of their support of social order and cohesion.

structuralism: an anthropological theory that teaches that human biology, specifically brain structure, drives culture.

symbolic anthropology (also called *interpretive anthropology*): an approach to anthropology that views culture as a system of symbols that people create, alter, and share with each other.

theory: a formal description of some phenomenon in the world that explains how that thing works.

unilinear cultural evolution: an early anthropological theory that states all cultures evolve from simple to complex along a single trajectory of progress.

Devotion 1

Communion as a Symbol

After taking the cup, he [Jesus] gave thanks and said, "Take this and divide it among you. For I tell you I will not drink again of the fruit of the vine until the kingdom of God comes." And he took bread, gave thanks and broke it, and gave it to them, saying, "This is my body given for you; do this in remembrance of me." (Luke 22:17–19)

Before he was crucified, Jesus shared a last meal with his disciples. He gave them wine and bread and told them to repeat this ritual in remembrance of him. Ever since, Christians have shared the cup and the bread with each other in the ritual of communion.

Christians disagree about what communion means on a spiritual level. Some believe it is a sacrament that delivers grace to the believer, and others believe it is only a symbol of Christ's sacrifice for us. Some believe the bread and wine are actually transformed into the body and blood of Jesus, and others believe the bread and wine are just bread and wine.

Symbolic anthropologists would analyze communion as a social drama in which people use symbols to communicate important truths. The bread and wine are symbols of Jesus's life and death, used in a religious ritual that is important to Christians of all times and places. The words used in prayer and in the story of the Last Supper are linguistic symbols that give meaning to the ritual. In anthropological perspective, communion is a social drama that uses symbols to strengthen the solidarity of the group and promote a social order. Perhaps Jesus gave us this ritual, knowing that while Christians would have different theological understandings, by participating in the ritual together, we would become more unified in him. Thus, despite theological disagreements, Christians may agree that communion serves a cultural function that is important for the strength of the church as the body of Christ.

Devotion 2

Injustice and Theory

For scoundrels are found among my people; they take over the goods of others. Like fowlers they set a trap; they catch human beings. Like a cage full of birds, their houses are full of treachery; therefore they have become great and rich, they have grown fat and sleek. They know no limits in deeds of wickedness; they do not judge with justice the cause of the orphan, to make it prosper, and they do not defend the rights of the needy. (Jer. 5:26–28 NRSV)

The prophet Jeremiah describes God's anger toward the Israelites, predicting downfall and exile. This passage describes Israel's society as marked by inequality and injustice. Some people are very wealthy, and they ignore those who are poor. Some even entrap and exploit the poor. The most vulnerable members of society are not cared for, not even in public institutions devoted to justice.

If an anthropologist could do fieldwork among the Israelites at this time, she or he might rely on different theories to analyze the culture. Cultural materialism could help explain why social stratification had reached such an extreme point and would look for environmental and ecological factors that shaped social organization. Structural-functionalism could help explain how injustice stabilized society. Extremes of wealth and exploitation of the poor is wrong and unpleasant, but it can keep everyone in their places and preserve order. Feminist theory could raise questions about gender: maybe the female orphans are treated differently than the male orphans, or maybe the human beings caught in traps for exploitation and theft are mostly male, or mostly female.

Prophetic writings inspire Christians today to address injustice and inequality in their own nations and around the world. Yet even Christians working against injustice can do more harm than good when lacking an understanding of how social problems link to other aspects of social life and culture. Anthropological theory can enrich our understanding of how injustice becomes embedded in a culture and how it can be changed, thereby helping a believer change the world with knowledge and strategy. As the writer of Proverbs taught, "It is not good to have zeal without knowledge" (Prov. 19:2).

12

Anthropology in Action

After studying this chapter, you should be able to:

1. Articulate the relevance of anthropology for Christian life.
2. Describe multiple applications of anthropology to work and service situations.
3. Express the importance of anthropology to the global church.
4. Describe some of the historic and contemporary connections between anthropology and missions.

Introduction

For the rest of their lives, people who took a single anthropology course in college often remember it as one of the most interesting. They may remember their professor's particular interest in Yąnomamö violence, or Melanesian museum curation, or Mexican medicinal plants. Anthropology is interesting, to be sure, but its importance is much greater than random knowledge of distant places. Whether students are studying anthropology for a major, general education, part of a seminary program, or elective credit, they need a clear vision of why anthropology is important and how it can benefit their lives.

Often, even after someone discovers anthropology, engages the questions and methods, and studies deeply, the question remains: *what can I do with this?* This question plagues many areas of academic study. What can someone do with a major in philosophy besides be a philosopher? What good is the study of history when it comes time to find a job? But students who pursue anthropology often face the double hurdle of first explaining to others what anthropology is, and then trying to figure out what they might do with it. The fact is, like these other seemingly impractical fields of study, anthropology provides critical skills and perspectives for virtually any path a person chooses to follow.[1] Anthropology is unique, however, in being centered on diversity, culture, and human difference. For this reason, anthropology has relevance for everyone and particularly for Christians.

Many Christian colleges and seminaries offer anthropology as part of a missions studies program. The connection of cultural anthropology with cross-cultural missions is valuable; we hope every missionary preparation program includes anthropology! The vast majority of Christians, however, will not find a calling in cross-cultural missions but will spend their lives invested in everyday activities such as working a job, raising a family, caring for elderly parents, volunteering in a local church, and living out their Christian witness in a context similar to the one in which they were raised. What does anthropology offer them?

This chapter addresses the basic question, "What difference does anthropology make?" First, we describe anthropology's benefit to job seekers and college graduates. Then, we explore anthropology's usefulness in everyday life. Third, we consider the global church and discuss how anthropology contributes to the ability of Christians to engage what has always been a cross-cultural faith. Finally, we engage the intersections of anthropology, ministry, and missions, particularly in terms of new paradigms of mission in the church today.

Anthropology at Work

It may not seem that knowledge of pastoralism (chap. 6) or the ability to distinguish patrilineality from matrilineality (chap. 8) would relate to a job working in electrical engineering or nursing, yet these jobs, and most others, involve working with people. Anthropology is fundamentally about people, how they see the world, and why they do what they do. Most students of anthropology, at both the undergraduate and graduate levels, work outside the academy, applying their research methods and understandings of culture to a wide range of professional concerns.

1. The American Anthropological Association (www.aaanet.org) has two career DVDs: *Anthropology: Real People, Real Careers* (Washington, DC: American Anthropological Association, 2006), and *Beyond Ethnography: Corporate and Design Anthropology* (Washington, DC: American Anthropological Association, 2008).

The electrical engineer may need to determine how a particular product—say, a cell phone—should work. Which features will be most important for people? What sort of shape will be most appealing? Ken Banks, a development expert with an undergraduate major in anthropology, tells the story of how anthropologists working for mobile phone companies used participant observation to better understand how people in various developing nations use phones. Ideas such as putting a flashlight on the phone, or enabling the phone to have multiple electronic phone books so that several users can share it came directly out of ethnographic studies of daily life in these communities. Corporations from Intel to Xerox have employed people with anthropological training to figure out aspects of social life and behavior that remain invisible to other methods of study. While some might sit back within the four walls of an office, working out product design or marketing strategies, trying to anticipate all the relevant issues or possibilities among potential consumers, "an anthropologist would immerse themselves in the subject and try to understand it from 'within.'"[2]

This willingness and ability to look at circumstances from "within" sets the anthropologically minded person apart. Ethnographic journalist Anne Fadiman chronicled a heart-wrenching series of cultural misunderstandings and mistakes in her book *The Spirit Catches You and You Fall Down*.[3] She described a situation in which medical professionals in Merced, California, misinterpreted the responses of a Hmong family regarding their daughter's treatment for epilepsy. Fadiman did fieldwork in this community of Southeast Asian immigrants about which most U.S. Americans know very little, and found that their reluctance to trust medical care, their unwillingness to obey all the physicians' medical orders, and other seemingly irrational behavior made sense when seen in terms of Hmong history, society, and culture. She discovered how the actions interpreted by the medical community as "noncompliance" and even child abuse were rooted in the parents' deep and profound love for their daughter and their commitment to her well-being, expressed through their cultural norms and understandings.

Fadiman also considered the views of the physicians and medical staff who cared for the little girl. Seeing their world from within, she chronicled how virtually all of them desperately wanted what was best for the patient. For the most part, they performed their jobs with distinction and tried hard to do what they felt was right for their patient. She also saw how their training, the institutional contexts in which they worked, and their deeply held cultural assumptions made it very difficult for most of them to understand or

2. Ken Banks, "Anthropology's Technology-Driven Renaissance," *PC World Magazine*, July 17, 2008, www.pcworld.com/businesscenter/article/148564/anthropologys_technologydriven_renaissance.html (accessed June 5, 2009).

3. Anne Fadiman, *The Spirit Catches You and You Fall Down: A Hmong Child, Her American Doctors, and the Collision of Two Cultures* (New York: Farrar, Straus & Giroux, 1997).

Anthropology and Academics

Most anthropology students do not become professors of anthropology, but some do. Christians who pursue doctoral study in anthropology follow a variety of paths toward meaningful service and careers.

Some Christian anthropologists do basic research and teach in secular universities and colleges. Others teach in Christian colleges, universities, seminaries, and missions training schools. Many of these anthropologists choose religion as their primary area for research. For instance, I (Brian) studied how Philippine Christians interpret and practice their Southern Baptist faith in light of the particular local context in which they live. Others, including me (Jenell), study nonreligious dimensions of culture, such as political activism among African American women.

Many Christian anthropologists apply anthropology to solving contemporary social problems. Some devote their careers to international development or the alleviation of poverty. Others work in missions, as missionaries or teachers. Anthropology is especially useful in missions work related to Bible translation, language preservation, development, and church planting. Some missionary anthropologists develop dual-track careers. One track involves their missions work, and the other includes ethnographic research and publishing in the secular academy. Thomas Headland, for example, spent years researching and doing missions among the Agta of the Philippines. His work is important to the Agta themselves and to his organization (SIL International), and his ethnographic writings are important to secular anthropologists who study hunter-gatherers, tropical forests, the Agta, or upland minority groups elsewhere in the world.

The Network of Christian Anthropologists is a group that connects Christian anthropologists in collegial relationships and spiritual support. The Network meets annually at the American Anthropological Association meetings, and members communicate throughout the year on a listserv and Facebook page. The Network provides a valuable forum for discussing anthropological issues with Christian perspectives.[1]

1. Information about fishnet, the listserv for Christian anthropologists, is at https://lists.bethel.edu/mailman/listinfo/fishnet. The Facebook group is called "Network of Christian Anthropologists."

have compassion toward a family that seemed to be undermining their best efforts to treat the patient. Their inability to listen to and trust the judgment of those who knew the patient best, the parents, eventually undermined much of their good medical work.

In the story, a few social workers and physicians with anthropological instincts intervened when they began to perceive the grave consequences of cultural misunderstandings. Unfortunately, too few of those involved had such insight. At many points, a nurse or physician with anthropological training might have asked a key question, worked with the family differently, or anticipated a misunderstanding that could have prevented the tragic outcome. Had someone in the Hmong family studied anthropology, that person might have been better able to consider the perspective of the medical personnel, or explain the traditions and assumptions of the Hmong community, rather than becoming fearful or hostile in the face of what appeared, to the Hmong parents, to be illogical or irrational medical advice.

Cultural relativism—the anthropological tenet that people's ideas and behaviors make sense when viewed from their culture's perspective—benefits virtually every occupation, calling, or context.

Adam Kis applies anthropology as country director for a relief agency in Central Africa. Here he conducts ethnographic interviews in Malawi.
Photo: Adam Kis

Anthropology in Everyday Life

Graduates who studied anthropology often report that, in addition to career and service, anthropology shaped them in ways beneficial to their everyday lives. One anthropology major from Bethel University in Minnesota later became a father, and his daughter developed autism. He used his basic linguistics knowledge to teach himself to listen to her attempts to speak and to communicate better with her. He used a fieldwork approach in his relationship with his daughter, trying to see the world from her perspective rather than simply judging or misunderstanding her based on his nonautistic perspective. He says that though he chose anthropology based upon its potential for public service and career, he's much more grateful for how anthropology shaped him as a father.

Fieldwork skills, anthropological values, and knowledge of theory are practically useful in many ways in everyday life. A married couple may analyze their own culture, questioning how they've been shaped by cultural expectations for romance and intimacy. Parents who are mystified by their child's behavior might use anthropological sensibilities to investigate the school, playgroup, or social networks in which their child participates. Neighbors who cannot understand why the people across the street eat, socialize, or speak as they do might first pursue a fuller perspective in the cultural or social background. This does not mean that every problem has a solution found in ethnographic analysis, but beginning with a posture of cultural relativism may provide insight not otherwise available. Seemingly irrational behavior may have a meaning or purpose that can be understood when viewed from the "insider's" point of view; this opens up possibilities for communication and understanding that might otherwise be lost.

Anthropology in Ministry

Anyone planning to be in ministry, whether as a professional or lay leader, will undoubtedly have the challenge and opportunity to minister in diverse contexts. The church is more complex today than ever before. In addition to denominational divisions (Methodists, Lutherans, Presbyterians of various sorts, etc.), associational differences (e.g., various Baptists or Congregationalists), and nondenominational congregations, virtually every community with a significant Christian presence has a variety of worship styles, organizational forms, and even ethnic constituencies. The United States and other countries with traditions of immigration such as Brazil, Australia, Canada, and the United Kingdom have congregations speaking Spanish, Thai, Haitian Creole, and many other languages; these congregations are often among the fastest-growing churches. This diversity adds to that of long-established Christian communities oriented toward specific racial majorities and minorities.

It is not enough for Christians to be well intentioned when working to build bridges between culturally diverse believers. In the absence of skills and abilities, good intentions often wither because of frustration and failure. In the case of black evangelicals and white evangelicals in the United States, it has been well documented by sociologists and anthropologists that in spite of the high degree of theological agreement between the two communities, cultural misunderstandings and an inability of both communities to understand the views of the other lead to continued mistrust and misunderstanding.[4] Efforts to create racially or culturally diverse congregations, such as mergers between black and white churches or congregations focused on "racial reconciliation," may succeed or fail in part based on the ability of leaders and congregants to recognize and respond to areas of cultural conflict.[5]

Pastors, worship leaders, Sunday school teachers, and committee leaders with anthropological perspectives will be well positioned to lead Christians past misunderstanding toward real reconciliation and fellowship. Billy Graham, who started his ministry just as the civil rights movement was beginning to take shape in the American South, was a leader among white evangelicals

4. Christian Smith and Michael Emerson, *Divided by Faith: Evangelical Religion and the Problem of Race in America* (London: Oxford University Press, 2000).
5. Kersten Bayt Priest and Robert Priest, "Divergent Worship Practices in the Sunday Morning Hour: Analysis of an 'Interracial' Church Merger Attempt," in *This Side of Heaven: Race, Ethnicity, and the Christian Faith*, ed. Alvaro Nieves and Robert J. Priest (New York: Oxford University Press, 2007), 275–92; also Brian M. Howell, "Power and Reconciliation in an Urban Church: The Case of New City Fellowship," in *This Side of Heaven*, 293–309.

in supporting the movement. He integrated his rallies and leadership when many white evangelicals were still resisting the end of segregation. At the same time, Graham has publicly said he wishes he had spoken earlier and more forcefully in support of Martin Luther King Jr. and the movement for racial equality. As an anthropology major from Wheaton College, Graham was well positioned to see how the symbolic power of physical segregation could never be reconciled with the message of equality before God in the gospel.

The predisposition to engage culture, inequality, and difference with an attitude of understanding, investigation, and interest is not only relevant to racial divisions or cultural difference. Many pastors work in a context similar to their own background, but if they have attended college and seminary, they may find that higher education creates a social class distinction between them and their parishioners. Using anthropological techniques and perspectives to investigate the context provides a way back into a community from which the pastor has been separated by the new social identity he or she has taken on. Anyone considering youth ministry probably understands that, in the United States, where each generation is encouraged to differentiate itself from the previous one, there are significant differences between the cultural contexts of youth and those even just ten years older. Moreover, many ministries involve connecting with *subcultures*, groups within a larger culture that define themselves (or are defined by others) in opposition or in distinction to the majority. Harold Recinos, a professor and United Methodist minister who also has a doctorate in cultural anthropology, urges pastors to practice *pastoral anthropology*: the use of ethnographic techniques to learn about the community where their church is located, the demographics of church members, and the social and spiritual needs of both communities.[6]

Anthropology and the Global Church

Lamin Sanneh was born into a Muslim family of *Nyanchos*, an ancient royal line in the West African country of The Gambia. As a teenager, Sanneh was intrigued by reading about Jesus in the Koran, and he began a search to understand the man Muslims consider a prophet. Eventually he gave his life to Christ and, after studying in London, later became professor of world Christianity at Yale University.

Sanneh understands, both personally and academically, the multicultural nature of the gospel. Sanneh writes and speaks about the power of the gospel to influence local cultures. Unlike Islam, which mandates a holy language and officially endorses specific cultural practices rooted in the Arabian societies in

6. Harold Recinos, *Jesus Weeps: Global Encounters on Our Doorstep* (Nashville: Abingdon, 1992).

Anthropological Study of a Congregation

Peter Cha is Professor of Pastoral Theology at Trinity Evangelical Divinity School. He used anthropological perspectives and ethnographic fieldwork to understand a question of interest in pastoral theology.

The Korean American immigrant community is fairly young, with many immigrants having come to the United States since 1965. For Korean Americans who are Christian, the church is an important source of social and spiritual support. But tensions between first- and second-generation immigrants are breaking the unity of the immigrant church. Many first-generation Korean immigrants speak Korean and want to preserve their culture, language, and ways of honoring family (obedience and submission). Many second-generation Koreans, however, speak English, are pursuing cultural assimilation, and have redefined Korean Confucian-based family values. A number of these U.S. born or raised Koreans are leaving immigrant churches to form their own churches or to join nonethnic-specific American churches.

Cha did fieldwork in a Chicago-area Korean immigrant church that was successfully keeping its second-generation members. He found that, in this church, Koreans vigilantly engaged with their ethnic culture, but in a creative, adaptive way, not simply in order to preserve the culture as it existed at one time. People of different generations learned to relate with one another not only spiritually but culturally as well. First-generation immigrants learned to understand and value the younger generation's need to assimilate, speak English, and alter traditional Korean practices. Second-generation members learned to value their parents' generation's love for Korean language and tradition.

Cha's fieldwork shows how intensive research in a specific setting can produce a case study that has broad relevance for other communities. It also shows how professionals in various fields can use anthropological methods and concepts. In this case, pastors and theologians can use anthropology to better understand congregations.[1]

1. Peter Cha, "Constructing New Intergenerational Ties, Cultures, and Identities among Korean American Christians: A Congregational Case Study," in *This Side of Heaven*, 259–74.

which it was born, Christianity quickly broke away from its Jewish beginnings to become a religion at home in every language, culture, and context in which it was accepted. The first work of the Spirit at Pentecost was to translate the gospel into the languages of the world. The apostles then set out translating the gospel into multiple cultural contexts, a process that continues today. Sanneh writes,

> Christianity's translated status exempted Christians from binding adherence to a founding culture. . . . As the religion resounded with the idioms and styles of new converts, it became multilingual and multicultural. Believers responded with the unprecedented facility of the mother tongue, and by that step broke the back of cultural chauvinism as, for example, between Jew and Gentile. Christianity's indigenous potential was activated, and the frontier beckoned.[7]

The activation of this "indigenous potential" has spread the church throughout the world. Although some contexts have remained resistant to

7. Lamin Sanneh, *Disciples of All Nations: Pillars of World Christianity* (New York: Oxford University Press, 2008), 27.

the gospel message, throughout sub-Saharan Africa, Latin America, and parts of Asia, Christianity has grown to become the majority religion. Today most Christians live outside Europe or North America and speak a language other than English. How does—or should—that growth affect the church as a whole?

Sociologist Robert Wuthnow has noted that although scholars of world Christianity often say the "center of gravity" has shifted from the countries of the northern and western hemispheres to the southern and eastern world (sometimes called the "Global South"), the shift has been far more in numbers than in influence. Churches of northern countries remain far wealthier, with greater educational, publishing, and media resources, and have a far stronger role in theological discussions than do the churches of the Global South. The fact that most Christians live in Africa and Asia does not necessarily mean that Christians in the United States or Canada have a meaningful connection with them.[8]

Wuthnow argues that simply talking about a shift of power or gravity is not the best way to think about the church anyway. The church is not a club in which the majority rules. The church is, following the biblical metaphor, a body in which each part is vital. As Wuthnow says:

> A story that focuses on the withering of one appendage and the strengthening of another makes no sense. A better story acknowledges each limb or organ's dependence on others. In this story, global Christianity emerges less as a narrative about shifting centers of gravity and more about opportunities for mutual edification and interaction.[9]

Whether those interactions result in edification depends on how they happen. Students of anthropology can use their knowledge and perspective to bless the church as a whole. Understanding the nature of language, the cultural construction of concepts such as gender and race, the material and ecological reasons for cultural practices, and the processes of cultural change will enhance the ability of people across the global church to have mutually edifying interactions.

Anthropology and Missions

Connections between missions and anthropology go back to the very foundations of the discipline (see chap. 1), when some of the first professional

---

8. Robert Wuthnow, *Boundless Faith: The Global Outreach of American Churches* (Berkeley: University of California Press, 2009), 39–47, 59–61.

9. Ibid., 61.

Is Cultural Diversity a Blessing or a Curse?

Culture existed in the beginning. When God created humans in the garden, living in perfect unity with God and each other, they expressed that perfect unity in the cultural modes of language and culture. We might think that when God redeems the world we could return to that first culture. Doesn't cultural difference produce conflict? Wouldn't a single culture and language finally bring the unity God desired? Though humanity may have started with one culture, the Bible gives us a different vision for the future.

At the tower of Babel, humans came together to proclaim themselves equal to God. Moreover, they willfully disobeyed God's command to fill and subdue the earth. When God scattered them, he confused their language not because linguistic diversity is a curse, but because he knew that would be the way to get people to obey.

The mirror image of the Babel event came centuries later as God redeemed the nations, sending the Holy Spirit to initiate the church in Jerusalem. There,

with the people of the nations gathered for Passover, the Holy Spirit came upon the disciples to preach the gospel of Jesus to the diverse assembly. What is significant is that God did not give each person the ability to understand the Galilean Aramaic of the apostles. Instead, they declared that "we hear them declaring the wonders of God in our own tongues" (Acts 2:11).

God does not redeem humanity by bringing us back together into a single language or culture. Instead, God blesses cultural diversity by sending the gospel out in the diverse languages of the world. Diversity is not a curse but a blessing to be encouraged, embraced, and enjoyed. Revelation describes an ultimate image of unity in diversity as every "nation, tribe, people and language, [will be] standing before the throne and in front of the Lamb. . . . saying: 'Praise and glory and wisdom and thanks and honor and power and strength be to our God for ever and ever. Amen!'" (Rev. 7:9, 12).

anthropologists served as missionaries.[10] For over a hundred years, Christian missionaries have developed the interrelationships of anthropology and missions work. Linguists such as Ken Pike and Eugene Nida were widely respected in anthropological linguistics for their Bible translation and other scholarship. Later missionary anthropologists such as Paul Hiebert, R. Daniel Shaw, Charles Kraft, Miriam Adeney, and Marvin Mayers (among others) served as influential members of the missionary community, writing articles and books that became widely influential in missionary training programs.

Anthropology in mission work focuses largely on cross-cultural communication and the translation of the gospel. *Contextualization*, along with companion terms such as "indigenization," "inculturation," and "accommodation," refers to fitting the gospel with the language, idioms, customs, and traditions of a culture so that Christianity becomes organically woven in with the context. When this term was first promoted in the 1970s, many theologians and missionary leaders objected. They argued that missionaries who took culture seriously—adapting the way they communicated the gospel—risked polluting or distorting the gospel message. What they did not

10. See James Clifford, *Person and Myth: Maurice Leenhardt in the Melanesian World* (Durham, NC: Duke University Press, 1992).

see was how every expression of the gospel reflects culture and history. While Scripture remains authoritative for Christians everywhere, Christianity—the expression of following Christ—always reflects cultural context (see chap. 2). The question, for missionary anthropologists, was not whether the gospel would be part of culture, but whose culture it would be part of. Melanesian Christians, for instance, could not become "just Christians." If they rejected their own cultural context as "un-Christian," they simply ended up with a foreign, often American culture in its place. The anthropological emphasis on contextualization suggests that missionaries and church leaders should encourage local believers to listen to the Holy Spirit and express Christian faithfulness in ways that reflect their own cultures and histories.

Interestingly, while the concept was first proposed as a way to encourage missionaries to dissociate the message of the gospel from the (generally Western) cultural context in which the missionary had learned it, it has become equally (or more) important for non-Western Christians struggling to reconcile their own cultural contexts with Christian faith. Missionary anthropologist Darrell Whiteman tells of a Thai student who, after learning about anthropology and contextualization, said, "Now that I have been studying contextualization and have discovered how the Gospel relates to culture, I am realizing that I can be both Christian and Thai."[11] Many Christians throughout the world once thought that to be Christian was to wear Western clothes, sing European hymns, and eat with a fork and spoon. Anthropologically informed understandings of culture and society have encouraged new generations of Christians around the world to think about how a relationship with God should be lived out in their own context and how that relationship might transform their culture. The contextualization concept has more recently been critiqued as being insufficiently attentive to issues of power, colonialism, and history, but there is no doubt that the concept has proved extremely important in missionary anthropology and the health of the church around the world.[12]

Anthropological contributions to missionary method and theory pushed many North American missionaries and missionary training programs away from paternalistic and culturally imperialistic means of communication. Paul Hiebert, who spent six years as a missionary in India before earning his PhD in anthropology, wrote, "It is possible for missionaries, like others, to go to another culture as tourists, noticing its strangeness but never entering and identifying with its world."[13] Only when we enter anthropologically, he

11. Darrell Whiteman, "Contextualization: The Theory, the Gap, the Challenge," *International Bulletin of Missionary Research* 21, no. 1 (1997): 3.

12. For a critique of the contextualization concept, see Brian M. Howell, "Introduction" in *Power and Identity in the Global Church: Six Contemporary Cases*, ed. Brian M. Howell and Edwin Zehner (Pasadena, CA: William Carey Library Press, 2009), 1–42.

13. Paul Hiebert, *Cultural Anthropology* (Grand Rapids: Baker Books, 1982), xxii. Hiebert uses the word "incarnational" to describe his favored approach to missions. We substi-

argued, can we "love humans in other cultures as people—to see them as human beings like ourselves."[14]

This is not only true for career missionaries. The first experience that many North American Christians have of missionary work, or even significant cultural difference, occurs during a short-term mission trip. These trips, generally lasting two weeks or less, sometimes are considered life changing for participants because they learn to see God through eyes of people unlike themselves. Christians from around the world who engage in short-term service work often encounter communities with great passion for the gospel in spite of political opposition, material deprivation, or social inequality.

At the same time, these trips can be confusing and frustrating. Having had just a glimpse of another Christian community, many come back wondering how to make sense of what they saw. Worse yet, after two weeks in another culture, short-term missionaries may think they have a very *clear* understanding of that place. The trip may provide a false sense of understanding and connection when a great deal more time and engagement is necessary for real knowledge. A short trip is often just long enough to have stereotypes reinforced, prejudices confirmed, or judgments strengthened. Truly connecting with people in another culture in the course of a two-week trip requires an understanding of the context and an ability to engage people in ways that fit with the culture of the hosts rather than the preferences of the guests.[15]

Even for short cross-cultural experiences, anthropology supplies ways of thinking about and seeing the world that enhance understanding of differences and similarities. Anthropology inspires us to ask more questions about what is going on, to investigate more deeply, and to embrace the unfamiliar in place of criticism without understanding. Regardless of the length of the trip, an anthropologically astute short-term missionary can learn to get beneath surface observations, asking questions and seeking to understand the context from within. Most of all, those with an anthropologically trained outlook who take a trip into another cultural context will be better positioned to see how their own culture has profoundly shaped their faith.

---

tute the word "anthropological," which we believe conveys the same intent without the theological problems associated with the term "incarnational" when used to describe a missionary methodology.

14. Ibid.

15. For some recent research on short-term missions that explores the challenges and solutions for those who want to travel in this way, see the theme issue of the journal *Missiology* from October 2006. See also Robert J. Priest, ed., *Effective Engagement in Short-Term Missions: Doing It Right!* (Pasadena, CA: William Carey Library Press, 2008); also see Brian Howell, "Mission to Nowhere: Putting Short-Term Missions into Context," *International Bulletin of Missionary Research* 33, no. 4 (2009): 206–11.

North American short term missionaries at work on a building project in the Dominican Republic.
Photo: Brian Howell

The Future of Christians in Anthropology

Though God exists outside culture, we do not. As we noted in chapter 2, Christians only experience God in specific times and places. As the church becomes more diverse, different cultural manifestations of Christ's body are becoming more evident to more Christians. Globalization brings us into contact with cultural influences of all sorts, Christian and non-Christian. Cross-cultural contact will no longer be (and largely no longer is) the exclusive purview of missionaries and jet-setters. Anthropology should continue to play a role in preparing us for the future. As Christians study anthropology, we can bring our insights to the wider church and help everyone in the coming changes.

Christians can also contribute to anthropology itself. While an earlier generation often found professional anthropology and the academy generally hostile to Christianity, there is good reason to believe that the environment is changing. As perspectives of various sorts—racial, gender, ethnic, sexual—are acknowledged and even celebrated in the academy, Christians have been able to offer something to the conversation. Along with other explicitly religious perspectives such as Buddhism and Islam, Christianity can gain a seat at the table when Christians come as well-trained, creative, and skilled scholars who identify their religious perspective as relevant to their work.

We hope that as Christian college students, seminarians, prospective missionaries, and other interested people encounter anthropology here or elsewhere, they will encounter new ways to love God and his people more deeply, fully, and compassionately with all their strength, hearts, and minds.

Terms

contextualization: fitting the gospel with the language, idioms, customs, and traditions of a culture so that Christianity becomes organically woven in with the context.

pastoral anthropology: the use of ethnographic techniques to learn about the community where a church is located, the demographics of church members, and the social and spiritual needs of both communities.

subculture: a group within a larger culture that defines itself (or is defined by others) in opposition or in distinction to the majority.

Devotion 1

The Gospel in Culture

When the day of Pentecost had come, they were all together in one place. And suddenly from heaven there came a sound like the rush of a violent wind, and it filled the entire house where they were sitting. Divided tongues, as of fire, appeared among them, and a tongue rested on each of them. All of them were filled with the Holy Spirit and began to speak in other languages, as the Spirit gave them ability. Now there were devout Jews from every nation under heaven living in Jerusalem. And at this sound the crowd gathered and was bewildered, because each one heard them speaking in the native language of each. (Acts 2:1–6 NRSV)

The first work of the Holy Spirit, at Pentecost, was to speak the good news in a variety of languages. People from Mesopotamia, Judea, Cappadocia, Asia, Egypt, Libya, Rome, and other places each heard about God's deeds of power in the language they knew best. The Holy Spirit comes to us in our own cultures, and this story shows the Holy Spirit working a miracle in order to communicate clearly with each person.

Lamin Sanneh says that after the Holy Spirit translated the gospel into languages by miracle, the apostles set out to translate the gospel into cultures through mission. We continue that work today when we share the gospel with people of other cultures, appropriately translating the good news into linguistic and cultural terms that make sense in particular contexts. We also continue the work when we learn from other cultures, gaining insight into how our own culture shapes our understanding of the gospel.

Devotion 2

Anthropology in Jesus's Ministry

A man with leprosy came to him [Jesus] and begged him on his knees, "If you are willing, you can make me clean." Jesus was indignant. He reached out his hand and touched the man. "I am willing," he said. "Be clean!" (Mark 1:40–41)

Jesus wasn't an anthropologist, but his ministry shows why elements of the ethnographic method are so important. Jesus lived among the people he was trying to reach, sharing their daily lives. He taught them in locations familiar to them and addressed the issues that were important to them. In this case, Jesus was emotionally moved by the person he encountered, and he reached out to touch him.

Anthropologists approach people similarly, living among them and coming to understand and value their concerns. Practicing the ethnographic method can lead to a greater ability to listen, perceive, understand, and communicate effectively. It can also lead to compassion, as the anthropologist comes to really understand another person's context by living in it.

The skills that characterize an effective anthropologist also mark the effective Christian—living, talking, communicating, and caring for people in their own contexts in a way that leads to compassion.

Index

response to globalization, 217–21
  on sexual diversity, 101
church life, and anthropology, 5
Cinderella, 96
citizenship, 66, 79
civilization, 233
"civilizing mission," 209
civil rights, 69
Claiborne, Shane, 219
clan affiliation, 161
class, 66, 70, 80–81, 85, 88, 229
  and culture, 81–83
Clifford, James, 241
Clinton, Bill, 213
clothing, in church, 187
code switching, 59, 62
coercive power, 133, 136, 137, 145, 149
Cofán, 147
cognatic descent, 155–56, 159–60, 170, 173
Collins, Francis S., 8
colonialism, 10, 16, 57, 72, 147, 207–8, 209–12,
  220, 222, 224, 229, 257
"colored," 73
Columbia University, 233
commodification, 204–5, 216, 222
communication, 41, 257
communication technologies, 30
communion, as a symbol, 245–46
community development, 5
Comprehensive Globalization Movement
  (CGM), 219
conflict resolution
  of bands, 141
  of kingdoms, 145
  of states, 147
  of tribes, 143
consanguinial kin, 163, 170
constructivism. See instrumentalism
contextualization, 17, 256–57, 260
conversation, culture as, 40–42
Copernicus, 227
cosmology, 9
cosmopolitans, 216
counterhegemony, 135–36, 149
cousin marriage, 163–64, 169
cows, as sacred, 184–86
craft production, 18
creation, 41, 43–44
creoles, 56–59, 62
cricket, 214
Croats, 79

cross-cousin marriage, 163–64, 170
cross-cultural missions, 19, 248, 258
Crow, 100
cultural capital, 67, 85
cultural development, 28
cultural diversity, 17, 20, 127, 252, 256
cultural ecology, 235, 236, 237, 244
cultural hybridity, 213, 222
cultural Marxism, 239–40, 244
cultural materialism, 183–86, 199, 236–37, 244,
  246
Cultural Other, 14–15, 21, 33
cultural relativism, 26, 30–33, 42, 101, 250–51
cultural superiority, 29, 33–34, 42
cultural traits, 233, 244
culture, 15, 25–26, 27, 42, 61, 225
  as adaptive, 37
  as central concept, 15
  changes language, 52
  and class, 81–83
  as conversation, 40–42
  and gospel, 15, 260
  as integrated, 37–38
  as learned, 36–37
  metaphors for, 38–40
  as part of creation, 43–44
  as shared, 37
culture change, 204, 209–12
culture wars, 25
curse, of Genesis, 125, 130

Dalits, 81
Darwin, Charles, 28
Dawkins, Richard, 176
decolonization, 214, 222
democracy, 207, 219
denominations, 252
dependency theory, 208, 222
descent, 155–62, 170
descriptive linguistics, 47–49, 53, 62
design feature of language, 50, 62
deterritorialization, 215–17, 222
diachronic approach, 47, 62
dialects, 59, 62–63, 66
  social judgments of, 53–55
Diamond, Jared, 71
diaspora, 215, 222
diffusionism, 233, 244
Dilthey, Wilhelm, 232
discrimination, 66
divorce, 166

domestic anthropology, 218, 222
Douglas, Mary, 238
dowry, 166, 170
dramaturgical anthropology, 238
dual descent, 158–59, 170
Durkheim, Emile, 229–30, 234, 238

Eades, Diana, 53
Ecole Practique des Hautes Etudes, 15
ecological approach, 242, 244
economic anthropology, 4, 107, 127
economic exploitation, 220
economic reciprocity, 133
economics
  neoclassical, 124, 207
  and globalization, 205
Ecuador, 78, 111, 147
egalitarianism, 110–11, 140
Egypt, 126
Einstein, Albert, 227
Eliade, Mircea, 196
Elliot, Elisabeth 78n9
Elliot, Jim, 78n9
Ellison, Keith, 80
enculturation, 43
Engels, Friedrich, 233n13
English language, 53, 55–56, 58
epistemological relativism, 32, 42
Esau, 160
Esther House, 2
ethnic fair, 26–27, 30
ethnic inequality, 230
ethnicity, 67, 70, 76–80, 85
ethnic stratification, 53, 58
ethnoarchaeology, 6, 21
ethnocentrism, 26, 33–36, 42, 149, 182, 207
ethnocide, 112, 127
ethnographers, gender bias of, 92–94
ethnographic data, 228
ethnographic fieldwork, 4, 21, 215, 235, 241–42, 251
ethnographic interviews, 12, 21
ethnography, 10–13, 21
ethnos, 23
ethnoscience, 62
ethnosemantics, 52, 62
Eucharist, 186
eugenics, 29
European colonialism, 209–10
Euskara, 57
evangelicalism, 189

evangelism, and anthropology, 5
evolution, 8, 9, 16, 28, 243
evolutionary psychology, 237n20
excavation, 6, 21
exchange systems, 120–23, 127
extensive farming, 113, 127

Fadiman, Anne, 249
fall, 44, 129–30
falsification, 227, 244
family, in the Bible, 168–70
family systems, 153–70
Female Genital Mutilation (FGM), 99, 104
femininity, 95–98
feminist theory, 94, 240, 244, 246
fetishes, 183, 199
fictive kinship, 170
fieldwork, 10–13
Filipino-Americans, 213
Filipino language, 56
Firth, Raymond, 144
fishing, rituals of, 183
fissioning, 111, 127
Fleming, Peter, 78n9
flexible citizenship, 216
focus groups, 12, 21
food, globalization of, 205–6
foraging, 109–12, 125, 128–30, 141, 155
forensic anthropology, 8–9
forest ecosystem, 18
formalist theory (economics), 123–25, 128
formal sanctions, 136, 149
Franco, Francisco, 57
Frank, Andre Gunder, 208
Franke, John, 60
free markets, 207
French Revolution, 146
Fulani, 72
Fuller Theological Seminary, 3, 179
functionalism, 182–83, 196, 234–35, 242, 244

Gaelic, 78
Galileo, 227
Gambia, The, 253
Gandhi, Mahatma, 211, 218
Ganesh, 181–82
garbage, 7
Garo, 157–58
Gates, Henry Louis, Jr., 161
Geertz, Clifford, 176, 186, 188, 227, 238–39
gender, 66–67, 70–71, 88–98, 104, 255
  and inequality, 93, 102–3, 230

and language, 97
  as socially constructed, 89
  vs. sex, 88–91
  variations, 91–92
gender blenders, 90
"genderlects," 97
gender role, 89, 104
gender socialization, 94–98, 104
gender status, 89, 104
generalized reciprocity, 120–21, 128, 129
generosity, 129
genetics, 8, 9
Gennep, Arnold van, 191
genocide, 112, 128
geography, 10
geology, 9
Georgetown University, 213
German idealism, 28
German language, 55, 56
gift-giving, 121
glasses metaphor, 38–39
global church, 5, 18–21, 61
global evangelism, and colonialism, 220
globalization, 30, 203–22, 229, 259
  agriculture and, 120
  foraging in, 112
  horticulture in, 116
  pastoralism in, 118
"globalization from below," 219
global media, 218–20
"Global South," 255
God, names and metaphors of, 61
goddess religions, 158n3
Gods Must Be Crazy, The (film), 204
"going native," 13, 21
gospel
  and anthropology, 5
  and culture, 15, 260
gossip, 138
Graham, Billy, 84, 252–53
grammar, 49, 52, 62
Gramsci, Antonio, 135–37
"grassroots globalization," 219
gravitation, theory of, 227
Great Commission, 23
Greek language, 46, 60
Greek philosophy, 28
Greeks, religion of, 181–82
Greene, Katrina, 221
Grenz, Stanley, 60
Grounded Theory (GT), 228n4

Guatemalans, 79
Gullah, 56

"half-breeds," 75
Harris, Marvin, 184–86, 236
Headland, Thomas, 18, 236, 250
Hebrew culture, 156
Hegel, G. W. F., 28
hegemony, 134–37, 149, 210, 220, 224
Henson, Kevin, 90
Herdt, Gilbert, 101–2
hermeneutics, 9
Herskovits, Melville, 124
Hiebert, Paul, 256–58
hierarchy, 66, 68, 80, 144
Hill, Jane, 58
Hinduism, 81, 181
hip-hop, 216
Hispanic/Latino culture, 76, 79
historical linguistics, 46–47, 53, 62
historical particularism, 29–30, 42, 233, 244
historic turn, 239–40
history, 10, 257
Hmong, 249–50
holistic understanding, 13, 21
Holy Spirit, and cultural forms, 61
homosexuality, 88, 92, 99–102
honeymoon, 194
Hopi, 51
horticulture, 109, 112–16, 125, 128, 130, 141
households, 169
Human Genome Project, 8
human nature, 229
human origins, 9, 16
human rights, 146
Hundred Years' War, 146
hunting and gathering. See foraging
Huntington, Samuel, 206
Hutus, 210–11
Hymes, Dell, 51, 59
hypodescent, 73, 85

Ibaloi, 141
idiographic explanation, 227–28, 244
Ifugao, 141, 191
Ikalahan, 20–21, 113–14, 141–42, 197
Ilokano, 55
Ilongot, 141
image of God, 63, 90, 178, 198
immigration, 80, 252
imperialism, 209
incarnation, 41, 150, 173

Lee, Richard, 111–12
leisure, 44
lens metaphor, 38–39
leveling mechanism, 122
Levi-Strauss, Claude, 196, 237
lexicon, 52, 55, 62
liberation theology, 83
Liebow, Elliot, 10
life-cycle rituals, 191, 199
life history, 12, 22
liminal period, 192, 194, 199
Lincoln, Abraham, 195
linguistic determinism, 52
linguistic morphology, 46, 62
linguistic nationalism, 57–58, 62
linguistics, 5, 7–8, 22
Linnaeus, Carl, 73
localization, 216–19, 222–23
London School of Economics, 234
Lone Ranger, 95
Lord's Prayer, 190
lower barbarism, 233
Lucas, George, 181
Lutheranism, 186
Luther, Martin, 146

Maasai, 116–17, 142, 192
Macapagal-Arroyo, Gloria, 213
Macapagal, Diosdado, 213
magic, 178–80, 199
making culture, 41–42
Malawi, 251
Malaysian culture, 137
Malinowski, Bronislaw, 94, 183, 196, 234
mana, 181, 199
Manila, 27, 53
mapping, 12, 22
Marcus, George, 241
market economy, 119, 121n6, 122–23, 128
marriage, 44, 124, 162–68, 170, 190
marriage exchange, 164–67, 171
marital status, 88, 105–6
Marxism, 30, 208, 238–40
Marx, Karl, 81, 229–30, 231–33, 235, 239–40
masculinity, 90, 95, 97–98
master status, 68, 85
materialist approach, 30, 242, 244
matriarchy, 158, 171
matrilineal descent, 157–58, 171
Mayers, Marvin, 256
McCully, Ed, 78n9

McDonald's, McDonalization, 26–27, 206, 217, 223
McEwan-Fujita, Emily, 205
Mead, Margaret, 14, 93, 233
means of production, 229
Mecca, 193
medieval Europe, 66
Melanesia, 122, 133–34, 144, 183
"melting pot," 80
Meneses, Eloise Hiebert, 76, 243
Mennonites, 83
Mesoamerican, 18
methodological atheism, 237–38
Metropolitan Community Church, 101
Mexicans, 80
Mexico, 18, 96, 216
Missiology (journal), 15
missional theology, 83
missions, 10, 16–17, 248, 255–58
Mizoram, 157
"mock Spanish," 58–59
modernization theory, 207, 222
modesty, 98
Mohammed, 60
monarchy, 145, 147
money, 121
Mongols, 209
monocropping, 118–19, 128
monocultural, 39
monogamy, 168
monogenesis, 29, 42, 156, 171
monotheism, 182, 199
moral relativism, 32, 42
Morgan, Henry Lewis, 232
Mormonism, 80
morphemes, 48, 62
morphology, 48
Moses, 224
motherhood, 96
Mother Theresa, 219
Mound Builders, 6, 22
multicropping, 114, 128
multiculturalism, 25, 27
multilingual societies, 56, 58
multisited research, 215, 222
Murdock, George, 159
Murle, 165
Murray, Stephen, 100
Muslims, 60, 80, 193, 203, 221, 253
Mussolini, Benito, 135
myths, 195–96, 198

Namibia, 110, 140
Nandi, 142
Naomi, 166
National Institutes of Health (NIH), 8
nationalism, 208
nationality, 79
nations, 23
Native Americans, 56, 72, 100, 122, 144
naturalism, 237, 243, 244
Navajo, 78, 100
Nazis, 29, 134–35
Ndembu, 192
negative reciprocity, 121, 128
neoclassical economic theory, 207
neocolonialism, 212, 222
neoliberalism, 207, 222
neolocal residence, 168, 171
Nepal, 168
Network of Christian Anthropologists, 250
New Caledonia, 15
Newton, Issac, 226–27
Nida, Eugene, 49, 256
Niebuhr, H. Richard, 40
Niger, 99, 114
Nigeria, 31, 99, 158
nomadic pastoralism, 117, 125, 148
nomadic reciprocity, 128
nomothetic explanation, 227–28, 234, 244
nonunilineal descent. *See* cognatic descent
Northwest One (Washington, D.C.), 218
Norway, 217
Norwegian language, 56
Ntarangwi, Mwenda, 221
nuclear family, 155, 161, 168
Nuer, 117–18

objectivity and anthropological research, 241–42
official languages, 49, 62
Old Testament, culture in, 156–57
oligarchy, 146, 150
Ong, Aihwa, 216
open class system, 81–83, 85
oppression, 210–11
oral languages, 49
Ortner, Sherry, 239

Pakistan, 214
paleontology, 9
Papua, 113, 161
paradigms, 227
paralanguage, 50, 62

parallel-cousin marriage, 163–64, 171
parole, 50–51, 60
participant observation, 11–13, 22
pastoral anthropology, 253, 260
pastoralism, 109, 116–18, 125, 128, 130, 141
paternalism, 69
patriarchy, 157, 169, 171
patrilineal descent, 155–57, 160, 169, 171
Paul
    on adoption, 171–72
    on body of Christ, 200–201
    on economic equality, 126
    on ethnocentrism, 34
    on gender roles, 91
    on gossip, 138
    on households, 169
    on human origins, 9
    on politics, 148
    on social inequality, 86
Peace of Westphalia, 146
Pentecost, 254, 256, 260
perspectivalism, 240–42, 244
persuasive power, 133–34, 136, 150
Peruvians, 79
Philippines,
    Christians, 2–3, 11, 20, 231, 243
    culture of, 26
    families in, 153
    farming rituals of, 191
    gender in, 91–92, 95
    horticulture in, 113–14
    language in, 53–56
    postcolonialism of, 212–13
    ritual change in, 197
    tribes in, 141
philology, 47, 62
phonemes, 48, 62
phonemics, 48, 62
phonetics, 48, 62
phonology, 48, 62
physical anthropology, 5, 8–9, 22
pidgin, 56–57, 62
Pike, Kenneth, 48–49, 256
pilgrimage, 192–93
plantation systems, 72
pluralism, 30
plural marriage. *See* polygamy
Poland, 135
Polanyi, Karl, 124
political anthropology, 150
political organization, 138–48

Tobin, Sarah, 221
Tongans, 181
tower of Babel, 256
Townsend, William Cameron, 48
transhumant pastoralism, 117, 125, 129
transnational, 215, 223
Trevor-Roper, Hugh, 79
tribes, 139, 141–44, 149–51, 154
Trinity, 59
Trinity Evangelical Divinity School, 254
Trobriand Island, 183, 186
Turner, Victor, 191–92, 238–39
Tutsis, 210–11
two-spirit, 100–101, 105
Tylor, Edward B., 180–82, 232

Uganda, 221
unilineal descent systems, 155–59, 162, 171
unilinear cultural evolution, 28–29, 43, 181–82, 207, 232, 245
United Kingdom, 145
United States, 26
    Christian culture of, 34
    and cousin marriage, 163–64
    democratic system of, 146
    ethnicity in, 76–80
    gender inequality in, 102
    kinship system of, 156, 161
    as multilingual, 56
    Spanish in, 58
"untouchables," 81
upper savagery, 233
urban anthropology, 4
urbanization, 30
urban ministry, 2, 4
usufruct rights, 115, 129
Ute Reservation, 7
uxorilocal residence, 157, 171

violence, 97
Virgen de Guadalupe, 96
Vishnu, 181
Vulgate, 60

Wallerstein, Immanuel, 208
Waorani, 78, 111, 147–48
warfare, 133, 144
Washington, D.C., 2, 11
Washington, George, 195

water metaphor, 38
Waters, Mary, 77
Watson, James, 206, 217
wealth, 30, 67, 85, 129
Weber, Max, 67, 229, 230–31, 238
weddings, 193–94
Weiner, Annette, 94
West Africa, languages, 56
Western capitalism, 123
westernization, 206–7, 211, 223
Wheaton, Illinois, 70
Wheaton College, 16, 205, 253
White, Leslie, 235
Whiteman, Darrell, 257
Whorf, Benjamin, 51
Wiccans, 180
Wilson, Jonathan, 60–61
Winfrey, Oprah, 161
witchcraft, 178–80, 200
Wodaabe, 99
women, in the church, 88
Woods, Robert, 97
Woods, Tiger, 71
World Bank, 217
World Church of the Creator, 33
world-systems theory, 208, 223
worldview, 39, 227
World War II, 211
worship, 86, 178, 189, 190, 252
"writing culture," 241
Wuthnow, Robert, 255
Wycliffe Bible Translators, 7, 17, 48–49

xenophobia, 33, 43

Yakö, 158
Yale University, 253
Yanamamö, 116
Ybarrola, Steve, 57
Yoruba, 153
Youderian, Roger, 78n9
youth ministry, 253
Youth With a Mission, 1
Yucatec Mayan, 18
Yugoslavia, 9, 79, 141n7

Zambia, 191
Zulu nation, 209
Zuni, 100